Study Guide to Accompany

Introduction to
Child Development
Sixth Edition

John P. Dworetzky
Western Washington University

Prepared by

Ellen C. Huft
Glendale College
Glendale, Arizona

West Publishing Company
Minneapolis/St. Paul   New York   Los Angeles   San Francisco

WEST'S COMMITMENT TO THE ENVIRONMENT

In 1906, West Publishing Company began recycling materials left over from the production of books. This began a tradition of efficient and responsible use of resources. Today, 100% of our legal bound volumes are printed on acid-free, recycled paper consisting of 50% new paper pulp and 50% paper that has undergone a de-inking process. We also use vegetable-based inks to print all of our books. West recycles nearly 27,700,000 pounds of scrap paper annually—the equivalent of 229,300 trees. Since the 1960s, West has devised ways to capture and recycle waste inks, solvents, oils, and vapors created in the printing process. We also recycle plastics of all kinds, wood, glass, corrugated cardboard, and batteries, and have eliminated the use of polystyrene book packaging. We at West are proud of the longevity and the scope of our commitment to the environment.

West pocket parts and advance sheets are printed on recyclable paper and can be collected and recycled with newspapers. Staples do not have to be removed. Bound volumes can be recycled after removing the cover.

Production, Prepress, Printing and Binding by West Publishing Company.

 TEXT IS PRINTED ON 10% POST CONSUMER RECYCLED PAPER    Printed with **Printwise** Environmentally Advanced Water Washable Ink

ISBN 0–314–20115–7

TABLE OF CONTENTS

# O THE STUDENT

DEAR STUDENT:

This study guide was written with the intention of helping you to make the best use of your study time and to have the best results. It was designed to help you to concentrate on the key issues of your interests, further your knowledge, and help you achieve the best grades possible.

■■■■

A MATTER OF TIME . . . .

Knowing that you are busy, the study tips I've recommended are tried and true and will definitely help you save time *and* learn the material. As a teacher and perennial student, I've approached studying from many angles. I offer you the result of careful investigation, reports from my own students, and field-testing by fellow students at every post-secondary level.

Perhaps the best place to start is with the time you have to manage. Thinking in terms of one week, you have 168 hours to budget. Sleeping will use 56 of these hours if you need eight hours a night. Eating can easily use 20 hours if someone else helps to prepare the meals or more if you have to prepare and clean up afterwards, especially if you have young children. Assuming that you have a family and social life, you'll want to save time for the people you care about, which can take minutes or hours at a time, depending on how big the demands are. For now, let's guess at 20 hours a week. If you are a full time student, that's five three-hour classes. You'll spend 15 hours in class (more if you have a lab-course) and discover you'll find you need at least nine hours per class; that's 45 hours of study and homework per week. You may want to budget more or less time depending on the classes you chose to keep up with the reading and test preparation! According to my arithmetic that leaves you with 12 hours a week for travel to school, day dreaming, personal care, shopping, exercise, and relaxation (all of which I recommend for mental health). Chart your own time compared to what I've suggested here, and see how you can juggle the busy hours you have.

Your Weekly Schedule

SLEEPING	_____	per week
EATING	_____	add prep and clean up
HOURS IN CLASS	_____	3 hrs. for each class
HOMEWORK	_____	9 hrs for each class
MISC.	_____	house and car care, shopping, travel, social events, family, exercise, relaxation
TOTAL	168 hrs.	

If you've never looked at a week's time like this, you may be surprised at how full your weeks are! You may now be aware that there are places from which you can steal time when the going gets tough. Getting help with meals, clean up, shopping, laundry, car maintenance, yard work, and ignoring the housework have been most helpful to me. Our "restaurant" closes one evening a week for a bring-in-pizza or other treat. Don't forget to ask for help; you might even get some! Often, exercise or relaxation time is combined with family or dating time. Balancing school schedules so you have both heavy and light homework classes in the same semester, rather than saving the worst until the last semester, help to keep you from overloading. If you have a job as well, you'll want to take fewer hours of class work and homework. Since no two weeks tend to require the same effort, you can put time in the bank for loved ones with an IOU when extra tight demands come along. Don't worry! They'll remind you and even think of fun things to do during the breaks from school.

■ ■ ■ ■   ◀
                                                                                                        ◀
                                                                                                        ◀
A GUIDE FOR STUDYING   ◀

Now, let's get to the study tips themselves:

Scan the book. Get an idea of the scope of the course. Read the table of contents, leaf through the pages, pictures, illustrations and notice the format of the chapters.

Take a good look at the syllabus your teacher has given you, so you can see the pace of the course, when the tests are to be given, what the rules are for written work, hand-in dates, and any other pertinent information that may be school policy or that of your specific class. Some teachers get really miffed if the students don't read and understand the syllabus. Some even include a question or two on the first test to make sure you've read it!

Scan this study guide. Notice the Learning Objectives section that alerts you to what you'll need to know from each chapter.

Pay attention to the Chapter Outlines. They've been created to help you organize and connect information in meaningful ways. As you go along, do the outlines yourself. You'll be surprised how much it helps. At the end of this section, I've written more about outlining the chapters.

Learn the list of Important Names, Terms, and Concepts for each chapter. Use them for quick reminders for getting in the mood for tests.

Notice the Guided Review that will help you to concentrate and remember what you've read. As you do the Guided Review, use the book when you need to if you really can't remember, and jot down page numbers for further reference.

Last, note the Practice Tests at the end of each chapter that will give you an idea of what you've remembered of the reading, as well as what needs to be reviewed more fully. Don't peek at the study guide or text for the answers until you're all finished with the test. If testing makes you nervous, practicing as you study can really help reduce your anxiety!

Now that you've scanned everything, begin reading the assignment. Pause at the end of each section, or every three or four paragraphs, look up from the book, and ask yourself what you've read. What are the key terms, the important concepts, and the contributions made by important people? Check with the study guide and fill in the Guided Review to help you pinpoint what you are expected to know. Be sure to correct any mistakes. Better now than at test time!

Programming all of your memories helps. Visual memories of reading the book are good, adding tactile memory by writing exercise helps more, and saying certain important things out loud gives you auditory memory as well. A triple whammy! Listen for the instructor's lecture cues to alert you to important information. These cues often let you know what will appear on the test.

Always read the chapter before you go to class. This will allow you to know what questions to ask as well as what points the instructor emphasizes.

Finish the chapter, a few paragraphs, or a section at a time. Take a few minutes' break to stretch, get a drink of water, or look out the window every thirty minutes or so. Your eyes will tire less quickly, and you'll be able to concentrate better when you go back to studying. Talk to yourself about what you're reading -- or if you'd rather, tell your pet. S/he will love you for it! Just for fun, I've included a mystery group of people to talk to if your pet doesn't cooperate.

Take the practice tests. These questions are not necessarily typical of the kinds you'll find on an in-class test. Here, your tests include only multiple-choice items so you'll be prepared for whatever comes! You'll know from the results how much more reviewing you'll need before you take the test in class. Be sure to correct any mistakes. You'll notice the questions in your study guide are constructed to reinforce the information, more than to test your memory since you have the book handy. If you know the answers to the questions, however, you'll pass the tests in class!

As you prepare to take a test, highlight the information in the text you feel the instructor will consider important enough for a question. Highlight the other points brought up by your instructor. Some students use a different highlight color for material discussed by the professor.

Review the Summary in the text both before and after you read the chapter to alert you to key issues.

On Outlining the Chapter: One of the most time saving devices I've found is to write a detailed outline of each assigned chapter as I read, as in step four. Not only does outlining help to organize and form links for remembering important material, it weeds out extraneous, albeit interesting, side line details. Thirdly, a detailed outline provides an economical way of studying for tests. Reviewing the outline allows you to test yourself on what you know and don't know. As you reread your outline, you'll recognize familiar material as well as see what you've forgotten as you've moved on to other topics. You can use the outline as a "cramming" tool, using the book only to look up those pieces of information you've ignored or forgotten. You'll be surprised at the time you'll save and how much you will retain for tests. Remember, cramming is useful as a review tool only after you've done the other steps. If you try to cram a whole chapter's material into memory in one sitting, you'll suffer "information overload" and lose much of it.

I've written typical, detailed outlines for you for the first few chapters. Thereafter, I have given you skeletal outlines for you to develop in more detail to cover all the chapter's information. Notice I've used the organization of the book as the core of the outline design. Well-organized books like this one almost write the outline for you! As you get used to the idea, you may develop your own outlining method. Feel free to use whatever works for you.

Be sure to leave blank spaces after every section to plug in additional lecture material so you'll have both text and lecture information together for test reviews.

ON TEST TAKING

Read the instructions carefully! You never know when the instructor will tell you to answer every other question only!

Make sure you have a complete test package. I'll never forget discovering that the last page was missing in one of mine after I had left the test-site. Check the number of questions so you can budget your time.

Read over any essay type questions but save them for last. Multiple choice questions may remind you of items to include in essay answers.

If you run into a tough question, pass it and come back to it later when your mind has been in the "child development" groove for a few minutes. A later question can often help to answer a previous one.

Read the questions and choices very carefully. Be careful of NOT, ALWAYS and NEVER items. Keep the question in mind. Read all of the choices carefully. The first sensible answer may not be the best one.

"All of the above" choices can be tricky. If you think one of the choices is wrong, look again at the remaining two for the best answer.

Answer all of the questions. An educated guess is better than no answer at all.

Rumor has it that instructors will have more "b" and "c" correct answers than "a" or "d", and that longest choices are more likely to be correct than the shorter ones. Unfortunately, instructors know of this rumor and so will be careful in the balance of answers. Be careful of rumors about your professor. Your instructor has heard them too, and will love to quietly do the unexpected.

On matching questions, do the ones you are sure of first. The rest may fall into place from sheer familiarity.

On essay questions, list the most important points you want to include in outline or brief form in the margin or on a separate piece of paper and write from that. This will help you stay on the subject. Your instructor probably is looking for a specific number of key points, and is very wise to padded answers. Use full sentences, the proper terminology, and check your grammar and spelling before you hand it in.

These aids have been of sure-fire help to me as a student and as a teacher in many college courses and I pass them on to you with my welcome to the child development course and my best wishes for your success.

OBSERVING CHILDREN'S BEHAVIOR

As you progress through this course you may have an opportunity (or an assignment) to conduct an empirical, objective observation of children's behavior and report your findings in a special report. You have no doubt watched children in a variety of settings in a casual way. In this exercise you will follow a design format and take extra care to report carefully only what you see without interpreting or guessing at why the behaviors occur. The following general suggestions are meant to be useful only with approval of your professor, who will no doubt give you specific help and guidelines.

Two terms, empiricism and objectivity, should be your watch words in your reports. Empirical reporting means that you only report what is observable and what could be observed by another person standing beside you. Objectivity in your report means that you describe the behavior(s) clearly and without bias, opinion or interpretation. "B is a mean kid and was mad at C" is interpretive. "B threw the sand bucket at C and called him a cabbage", gives more information, is more descriptive, and does not carry your subjectivity. Remember that mind reading is not permitted.

Ethical considerations are of importance as well. First of all, obtain permission to observe the child, or children, from the teacher or parents. Explain what you will be doing and why. Second, read the ethics section in the text and discuss it thoroughly in class to be sure you understand all that is involved. Use initials, numbers, or fictitious names rather than real names to insure confidentiality. Above all, the children's welfare comes first!

Resist interaction with the child(ren) unless your format involves an interview or a measurement activity. It is very difficult for you and the children to keep your objectivity if you observe and evaluate your own children's behavior. The same is true if the children you observe are those with whom you are involved in part-time care.

As you go through the study guide, you will see some suggested reports in some of the chapter learning objectives or practice tests. Some require reading of additional research while others recommend that you spend time observing a specific behavior or thinking through a problem situation. The following suggestions may give you some additional ideas, and help you organize and write your observation exercise.

Some data gathering designs will be more effective than others since you will be limited by time and equipment. Plan to spend at least three separate observation periods to insure that there is indeed consistency in the behavior of the child(ren) you target. B may be a terror the first day, and a lamb the next! In addition, those whom you observe will need to get used to your being in their otherwise familiar setting. Children may act differently because of your presence. Some child development facilities, such as schools or preschools, have observation laboratories where you can view children in play or learning activities through a one-way mirror, thus eliminating subject bias.

Charting the target behavior can be really a helpful way to make quick records. The children's initials would be placed on one axis, while typical behaviors would be coded on the other.

Direct observation in a natural setting can be conducted anywhere children or children and their parents or teachers are together. Parks, preschool and school playgrounds, and at the children's organized games, are good places to watch play styles and socialization, attachment behaviors, prosocial or competitive behaviors, and social learning. As you make your first visit to the site, you will want to observe long enough to choose one or two target children who are sure to be there when you can visit and to choose the target behavior. Be sure to describe the setting, the numbers of children and grown ups, and other pertinent information. Follow a paradigm that gives information about the antecedents to the target behavior as well as the reinforcements. Remember to get permission from the teacher or parent for your observation.

The Interview method can be a good data gathering tool if the interview is carefully constructed and given in exactly the same way to all of your target subjects. This can be used with members of the same age or sex group, or with samples of two groups for comparison, and can relate to a specific attitude, behavior or role. One of my students did a fine interview of three generations of parents, three from each of three age groups, and compared parenting styles using the textbook's description of the Schaefer dimensions. She found some surprises! Spend time formulating the questions so that they do not reflect or lead to bias. The interview should be done in person, giving the subject enough time to answer thoroughly and yourself time to record answers to questions carefully and completely. Never use correct names, but give the age and sex of subjects. The sum of your report should reflect similarities as well as differences. You may want to use simple statistics to describe the percentage of these differences and similarities. There are bound to be individual answers to be recorded, as well.

The Survey method is not as successful as the interview method. Many who promise faithfully to return your survey instrument by Monday will never get around to it. You can count on about a one-third to one-half return at best. In addition, there is always the problem of subject bias. We tend to answer these as we think the surveyor wants us to, or we forget details, or rush through the items without giving them much thought. I'd recommend the use of the survey only in the light of its limitations, and only if you have lots of time and a large population to survey.

Several books or chapters in books are available in your library to help give you ideas and guide lines. Your professor may have exact information sheets for part of your report, so be careful to get all of the information required. If you use an idea or a quote from a source other than your text be sure to include the credit in your bibliography.

ACKNOWLEDGMENTS

Even study guide authors need and appreciate the support of colleagues, students and family. I've been lucky to have help from all three. My students and colleagues at Glendale Community College have been marvelous in their feedback and encouragement. In addition, my thanks to Jan, Dennis, Clyde and all those who edited and formatted and encouraged at West Educational Publishing.

Words can't express my deep thanks to Karen and John Dworetzky for their reassurance and measureless help. I do wish you could meet them to know how terrific they are! By the way, Christopher and David are great too!

To Frank, and John, Trish, Rob and Fran who listened and cheered, comforted and steered me on course, and taught so me so much, and put up with me so patiently all these years, you deserve roses for your noses.

ELLiE

CHAPTER ONE

AN INTRODUCTION TO DEVELOPMENT: HISTORY AND RESEARCH

■ ■ ■ ■

LEARNING OBJECTIVES

One of the best ways you have of knowing what you know is to tell someone else. As suggested in the "Dear Student" section, educators know you learn best when you discuss what you read, see or hear with someone else. Often when you're alone your pet is a willing listener. Better yet, form a group of class-mates so you can study together. For those of you who have neither opportunity, I've invented a group of new friends from another planet called Latnem-Poleved for you to use as listeners. Don't be afraid, you won't be considered peculiar as long as you know with whom you are studying! Be able to discuss the following with your friends:

1. Show them how philosophers' questions lead to scientific investigations and how developmental psychology can trace its roots to the work of the 19th century naturalists.
2. Be sure to explain to them about G. Stanley Hall's efforts using Darwin's methods and views as he studied the development of children.
3. Be able to describe and give examples of the central issues which have emerged in the research into child development.
4. Show your friends the six dimensions of research and give them examples of each.
5. It is important that you understand the value and function of the experiment, for this is how we learn of the effects of different variables on behavior.
6. Describe the kinds of controls necessary; how we select subjects, and how we attempt to eliminate bias.
7. Use a simple example to illustrate how both observers and subjects show bias and explain how a double-blind design is used.
8. While you're at it, discuss the value of replication and expansion. You may want to use an example from the book or your lecture notes.
9. Describe the way a single subject is studied. Explain how the A-B-A and A-B-A-B design can be used. Remember the advantages and disadvantages of this type of study.

10.   Make sure they understand the difference between cause and correlation, and how correlations are used. They need to understand this or many of the studies reported in our media may mislead them.

11.   Show your listeners how age is used as a variable in cross-sectional and longitudinal research. Tell them of the advantages and disadvantages of each of these.

12.   Describe the time-lag and sequential designs and explain their advantages.

13.   As there are many theories of human development, be sure your friends understand what a theory is, the types of theories, and their problems and goals.

14.   Be sure to describe the problems and considerations we have about ethical issues as they come to bear in our research. They should know the difference between ethical and legal definitions.

If you know and can discuss these learning objectives, you can probably pass most essay questions posed by your instructor on a test. Remember to practice by telling someone else the answers to help you store the information into long term memory.

■ ■ ■ ■

CHAPTER OUTLINE

Don't panic at the length of this outline. When you make yours this detailed, you'll find it saves time and effort as you study for tests. Use the outline as you would a summary to help you remember what you've read and studied. This outline has been done for you except for a few sections. In subsequent chapters you will be asked to do more for yourself. Be sure to save room for lecture notes.

Chapter Preview: Here's a chance to think about your opinions on some salient issues regarding the development and welfare of children.

I.   The History of Human Development
    A.   The Dawn of History
        1.   A letter to his son from an Egyptian father, 1800 BC.
        2.   Appreciation for the qualitative uniqueness of childhood not seen before the 20th century
        3.   Children seen as only quantitatively different from adults
    B.   Scientific Approaches Into Child Development
        1.   John Locke (1632-1704)
            a.   "tabula rasa" --
        2.   Cultural differences discovered
            a.   Captain James Cook (1728-1779)
                (1)   Tahitian sex education
        3.   Jean Jacques Rousseau (1712-1778)
            a.   education should offset restrictions and corruption of institutions. "Natural Man" --
            b.   children should develop without strict controls
    C.   Empirical Efforts - The Beginning of Contemporary Developmental Psychology
        1.   The British Empiricists and Charles Darwin
            a.   systematically documented observations of the development of

animal species over time

- 2.   b.   Darwin's (1809-1882) methods used to compare development of animals to that of children and introduced concept of evolution

D.   The 20th Century
- 1.   G. Stanley Hall
  - a.   first to earn Ph.D. in Psychology
  - b.   founder of American Psychological Association
  - c.   first to study children in laboratory
    - (1)   perception, learning and memory
  - d.   impressed with Sigmund Freud's work
- 2.   Sigmund Freud (1856-1939) Vienna
  - a.   importance of early childhood experiences in shaping adult personality
  - b.   lectures at Clark University (1908) stimulated interest in early stage based child development
- 3.   Alfred Binet (1857-1911) France
  - a.   first intelligence tests to separate slow learners from normals in French schools
- 4.   Arnold Gesell (1880-1961) United States
  - a.   comparison of age related differences in variety of functions
- 5.   Jean Piaget post World War I
  - a.   cognitive Development
- 6.   John Watson United States
  - a.   founder of behaviorism
- 7.   Post World War II baby boom
  - a.   resurgence of interest in child development
- 8.   Developmental psychology defined --
  - a.   *Your turn--*

_____

_____

_____

_____

_____

II.   Central Issues in Development: changes in human behavior over time and as they relate to age

A.   Nature Vs Nurture -- *you do*

_____

B.   Stability vs. Change -- *good! do it on this too*

_____

C.   Continuity vs. Discontinuity -- *you're on a roll*

_____

III.   Research Methods -- Systematic and Objective Methods of Observing, Describing and Recording Events

A.   Six dimensions of developmental research
Fill in a brief description of each to help you keep them straight. You'll need more room than this, of course. An example will help.
- 1.   Descriptive vs. explanatory
- 2.   Naturalistic vs. manipulative

      3.   Historical vs. ahistorical
      4.   Theoretical vs. serendipitous
      5.   Basic vs. applied
      6.   Single subject vs. group

B.   Experimental Methods

      1.   Choose a testable issue to form hypothesis or statement
           a.   selection of behavior to be measured
      2.   Select format of study
           a.   methods of selection. Which dimensional approach best. What population, etc.
      3.   Definitions of terms
           a.   reliability of measurements and observations
      4.   The Controls
           a.   selection of the experimental group and the control group comparison
           b.   random selection of subjects to each group
           c.   all variables held constant except for variable not shared
               (1)   independent variable - the one the experimenter manipulates - not shared by both groups
               (2)   dependent variable - the resulting change in behavior of the subjects in experimental group compared to the control group subjects
      5.   Observer bias and subject bias
           a.   what you believe or expect is what you get
           b.   performance for sake of experiment or experimenter
           c.   methods to avoid bias
               (1)   double blind controls
               (2)   interobserver reliability
      6.   The results of the experiment
           a.   statistical analysis and comparison
      7.   Replication and expansion
           a.   if it hasn't happened twice, it hasn't happened!
           b.   variations on the theme, questions generated
           c.   analysis of study on the six dimensions
      8.   Single subject design
           a.   use of time as control
           b   A-B-A design
           c.   A-B-A-B design

C.   Nonexperimental Methods

      1.   The Correlational Method
           a.   correlation vs. causation. Relationship! Be careful
           b.   prediction
           c.   often leads to doing scientific experiment to prove causation
      2.   Case Studies
           a.   a single individual
           b.   descriptive over time
           c.   the danger of generalization

D.   Using age as a variable
    1.   The longitudinal approach
        a.   repeated measurements of the same individual or group behavior over time
        b.   advantages and disadvantages. *You list them*

_____

_____

        c.   the Terman study
    2.   The cross-sectional approach
        a.   numbers of subjects of different ages measured at the same time
        b.   Advantages and disadvantages. *You list them*

_____

_____

    3.   Time lag design
        a.   control for cultural effects over time
        b.   different groups tested in different years, age held constant
    4.   Sequential design
        a.   combines the best elements of 1, 2, and 3

IV.   Building a Theory
    A.   A Jigsaw Puzzle
        1.   How to organize data, ideas and hypotheses to provide a more complete understanding of information or to explain or predict behavior

V.   Theories of Development
    A.   Environmental theories- historically seen in America
        1.   Learning and experience
    B.   Epigenetic theories- historically seen in Europe
        1.   Interaction between environment and subjects' genetic inheritance

VI.   Scope versus Precision
    A.   A theory's usefulness is measured in terms of its leading to accurate predictions
        1.   Too broad a scope (a Grand Theory) allows for less precision and less accurate predictions.
    B.   The complexity of human behavior and the goals of psychology
        1.   Human development is so broad and complex, and individuals so variable, we must limit our scope to retain precision, adding bit by bit to expand our theories through observation and experimentation
        2.   Goals: to develop a science with predictive power in spite of the complex variables of human systems

Application: The ethical and legal responsibilities of experimenting with children
    A.   Ethical standards for research
    B.   Related problems and the responsibilities of psychologists
    C.   The rights of children
    D.   The consent by proxy problem

At Issue: How Broad is the Scope of Child Research?
    1.   Contributions from other disciplines to the study of child development.
    2.   *YOU practice on the rest of this one.*

NAMES TO REMEMBER

Connect these to their accomplishments or theories:

John Locke -- children born a blank slate for the environment to shape.

Now it's your turn:

Captain James Cook
Jean Jacques Rousseau
The British Naturalists
Charles Darwin
G. Stanley Hall
Sigmund Freud
Alfred Binet
Arnold Gesell
Louis Terman

Jean Piaget
Margaret Mead
Albert Bandura
A.P.A.
National Commission for Protection of Human Subjects
John Dworetzky -- *(better get this one)*
Your Instructor -- *(Yup! You'd better get this one too!)*

TERMS AND CONCEPTS

Knowing these will make tests much easier. Go over this list as a "quickie" review.

developmental psychology
childhood
qualitative
quantitative
the scientific inquiry
psychology
naturalist
cognitive development
behaviorism
infantile sexuality
nature vs. nurture
stability vs. change
temperament theories
continuity vs. discontinuity
linear progression
nonlinear progression
the "baby-boom"

research methods
the dimensions of research
descriptive vs. explanatory
naturalistic vs. manipulative
historical vs. ahistorical
theoretical vs. serendipitous
basic vs. applied
single subject vs. group
the experimental design
definitions and reliability
variables
controlled variables
independent variable
dependent variable
experimental and control groups
observer and subject bias
double-blind

replication and expansion
single subject design
time, A-B-A, A-B-A-B designs
correlational method
correlation vs. causation
prediction vs. causation
case studies
cross-cultural research
longitudinal approach
cross-sectional approach

time-lag design
sequential design
cohort
a theory
environmental theories
epigenetic theories
ethical and legal aspects
psychological damage
informed consent
ethical standards

■ ■ ■ ■

GUIDED REVIEW

Look for the answers as you read two or three paragraphs at a time.

1. In the 18th century, John Locke proposed that children were born as if a __blank slate__ on which __culture__ would determine the behavior of the child.

2. Captain James Cook added support to this idea when his trip to __Tahiti__ revealed the local culture's attitude toward __sex__ education was very different from his home continent.

3. Jacques Rousseau proposed his philosophical ideas, saying that the goal of childhood education should be to offset the influences of __institutions__ that would interfere with the development of "__natural man__."

4. The 19th century brought improved efforts toward scientific observations by the __British Naturalists__. Their systematic recordings of change over time marked the beginning of contemporary __developmental psychology__.

5. In his recordings of nature, Charles Darwin, demonstrated the force of __time__ as a factor during which many __changes__ can occur. He referred to this process as __evolution__.

6. Real progress was made by G. Stanley Hall, who was the first to study children in a __laboratory__ He studied the topics of children's __perception, learning__, and __memory__.

7. Among Hall's accomplishments were that he was the first to earn a __Ph D__ in Psychology, and that he was the founder of the __American Psychology Association__.

8.   A new theory was proposed in the late 1800's and early 1900's, by Sigmund Freud, who declared that the years of __early__ __childhood__ were the foundation of the __adult__ personality. He introduced the idea of __infantile__ __sexuality__.

9.   A French researcher, __Alfred Binet__, developed the first tests to study intellectual differences in children.

10.   An American psychologist, __Arnold__ __Gesell__, systematically compared age-related differences in social, motor, emotional and physical development among children.

11.   While __Jean__ __Piaget__ studied children's cognitive development, __John__ __Watson__, the founder of American behaviorism, was writing and lecturing about child psychology and parenting.

12.   The __baby__ __boom__ after World War II reversed the previously downward trend of interest in child development, placing a greater emphasis on the __scientific__ approach.

13.   Three major issues emerged as empirical methods were applied to child development. They were __nature__ vs. __nurture__, __stability__ vs. __change__, and __continuity__ vs. __discontinuity__.

14.   A most important finding in the nature vs. nurture issue is that it is the __interaction__ between the __two__ that determines development.

15.   In the developmental issue of __stability__ vs. __change__, certain behavioral characteristics are seen as relatively consistent over time, while others are seen as __changing__ throughout the life span. In the issue of __continuity__ vs. __discontinuity__ development is characterized either as a linear progression, or as occurring in __abrupt__ __shifts__.

16.   The six dimensions of developmental research illustrate the systematic methods of : __observing__, __recording__, and __describing__ events used in all psychological research.

17.   __Experiments__ are conducted so that scientists can determine the effects of different variables on __behavior__.

18.   The first step in an experiment is to choose a __testable issue__.

19.   Terminology used in an experiment must be clearly __defined__. In addition, to avoid subjective interpretations of the behaviors, __comparisons__ are made of two or more observers' recordings and measurements. This technique gives us __interobserver reliability__.

20.   If the study involves the use of two groups of subjects, one group will be called the __control__ group, the other the __experimental__ group. The division of subjects into these

groups must be done __randomly__ to allow each group to be compared to the other.

21. All variables are held constant for each group except one. If there is a difference in behavior between the two groups, at the end of the experiment, the only variable responsible for the difference would be the one that the two groups __didn't__ __share__. This variable is known as the __indep.__ __variable__.

22. Both __observers__ and __subjects__ may show bias in the experiment according to their __expectations__. To control for either bias, a __double__ __blind__ experiment is conducted so that neither subjects nor observers know who is in which group.

23. The __statistical__ __analysis__ of the compared behaviors will show mathematically if the difference between the two groups is significant. The behavior of the subjects in the groups is known as the __dependent variable__.

24. "If it hasn't happened twice, it hasn't happened" illustrates the need for __replication__.

25. If our experiment generates more questions than we addressed, we will want to __expand__ our research.

26. Time is the control in __single__ __subject__ experiments.

27. Introducing a stimulus, observing the subject's behavior, then withholding the stimulus and watching to see if there is a change in the behavior, is called the __ABA__ design. Reintroducing that stimulus and observing the resulting behavior will verify the above design and is known as the __ABAB__ design.

28. Although surveys and questionnaires are ways of gathering information, it is important to note that there are flaws in this design as a scientifically __valid__ method. Three reasons for this are
    1. __respondents may show bias__,
    2. __questioning methods may influence subj. answers__, and
    3. __sample pop may not represent whole pop.__

29. A __correlation__ is a relationship between two variables.

30. It is important to recognize that we cannot assume __causation__ because of this __correlation__.

31. Correlations allow us to make __predictions__ and give us __information__ which may be verified by conducting a scientific __experiment__.

32. Age as a variable has been used in the two basic methods of research known as the __longitudinal__ and __cross__ __sectional__ approaches.

33. In __cross__ __sectional__ research, large numbers of subjects close in age, or

__cohorts__ can be observed and measured at one time. These studies are limited in that they don't consider earlier __history__ variables which affect the subjects studied.

34. __Longitudinal__ research studies the same individuals by making repeated measurements over several years or life stages. These are limited by the expense and __loss__ of subjects over the long study period.

35. Efforts to eliminate problems in earlier designs include time-lag research, which helps control for cultural effects or variations over time, and the __Sequential__ design, which combines the best of __Cross__ __sectional__ , __longitudinal__ and __time__ __lag__ designs.

36. Data, ideas and hypotheses which have been organized to explain a body of information are called __theories__ .

37. Human development theory is challenged to develop accurate predictability because it is the study of __complex__ systems rather than that of __fundamental__ forces such as physicists address.

38. To protect children's rights during the studies, professionals must follow __ethical__ __principals__ such as we see in the Application section.

39. Two major issues here are the prevention of __psychological damage__ to children, and the discretion of parents when they give __informed__ __consent__ by proxy.

40. A short definition of developmental psychology is that it is the study of __age related differences in behavior__ .

■■■

PRACTICE TEST 1

1. Until the twentieth century, childhood was seen as a time which was
   a. unique and special in human development
   b. an exceptional period of human need
   c. only quantitatively different from adulthood
   d. a matter of dependence and/or neglect

2. The roots of developmental psychology are found in the works of
   a. John Locke
   b. Jean Jacques Rousseau
   c. Captain James Cook
   d. philosophers whose questions sparked empirical investigations

3.   Empirical efforts to record the development of living creatures including humans are credited to
   a.   18 century philosophers
   b.   the British naturalists and Charles Darwin
   c.   G. Stanley Hall
   d.   John Watson

4.   The first developmental psychologist is considered to be
   a.   John Watson.
   b.   G. Stanley Hall.
   c.   Sigmund Freud
   d.   Charles Darwin.

5.   Sigmund Freud's dynamic theories of early childhood and _____ sparked a new interest in how children's development related to adulthood.
   a.   intellectual development
   b.   infantile sexuality
   c.   physical and emotional development
   d.   social progress

6.   Alfred Binet, Arnold Gesell, Jean Piaget and John Watson investigated _____, _____, _____, and _____, respectively.
   a.   intelligence, motor and physical development, cognition, child rearing practices.
   b.   intelligence, cognition, child rearing practices, motor and physical development.
   c.   motor and physical development, intelligence, child rearing practices, cognition.
   d.   child rearing practices, intelligence, motor and physical development, cognition.

7.   Basic research advances _____, while applied research advances _____.
   a.   technology, knowledge
   b   descriptions of what has occurred, explanations of how it occurred
   c   new knowledge, the application of knowledge to technology
   d.   laboratory observations, observations in a natural setting.

8.   The first task in a properly constructed experiment is to
   a   choose a testable issue.
   b.   choose a testable group
   c.   choose a testable variable
   d.   Replicate and expand a testable subject.

9.   Bias is a concern of the conscientious experimenter and can be seen in _____ and _____.
   a.   the unshared variable; the resulting behavior
   b.   the observer(s); the subject(s)
   c.   the control group; the experimental group
   d.   a group study; in a single subject study.

10.   If there is a difference between the experimental and control groups at the end of our experiment, the reason would be

a.   the subject bias has not been eliminated
b.   observer bias has not been controlled for
c.   the result of the one variable both groups had not shared
d.   all of the above

11.   A single subject design uses ___ as a control.
a.   statistics
b.   manipulation of the subject
c.   time
d.   expansion

12.   A correlation is a relationship between variables or events which
a.   explains the cause of the variables
b.   is a cause and effect statement
c.   allows predictions to be made
d.   is always a coincidence

13.   Longitudinal studies _____, while cross sectional studies _____.
a.   measure the same individuals over a long period of time; measure large numbers of subjects at the same time.
b.   are not concerned about early development of the subjects; tend to lose subjects during the time of study.
c.   involve old people only; involve only children
d.   are less expensive than cross sectional; are more subject to societal events than longitudinal

14.   Environmental theories are those which explain or predict behavior based on
a.   the person's learning and past experience
b.   the genetic inheritance of the subject
c.   both a and b.
d.   neither a nor b.

15.   Contributions from other disciplines enhance our knowledge. They
a.   include anthropologists, biologists, physicians, and other social and natural scientists
b.   are frequently scientifically verified
c.   provide developmental scientists opportunities to broaden their scope of research
d.   all of these

■ ■ ■ ■

PRACTICE TEST 2

1.   Prior to the 20th century, childhood was seen as
a.   a special developmental time

b. the time of personality development

c. a time of scientific study of parenting

d. no special period except for educational needs

2. John Locke preceded behaviorism with his notion that individuals were born

 a. evil.

 b. a blank slate.

 c. inherently good.

 d. to change as they learned to control their world.

3. G. Stanley Hall was the first to

 a. study children's thought processes in a laboratory.

 b. earn a Ph.D. in psychology.

 c. found the American Psychological Association.

 d. all of the above.

4. Empirical studies of human development promoted three major issues. They are

 a. nature vs. nurture

 b. stability vs. change

 c. continuity vs. discontinuity

 d. all of these (I know, much too easy)

5. Sigmund Freud and Alfred Binet had quite different interests in child development. Freud's dynamic theory addressed _____, while Binet's concern was _____.

 a. sexuality; cultural influences.

 b. behaviors learned in the environment; intelligence

 c. early childhood experiences; intellectual functions

 d. Rites of Venus; neurotic behaviors

6. The following is an example of naturalistic vs. manipulative research:

 a. understanding the cause of AIDS; finding a cure for AIDS

 b. watching ape behavior in the wild; controlling ape behavior in the laboratory.

 c. studying groups averages second grade reading scores; studying the development of one second grader's reading improvement

 d. developing a computerized reading score analyzer; recording children's phonic lessons

7. "If a tree falls in the forest, does it make a noise?" This is an illustration of the

 a. need for careful definitions of terms

 b. need for a tape recorder

 c. need for a controlled variable

 d. need for a case study

8. The purpose of the control group in an experiment is

 a. to control for age, and sex bias

 b. to provide a comparison to the experimental group

    c.   to control for subject bias
    d.   both a and b

9.   Observer and subject bias can be controlled in an experiment by
    a.   conducting a double blind experiment
    b.   doing a statistical analysis
    c.   manipulating the variables
    d.   expanding the experiment

10.   In the text book experiment, the degree of violence in the cartoons shown to the two groups was the _____ variable, while the amount of aggressive behaviors shown by the children in each group after seeing the cartoons was called the _____ variable.
    a.   independent; dependent
    b.   dependent; independent
    c.   extraneous; dependent
    d.   extraneous; independent

11.   A design which would illustrate a single subject study, could be expressed in terms of time and the conditions under which behavior occurs. It could be described in the following two ways
    a.   A-B-A and A-B-A-B.
    b.   K-X-Y-Z and W-X-Y-Z.
    c.   K-O-O-L and W-A-R-M.
    d.   T-L-C and T-C-B.

12.   What term is used by experimenters when two variables or events occur in the same space or time?
    a.   causation
    b.   coincidence
    c.   a fluke
    d.   correlation

13.   An example of a longitudinal study would be _____, while an example of the cross sectional study is _____.
    a.   intelligence test scores in childhood as they relate to later life; independent studies of three different age groups of toddlers
    b.   the effect of violent cartoons on children; the effect of vitamin therapy on the elderly
    c.   the independence of 2 year olds; the independence of 6 year olds
    d.   the effect of an alcoholic adult on his/her relationships; the effect of an alcoholic parent on the children

14.   A theory which emphasizes the interaction between a person's environment and his genetic heritage would be called:
    a.   personality theory
    b.   psychoanalytic theory
    c.   epigenetic theory
    d.   environmental theory

15. Ethical practices in using a child in an experiment
    a. require parental consent
    b. require informed parental consent
    c. require written, informed parental consent
    a. require a legally approved, written, informed consent

ANSWER SECTION

Guided Review

1. blank slate, culture or environment
2. Tahiti, sex
3. institutions, "natural man"
4. British naturalists, developmental psychology
5. time, changes, evolution
6. laboratory, perception, learning, memory
7. Ph.D., American Psychological Association
8. early childhood, adult, infantile sexuality
9. Alfred Binet
10. Arnold Gesell
11. Jean Piaget, John Watson
12. baby boom, scientific
13. nature vs. nurture, stability vs. change, continuity vs. discontinuity
14. interaction, two
15. stability, change, changing, continuity, discontinuity, abrupt shifts
16. observing, recording, describing
17. experiments, behavior
18. testable issue
19. defined, comparisons, interobserver reliability
20. control, experimental, randomly
21. didn't share, independent variable
22. observers, subjects, expectations, double blind
23. statistical analysis. dependent variable
24. replication
25. expand
26. single subject
27. A-B-A, A-B-A-B
28. valid; (1) repondents may show bias, (2) questioning methods may influence subjects' answers, (3) sample population may not represent population as a whole
29. correlation
30. causation, correlation
31. predictions, information, experiment
32. longitudinal, cross sectional
33. cross sectional, cohorts, historical
34. longitudinal, loss
35. sequential, cross sectional, longitudinal, time lag
36. theories
37. complex, fundamental
38. ethical principles
39. psychological damage, informed consent
40. age related differences in behavior

<u>*Practice Test 1*</u>

1.	c	9.	b
2.	d	10.	c
3.	b	11.	c
4.	b	12.	c
5.	b	13.	a
6.	a	14.	a
7.	c	15.	d
8.	a		

<u>*Practice Test 2*</u>

1.	d	9.	a
2.	b	10.	a
3.	d	11.	a
4.	d	12.	d
5.	c	13.	a
6.	b	14.	c
7.	a	15.	b
8.	d		

CHAPTER TWO

INHERITANCE AND THE BIOLOGICAL FOUNDATIONS OF DEVELOPMENT

■ ■ ■ ■

◀
◀
◀

LEARNING OBJECTIVES

Your friends from that other galaxy are still here. (Have you spelled Latnem-Poleved backwards yet?) Be ready to explain these concepts to them, and ask them about their world. Of course, if you'd rather, get a study group together to practice the vocabulary, and to discuss the issues presented. Use any method that helps you remember!

1. Explain the relative importance of nature versus nurture and why it is a major issue in developmental psychology.
2. Describe the first life on this planet and the presence of chemicals which allowed life to emerge.
3. Discuss our concept of the double helix of DNA. Explain about the DNA code, where it is found, and how it splits. Remember the importance of the fact that it replicates itself. Describe the sections of DNA called genes.
4. Tell them what you know of Charles Darwin and his work on natural selection and diversification. Explain what these terms mean. Be sure to tell them about his view of changes over time and the kind of effect he had on the future discipline of developmental psychology. Define for them what science has discovered about differential reproduction.
5. Notice the findings of anthropologists and geologists dating the emergence of various forms of life on the earth. Like many children, some grown ups may believe that early man and dinosaurs existed at the same time.
6. Describe the numbers of genes we have and how they are arranged and transmitted to the next generation. Tell them how gametes divide differently than body cells, and why it works out so well that way.
7. Talk about Gregor Mendel's contributions to our knowledge of the simple laws of inheritance, including homozygosity, heterozygosity, dominance and recessiveness, phenotypes and genotypes. Get ready! They'll ask how his ideas on garden peas relate to human beings.
8. Be sure to understand about sex-linked disorders and how they occur.
9. Some of your listeners may not know about the ambitious Human Genome Project to map every gene on each human chromosome. Be sure to discuss this project. Many ideas, both pro and con, will

be generated by the possibilities inherent in this project.

10. Explain the complex genetic interactions which take place in humans, and the possible ramifications. Discover modifier genes, and polygenetic inheritance, how PKU occurs, and how other genetic imprinting results in abnormalities.

11. It is important to understand chromosome problems. Down syndrome and fragile X are two examples. You have examples of modern research in the discussion in the text.

12. Screening tests have been used to detect a variety of chromosome and genetic defects. Be familiar with them so you can discuss them and the treatments for repair of defective genes.

13. A good example of the importance of genetics can be shown in the interest in genetic planning and sperm banks. Talk about the problems which have occurred in the one discussed in the text.

14. Talk to them about inherited behaviors. Describe canalized behaviors and sensitive periods. Give them examples. It'll help you all.

15. Compare the practice of positive and negative eugenics and they are still practiced in the present. You may want to do some research on their success in agriculture and animal husbandry.

16. Be sure to find a group to talk about questions raised in the For Discussion section at the end of the chapter. I'm willing to bet you'll have some interesting opinions and something to think about.

■ ■ ■ ■

CHAPTER OUTLINE

In this outline, you get some more practice! Although most of the outline is complete, you are asked to find the information to complete parts of it. Remember, the better you get at this, the more time you'll save!

Chapter Preview: How to build a human being: a look into the future.
Do we really want to manufacture a human being? What ethical considerations occur to you?

I. DNA The essence of Life
    A. John Watson, Francis Crick, Maurice Wilkins, 1953
        1. Nobel Prize for discovery of structure of DNA
        2. The double helix- the twisted ladder of genetics
    B. A,T,G,C, adenine, thymine, cytosine, guanine
        1. Fixed horizontal pairing rule
        2. No rule for vertical sequence
        3. Each section of helix determines code for animal or plant, called gene.
        4. Identical in every cell of that organism
        5. DNA replicates itself; this property distinguishes biology from chemistry
II. Nature - Nurture Revisited: "The Boys From Brazil"
    A. A Clone: an exact replica of an organism derived from one of its cells
    B. The Fictional Novel "The Boys from Brazil" offers nature vs. nurture discussion
        1. Nazi scientist creates clones of Adolf Hitler hoping for similar leader for Nazi Reich
        2. What would happen if it worked? Why wouldn't it work?
           Here's your chance! You fill in three or four items here:
           a. _____
           b. _____

c. _____

d. _____

III. The Evolution of Life
  A. The creation of a Stable Code of DNA
    1. To be stable must:
      a. be able to replicate and pass on copies of itself
      b. code for an external cell membrane that is long lasting and strong
      c. obtain energy from the environment
        (1) energy from process of fermentation
      d. be favored by environment, survive to reproduce--called differential reproduction leading to increased favored codes
  B. Charles Darwin -- considered mid 19th century founder of modern evolutionary biology
    1. Natural selection through natural forces
  C. Diversification and Mutation
    1. Diversification is second major force (natural selection first)
    2. Provides variety within species
    3. Gross as well as minor changes
    4. Error in translation or structure of DNA
      a. point mutation
        (1) replacement of one base by another
        (2) haphazard
        (3) although small, most often has negative effects
          (a) E.g.; a form of bladder cancer
          (b) any code made superior by mutation favored during natural selection
      b. cause of mutations
      Here's another chance for you -- 4 classes of causes
        (1) _____
        (2) _____
        (3) _____
        (4) _____
  D. The Evolution of Modern Humans
    You can summarize Table 2.1 This is worth studying!

IV. Chromosomes and Inheritance
  A. The Nucleus of the Living Cell -- Our Genetic Heritage
    1. Chromosomes- the "colored body"
      a. In humans, 46 total, 23 pairs
      b. made from strands of DNA
      c. genetic code for entire body- differs for each animal and plant

B.   Sex Cells, (Sperm and Egg Cells) -- Gametes
    1.   Contain only 23 chromosomes each
    2.   Divide through meiosis (rather than mitosis)
       a.   when united form 23 pairs so each body cell will have 46
C.   Karyotypes
    1.   Pictured arrangement of chromosome pairs for study
    2.   First 22 pairs called autosomes
    3.   23rd pair called sex chromosomes
       a.   like autosomes except carry sex determining codes
       b.   XX female, one X from mother, one X from father
       c.   XY male, X from mother, Y from father
       d.   male determines sex of child
D.   Mendel's Laws
    1.   Gregor Mendel, mid 1800's
       a.   Observations of traits in crossing garden peas
    2.   Formulated ideas on simple inheritance:
       a.   Alleles -- parental genes affecting the same traits; dominant alleles-- visible, expressed
          recessive alleles-- carried not expressed
          double recessive -- are expressed
          Here's a chance to practice
          homozygous _____
          heterozygous_____
          codominance_____
          phenotype_____
          genotype_____
    3.   Mendel's laws helpful in understanding some traits in humans
      Another chance for you to shine: Give three good examples
       a.   _____
       b.   _____
       c.   _____
    4.   Sex-linked inheritance
       a.   located on 23rd pair of chromosomes
       b.   examples: hemophilia, red-green color blindness, baldness, etc.
         (1)   carried on X, expressed in male
         (2)   Y smaller, doesn't carry as many genes
V.   Complex Genetic Interactions
   A.   Modifier Genes determine how other genes are expressed
     1.   E.g.: phenylketonuria- PKU
     2.   genetic imprinting
       many possibilities. *You find two*
       a.   _____
       b.   _____
   B.   Genetic and Ontogenetic Disorders: missing or added parts to chromosome; monosomies, trisomies, multisomies see Table 2.3
     1.   Down syndrome

       a.   a trisomy on the twenty-first autosome

       b.   physical symptoms

          (a) _____

          (b) _____

       c.   intellectual disability range

       d.   possible causes

          (a) _____

          (b) _____

       e.   association with Alzheimers disease

C.   Other Chromosomal Abnormalities

    1.   Fragile X syndrome

       a.   translocation of genetic information

       b.   symptoms; males

          (a) _____

       c.   symptoms; females

          (a) _____

D.   Detection of Prenatal Defects

    1.   Amniocentesis

       a.   performed if necessary between the 14th and 16th week, for diagnosis of possible abnormality

       b.   some danger involved

       c.   obtain karyotype

    2.   Chorionic Villi Sampling

       a.   can be performed at 10 weeks

       b.   _____

    3.   Flow cytometry with fluorescent insitu hybridization

       a.   "flow with FISH"

       b.   _____

    4.   blood tests

    5.   preimplantation diagnosis

E.   Gene Disorders

    1.   Genetic Counseling

       a.   the family tree

       b.   screening for sex linked trait

    2.   Screening and Treatment of Inherited Disorders

       a.   availability of test

          (1)   Tay-Sachs disease

          (2)   Sickle-cell anemia

          (3)   PKU

          (4)   cystic fibrosis

    3.   Future Outlook

       a.   *This is especially important to you. You do!*

          _____

          _____

          _____

VI.   The Inheritance of Behavior

A.   Polygenetic Inheritance
      1.   several genes work together to determine or modify characteristics
B.   Reflexes
      1.   Reactions to stimuli that are built in
         a.   coughing, blinking, swallowing, breathing
C.   Canalized Behaviors
      1.   An inherited ability to learn particular behaviors
      2.   Using inherited special physical structures to make the behaviors possible
      3.   The learning of these behaviors is almost inevitable
      4.   Can be very strongly or weakly canalized
         a.   Examples in humans: unique language invented to communicate, invention and use of tools
D.   Sensitive Periods
      1.   A prime time in development when an environmental influence is most likely to have an effect on behavior
      2.   Examples:
         a.   possibly sexual roles and preferences
         b.   research shows a sensitive period at 8 to 9 years when viewing violence is likely to influence later violent behavior

Applications--Eugenics
A.   Positive Eugenics: Selective Breeding to Insure Selected Characteristics Deemed Ideal
      1.   E.g., Robert Graham sperm banks
B.   Negative Eugenics: Selective in terms of Eliminating Genetic Defects
      1.   U.S. and other countries
      2.   Robert McIntire's proposal for good parents!
         Hmm! where does he belong?

At Issue: John Watson, co-discoverer of DNA heads the nearly world-wide research team to map the human genome. As you read this carefully, consider the various aspects and consequences, both beneficial and problematic.

NAMES TO REMEMBER

John Watson	Queen Victoria
Francis Crick	Dr. Langdon Down
Maurice Wilkins	C. H. Waddington
Adolf Hitler	Sir Francis Galton
Charles Darwin	Robert Graham
Dr. John Langdon	Roger McIntire
Gregor Mendel	Project SETI

■ ■ ■ ■

TERMS AND CONCEPTS

amino acids, molecules
DNA, deoxyribonucleic acid
gene
clone
nature
nurture
differential reproduction
natural selection
diversification
mutation
point mutation
hominid
primate
chromosome
nucleus
gamete
meiosis
mitosis
karyotype
autosome
sex chromosomes
alleles or allelic genes
dominant
recessive
double recessive
homozygous
heterozygous
phenotype

genotype
multisomies
monosomies
trisomies
Down Syndrome
Tay-Sach's disease
Sickle Cell anemia
genetic code
genetic engineering
genetic imprinting
codominance
sex linked disorder
Fragile X
Prader-Willi Syndrome
Angelman's syndrome
modifier genes
amniocentesis
chorionic villi sampling
flow with FISH
phenylketonuria
polygenic inheritance
canalization
innate
sensitive period
eugenics
positive eugenics
negative eugenics
sperm banks

■ ■ ■ ■

GUIDED REVIEW

1. Four chemicals, _adenine_, _guanine_, _cytosine_, and _thymine_, combine to form the unique _DNA_, which is found in all 60 _trillion_ cells in the human body.

2. The structure of DNA was discovered by James _Watson_ Francis _Crick_ and Maurice _Wilkins_, for which they were awarded the _Nobel_ _prize_ in

1953.

3.   A unique property of DNA is its ability to __make   copies__ of itself, a quality which sets this molecule apart from any other. This property, more than any other, distinguishes biology from __chemistry__.

4.   DNA is arranged in a code which is determined by the __vertical   sequence__ of the base pairs.

5.   Although the __horizontal__ joining of A and T, and C and G follows strict rules, the __vertical__ sequence does not.

6.   The vertical sections or __genes__ determine the protein of the individual organism and form the __blueprint__ for determining the specific characteristics.

7.   The fictional novel <u>The Boys From Brazil</u> suggests what could happen if a __clone__ could be created from a single cell of a living being.

8.   The twins of Adolf Hitler would at least __look__ like the original. However, even with the same genetic make-up, or __nature__ one could not know how the experiences in the environment, or __nurture__ could affect the different clones.

9.   The term __differential reproduction__ defines the survival of organisms whose genetic codes are favorable to the environment and are more likely to be __passed   on__ to the next generation.

10.   __Charles   Darwin__, the founder of modern evolutionary biology, built on this principle, and referred to this as __natural   selection__.

11.   According to Darwin, the great variety of characteristics within a species is due to the second major force in the evolution of life, called __diversification__

12.   The cause of this phenomenon is __mutation__, which usually results in __minor__ changes in the body or the organism.

13.   An error in the structure of DNA limited to the replacement of one base by another is called a __point   mutation__ and can have __negative__ results.

14.   Some external causes of mutations include __ionizing radiation, heat, chemicals__ and __viruses__.

15.   Table 2.1 indicates that __oxygen__ became a part of the earth's atmosphere as a result of a "lucky mutation" allowing certain bacteria to develop the process of __photosynthesis__

16.   Although humans are a members of the broad category of __primates__, modern man has been in existence for only about __100,000__ years.

17. Within the nucleus of each cell in the body lies the genetic material called _chromosomes_

18. In a human body cell there are ___46___ chromosomes or ___23___ pairs, whereas in the human sex cell there are ___23___ chromosomes as a result of ___meiosis___, which splits the pairs in half without replicating the missing half.

19. A photograph of stained pairs is called a ___karyotype___. The XX combination on the 23rd pair shows that the ___daughter___ has received an X from both the ___mother___ and ___father___. She and her brother could have received the sex determining chromosome only from their ___father___.

20. The second X chromosome in females provides a healthy back up allele for the female, but the Y chromosome cannot do this every time because the Y cannot carry as ___many genes___. Poor Ann Boleyn!

21. ___Gregor Mendell___ discovered and developed the basic laws of inheritance as he studied garden peas. He suggested that these characteristics were determined by ___dominant___ and ___recessive___ alleles.

22. His experiments revealed that there were pairs of alleles which are identical, called ___homozygous___ and those that are different, called ___heterozygous___

23. The observable characteristics which are expressed denote the ___phenotype___, while the actual genetic composition is the ___genotype___. Practice using the Punnett square to see this work.

24. Some human characteristics which follow Mendel's laws include eye ___color___, hair ___shape___, and blood ___type___.

25. Characteristics carried by the 23rd pair, which are usually expressed in one sex but not the other, are called ___sex___ - ___linked___.

26. Some sex-linked characteristics include ___baldness, hemophilia___ and ___red___ - ___green___ color blindness.

27. Variations in levels of different characteristics expressed by genes is determined by ___modifier genes___ such as seen in PKU.

28. Genetic anomalies, such as ___monosomies, multisomies___, and ___trisomies___, are seen when a problem arises in the structure of ___chromosomes___.

29. The best known chromosome disorder is a ___trisomy___ on the 21st autosome pair, which results in ___down syndrome___.

30. Mothers younger than ___20___ or older than ___35___, or fathers older than ___55___ are more at risk for having a baby with Down syndrome.

31.   In the United States there are at least __250,000__ individuals with Down syndrome. __40__ % of these have congenital __heart__ __defects__ .

32.   Although 80% of Down syndrome sufferers will reach age __50__ , they will invariably acquire __Alzheimer's disease__ , which suggests there is an association between the two diseases.

33.   Although about half of Down syndrome affected children will reach a reading level of the __second grade__ , they will remain intellectually impaired for their __lifetime__ .

34.   Second to Down syndrome as a cause of mental retardation is __Fragile X__ syndrome, a sex-linked disorder that results in __moderate__ retardation in males and __mild__ retardation in females.

35.   Genetic counseling relies on the use of family __health histories__ , and, since many disorders follow __Mendel's__ laws of inheritance, the counselors can predict the future occurrence of some disorders in the family.

36.   Screening tests, such as those used for the heritable disorders of __Tay Sach's__ disease, __PKU__ , and __Sickel Cell__ anemia, can identify parents or babies who may be carriers of the disorder.

37.   In addition to those above, cystic fibrosis may be detected using a test called __flow cytometry w/__ or "Flow w/ FISH" __fluorescent insitu hybridization__

38.   Only chromosome-related prenatal defects increase in likelihood in relationship to the mother's __age__ .

39.   When one describes behaviors which are inevitably learned and highly resistant to extinction, one is speaking of __canalized__ behaviors. Examples of this in humans would include the use of __tools__ and __talking__ or use of __language__ .

40.   A time when an organism is primed to learn best from an environmental influence is known as a __sensitive period__ .

41.   Since Galton's time, selective breeding or __eugenics__ has been continued to some degree through the controversial use of modern __sperm bank__ .

42.   Robert Graham's attempt to create an elite sperm bank ran into several problems, including
      (1)   __not enough elite donors__
      (2)   __those who did; were older than preferred__
      (3)   __poor screening of recipients__

■ ■ ■ ■

PRACTICE TEST 1

1. _____ is a molecule combined of four base molecules which determine the unique code for the proteins of each different plant or animal on earth.
    a. ABC
    b. KTAR
    c. DNA
    d. ERA

2. DNA's ability to replicate itself
    a. follows a strict rule for human beings
    b. happens in all molecules in chemistry
    c. never occurred
    d. marks the major difference between chemistry and biology

3. A twin created from a single body cell of a living being is a
    a. miniature adult
    b. clone
    c. common occurrence
    d. way to get nature and nurture together

4. _____'s theory of evolution introduced the theme of _____, which is, in essence, the basis of developmental theory.
    a. Urey and Miller's; DNA
    b. Watson, Crick and Wilkins'; positive eugenics
    c. Sir Francis Galton's; natural selection
    d. Charles Darwin; change over time

5. A second major force, called _____, is a useful explanation for the great variety seen within a given species.
    a. natural selection
    b. diversification
    c. evolution
    d. favorable trait selection

6. _____ similar to today's lemurs existed approximately _____ years ago.
    a. Bacteria; 50 million
    b. Humans; 50 million
    c. Primates; 50 million
    d. Amphibians; 50 million

7. On the _____ in _____ cell(s) in the organism lies the genetic code for the entire body.
    a. genes; the brain
    b. chromosomes; every

c.   chromosomes; gamete
d.   genes; the brain

8.   The first 22 pairs are called _____, while the 23rd pair are _____
      chromosomes. They can all be seen by the addition of a stain and a photographic process called
      the _____.
      a.   autosomes; sex; karyotype
      b.   sex; monosomes; X-ray
      c.   autosomes; single cell; X-ray
      d.   multisomes; monosomes; karyotype

9.   The sex of human offspring is determined by
      a.   the mother
      b.   a combination of mother's X and father's Y
      c.   the father
      d.   a 50-50 chance on the 20th pair

10.   Gregor Mendel discovered that some traits in the pea are _____ and some others are
      _____.
      a.   turned on, turned off
      b.   major genes, minor genes
      c.   dominant alleles, recessive alleles
      d.   both a and c

11.   The observable characteristics of a trait denotes the _____, while the actual genetic
      composition denotes the _____.
      a.   homozygous, heterozygous
      b.   double recessive, double recessive
      c.   genotype, phenotype
      d.   phenotype, genotype

12.   All sex-linked disorders
      a.   involve genes on the 23rd pair.
      b.   are only carried by the mother.
      c.   are only carried by the father.
      d.   are passed on to all members of the family.

13.   PKU is an example of how _____ genes can act on other genes to determine the levels at which
      they are expressed.
      a.   sex-linked
      b.   engineered
      c.   modifier
      d.   back-up

14.   The effects of abnormal genetic factors on development can be seen in the effects of an extra
      chromosome on the 21st pair, known as

a.   Down syndrome
b.   Huntington's Disease
c.   Alzheimer's Disease
d.   Wilson's Disease

15.   Although the cause of the trisomy is not understood, there is an association between Down syndrome and
a.   the father's age
b.   the mother's age
c.   errors in the father's sperm
d.   all of the above

16.   Although half of Down syndrome children can attain second grade reading levels,
a.   they improve steadily throughout their lives
b.   they remain intellectually impaired throughout their lives
c.   they are not capable of performing self care skills
d.   they all require institutional care.

17.   Amniocentesis may be performed if necessary during the ___ to ____ weeks to examine the _____ of the fetus.
a.   10th to 12th, structural development
b.   20th to 21, chromosomes
c.   14th to 16th, structural development
d.   14th to 16th, chromosomes

18.   The science of examining fetal genes is still in its early stages, however, genetic counselors can aid prospective parents by
a.   predicting potential genetic disorders by examining the family trees of both parents
b.   predicting sex-linked disorders and suggesting preselection of the sex of the child
c.   both a and b
d.   neither a nor b

19.   During the sensitive periods in the life of the organism
a.   an influence in the environment will have its most profound effect on its behavior.
b.   the organism is unaware of environmental influences.
c.   influences in the environment will have no effect on its behavior.
d.   violence viewed at 5 years old will produce violent behavior in adulthood.

■ ■ ■ ■

PRACTICE TEST 2

1.   As human beings we are combinations of our inherited characteristics and our experiences in our

environment. Said more succinctly, we are the products of the interaction of _____ and
_____.

    a.   nature, discipline.
    b.   our bodies, our minds.
    c.   our knowledge, how we use it.
    d.   nature, nurture.

2.   How the vertical sequence of the base pairs of molecules are arranged on the DNA double helix forms the code for
    a.   the proteins which determine each animal or plant.
    b.   the strict rule for combining the base molecules.
    c.   adenine, thymine, cytosine, guanine.
    d.   the sugar phosphates.

3.   The vertical sequence of the base pairs on DNA is coded into sections called:
    a.   proteins.
    b.   clones.
    c.   genes.
    d.   sex-linked characteristics.

4.   _____, the founder of modern evolutionary biology, proposed that the forces of _____ were responsible for the survival of creatures which were well suited and adapted to their environment.
    a.   Charles Darwin, natural selection.
    b.   Urey, Miller, chemical bases.
    c.   Watson, Crick, DNA.
    d.   Sir Francis Galton, Eugenics.

5.   An error in the translation of the DNA code when one base pair is replaced by another is called
    a.   a horrible mistake.
    b.   a beneficial mutation.
    c.   a point mutation.
    d.   natural selection.

6.   Mutations in a single individual member of a species may be caused by
    a.   ionizing radiation.
    b.   heat.
    c.   various chemicals and viruses.
    d.   all of the above

7.   Modern man has been in existence for _____. However, "hominid" predecessors to man may have existed for approximately _____ years
    a.   80 thousand; 1 to 2 million.
    b.   40 thousand; 3.6 billion.
    c.   15 thousand; 500 million.
    d.   100 thousand; 5 to 14 million.

8.   In the human body, _____ chromosomes are arranged in _____ pairs, except in the
      _____ cells which have _____ chromosomes
      a.   92; 46; gamete
      b.   23; 46; DNA
      c.   46; 23; gamete; 23
      d.   nucleus; 23; sperm and egg; 46

9.   Sex chromosomes differ from autosomes in that they
      a.   are shaped differently depending on which sex code is carried
      b.   also carry the gene to determine the sex of the organism
      c.   are referred to as X, female, and Y male
      d.   all of the above

10.   The fundamental laws of inheritance were discovered by _____ when he found that
      genes he called _____ can affect the same trait.
      a.   Charles Darwin; selective
      b.   Gregor Mendel; alleles
      c.   Watson, Crick; DNA
      d.   Gregor Mendel; gametes

11.   When the alleles in a pair are identical they are
      a.   homozygous
      b.   heterozygous
      c.   phenotype
      d.   genotype

12.   If two brown-eyed parents have a blue eyed child:
      a.   they can't! They will have only brown eyed children since the brown allele is dominant.
      b.   the child is an example of codominance.
      c.   each parent is heterozygous brown.
      d.   they should get a divorce on grounds of infidelity.

13.   Many of the most common sex-linked disorders are carried by _____ and expressed in

      _____.
      a.   males; females.
      b.   royalty; commoners.
      c.   females; males.
      d.   8% of men; 5% of women.

14.   Trisomies, multisomies, and monosomies, are _____ which result in developmental
      disorders such as _____.
      a.   abnormal chromosome pairings; Down, Turner's, and Kleinfelter's syndromes
      b.   gene disorders; Fragile X syndrome, Tay-Sachs disease, sickle cell anemia
      c.   gene disorders; XXYY, XXXY, XXXXYYY
      d.   all of the above

15.   Although 80% of victims of Down syndrome will reach 50 years of age, they are liable to suffer
        from
        a.   lung disease, liver, and pancreas diseases
        b.   fragile X syndrome
        c.   congenital defects, leukemia, Alzheimer's disease
        d.   sensory defects

16.   Males who receive a fragile X chromosome are usually _____, while females are usually
        _____.
        a.   moderately retarded; mildly retarded
        b.   moderately retarded; not retarded
        c.   not retarded; moderately retarded
        d.   less retarded; more retarded

17.   Certain screening tests that have been successful in detecting genetic disease include those for
        a.   Tay-Sach's disease
        b.   Sickle-cell anemia
        c.   PKU
        d.   all of the above

18.   A screening test called _____ has been used to find embryos carrying the
        gene for cystic fibrosis.
        a.   amniocentesis
        b.   flow with Fish
        c.   a blood test
        d.   preimplantation diagnosis

19.   Highly canalized behaviors
        a.   are the same as reflexes.
        b.   are learned very easily and resist extinction in the environment.
        c.   serve little purpose so are not studied in detail.
        d.   are the same as the sensitive period.

ANSWER SECTION

Guided Review

1.   adenine, thymine, cytosine, guanine, DNA, trillion
2.   Watson, Crick, Wilkins, Nobel Prize
3.   make copies, chemistry
4.   vertical sequence
5.   horizontal, vertical
6.   genes, blueprint
7.   clone
8.   look, nature, nurture
9.   differential reproduction, passed on
10.   Charles Darwin, natural selection
11.   diversification
12.   mutation, minor
13.   point mutation, disastrous or negative
14.   ionizing radiation, heat, chemicals, viruses
15.   oxygen, photosynthesis
16.   primates, 100,000
17.   chromosomes
18.   46, 23, 23, meiosis
19.   karyotype, daughter or female, mother, father, father
20.   many genes
21.   Gregor Mendel, dominant, recessive
22.   homozygous, heterozygous
23.   phenotype, genotype
24.   color, shape, type
25.   sex-linked
26.   baldness, hemophilia, red-green
27.   modifier genes
28.   monosomies, multisomies, trisomies, chromosomes
29.   trisomy, Down Syndrome
30.   20, 35, 55
31.   250,000, 40%, heart defects
32.   50, Alzheimer's disease
33.   second grade, lifetime
34.   Fragile X, moderate, mild
35,   health histories, Mendel's
36.   Tay-Sachs, PKU, Sickle-cell
37.   flow cytometry with fluorescent insitu hybridization, "flow with FISH"
38.   age
39.   canalized; tools, talking, language
40.   sensitive period
41.   eugenics, sperm banks

42.   *not enough elite donors, those who did donate were older than preferred, poor screening of recipients*

<u>Practice Test 1</u>

1.	c		11.	d
2.	d		12.	a
3.	b		13.	c
4.	d		14.	a
5.	b		15.	d
6.	c		16.	b
7.	b		17.	d
8.	a		18.	a
9.	c		19.	a
10.	d			

<u>Practice Test 2</u>

1.	d		11.	a
2.	a		12.	c
3.	c		13.	c
4.	a		14.	a
5.	c		15.	c
6.	d		16.	a
7.	d		17.	d
8.	c		18.	b
9.	d		19.	b
10.	b			

CHAPTER THREE

CONCEPTION, PRENATAL DEVELOPMENT, AND BIRTH

■ ■ ■ ■

◀
◀
◀

LEARNING OBJECTIVES

Your make-believe listeners are full of questions. Can you imagine how beings on other planets approach the issues of reproduction as discussed in this chapter? Ah well, back to earth. These are fascinating topics to compare notes with members of your study group. Be able to discuss the following:

1. Let them know how it takes two to tango! And tell them how the union of a male sperm and a female ova ensures diversity, thus giving our species the best chance of survival.
2. Describe the problems that may occur to prevent conception. Detail the effects of the woman's age, blocked or scarred fallopian tubes, the fat to lean tissue ratio, and even drinking milk in some cases.
3. As you explain the development of the fetus from zygote to neonate, be sure to include what happens as the baby is forming during the major periods after conception. See table 3.1. Discuss each period so they can see the changes during the different developmental phases.
4. Discuss how prospective parents can avoid many of the threats to the developing embryo or fetus. To paraphrase your author, think of the developing child in terms of the fact that he/she is the most complex chemical reaction known.
5. Explain the various teratogens and pathogens that may adversely affect the fetus.
6. You'll want to explain the labor and delivery processes. Be sure to include the stages of labor, and the birthing methods used to help the mother and the baby.
7. Be able to discuss the neonatal assessment methods used right after birth. Tell your listeners how the major methods are used.
8. Explain the studies of premature babies and what we've learned to help them get a good start. Discuss low birth weight babies and the risks involved, as well possible ways to avoid them.
9. Tell them about the ways multiple births occur and, for those of you who've had the experience, the joys and difficulties involved.
10. You'll want to provide information to them about the recommendations of the World Health Organization regarding family planning.

11. A lively discussion will probably occur when you talk to other mothers about the pros and cons of breast feeding.

12. Exciting new technologies of conception are in practice and being researched now. The discussion in the Application Section "A Brave New World" will provide another topic for an interesting discussion of ethical considerations.

■ ■ ■ ■

◀
◀

CHAPTER OUTLINE

◀

You'll be filling in more this time, so read carefully!

Chapter Preview: The Lamaze Method
I. Conception
    A. Diversity
        1. Millions of combinations through uniting of mother's and father's code insure better chance of surviving natural selection
    B. Conception
        1. Fertilization: normally takes place in the fallopian tubes. Only one sperm accepted by ovum
        2. Fertility of female
            a. 73% in women 25 yrs and younger
            b. 74% _____
            c. 61% _____
            d. 54% _____
                (1) older women fail to ovulate regularly
                (2) slowed down hormone levels
                (3) scarred or blocked fallopian tubes from past infections and endometriosis
            e. ratio of body fat to lean tissue
            f. the studies of the effect of galactose in milk on the human egg.
II. The Period of the Ovum: from conception to attachment in uterus. The first two weeks
    A. The Zygote: The Fertilized Ovum
        1. Fertilized ovum travels to uterus in 3 or 4 days
        2. Now called blastocyst and floats in uterus for approx. 48 hours
        3. Two layers form in blastocyst
            a. ectoderm-
            b. endoderm-
            c. developing later - mesoderm --
        4. Attaches to wall of uterus through outer cells (now called trophoblast cells) which penetrate lining of uterus forming nurturing connections
III. The Period of the Embryo: 2nd to 8th week- until Ossification
    A. Trophoblast signals mother's body "a baby is forming"
        1. Triggers "dampening" response in immune system to prevent mother's antibodies

from attacking embryo
    a.   "dampening" response effects on autoimmune diseases
  2.   1 of 300 abort because of immune system attack
    a.   problem helped by inoculating mother with husband's cells to make mother more sensitive to "baby forming" message.
  3.   Immunoglobulin protection for fetus
  4.   Rapid cellular division occurring

B.   Cellular Specialization - Differentiation
  1.   DNA code for entire body in each cell
  2.   Some parts of DNA active, others inactive depending on how and which cells are to be differentiated
  3.   Process not fully understood

C.   Auxiliary life-supporting structures developed
  1.   Umbilical Cord
    a.   major blood vessels which pass through placenta to and from mother
  2.   Placenta
    a.   semi-permeable membranes
    b.   nutrients and wastes pass through- no blood exchange
    c.   mother's antibodies can't pass through to attack as foreign body
    d.   allows immunoglobulins to enter embryo
        (1)   provides mother's disease resistance

D.   Physical Features
  1.   At 4 weeks 1/5th inch long _____
_____

E.   Spontaneous Abortion
  1.   Approx 31% _____
  2.   Assumed high proportion are abnormal embryos
  3.   Often mother not aware
  4.   95% women go on to have successful pregnancies

IV.   The period of the Fetus--8 weeks to birth. see table 3.1
  A. Changes in the Development of the Fetus
  1.   8 weeks : beginning of bone development = ossification
    a.   ___ 1 inch long, resembles human
  2.   5th month
    a.   _____
  3.   6th month
    a.   _____
  4.   7th month
    a.   _____
  5.   8th month
    a.   _____
  6.   9th month
    a.   _____

V.   Adverse Influences on Prenatal Development:
Psychologists concern for effect on child's development and the reactions of others to child's handicap and child's self esteem

A. Teratogens: Dangerous substances which enter the intrauterine environment
   1. Cigarette smoking in mother
      a. carbon monoxide levels in mother's blood increases
         (1) carbon monoxide chosen over oxygen and carried over placental barrier to embryo
         (2) Lack of oxygen suffocating to embryo, damage possible
            (a) can be expressed later in learning difficulties
      b. 3000+ chemicals in smoke
         (1) E.g.: nicotine constricts mother's capillaries, a further deprivation of oxygen
      c. may affect lung and heart development in fetus
      d. increased chance of placenta separation from womb leading to miscarriage;
      e. malformation of heart and other organs
      f. may contribute to Sudden Infant Death Syndrome
      g. lower birth weight
      h. 40% risk of fallopian tube pregnancy
   2. When fathers smoke
         (1) mother inhales second-hand smoke
         (2) can affect sperm production--fertility, abnormal sperm
   3. Alcohol: even small amounts for mother are huge for fetus
      a. fetal alcohol syndrome
         (1) _____
         (2) _____
         (3) _____
         (4) brain weight and damage to specific brain areas
            (a) _____
            (b) _____
            © _____
      b. no alcohol is better than some--no safe level
      c. occasional binge drinking dangerous too
      d. not all babies affected by either smoking or alcohol
         (1) choose to play the odds
         (2) risk quadrupled if mother uses both cigarettes and alcohol
   3. Caffeine--coffee, soft drinks, cocoa, etc.
      a. lower birth weights possible,
      b. higher probability of miscarriage and reduced fertility seen in some studies
      c. when in doubt - DON'T
   4. Other drugs
      a. Other addictive drugs- heroine, marijuana, cocaine, morphine etc.
         (1) if mother is addicted so is newborn
         (2) studies of father's use show potential danger to sperm as cocaine can bind to sperm
      b. other tranquilizers, antibiotics, anticonvulsives
         (1) _____
      c. over the counter medications _____
   5. Anesthesia and Analgesia, some antibiotics

      a   _____

      b.   _____

6. Trade off needs to be examined carefully. Take only when absolutely necessary.
7. Number of drugs typically taken during pregnancy -- 11
8. Environmental Hazards
   a. chemical wastes and pollution
      (1) _____
   b. heavy metals
      (1) _____
      (2) _____
   c. heat
      (1) _____
      (2) _____
   d. radiation
      (1) _____

B. Pathogens
   1. Toxoplasmosis
      a. _____
      b. _____
   2. Viruses
      a. Rubella in mother, first three months
         (1) effects on infant _____
      b. Cytomegalovirus
         (1) in female genital tract
         (2) _____
      c. Genital Herpes
         (1) _____
         (2) _____
         (3) _____
      d. Slow Viruses
         (1) _____
         (2) _____
      e. AIDS
         (1) _____
         (2) _____ Use extra room in your notes
   3. Rh Incompatibility
      a. _____
      b. _____
      c. _____
      d. treatment _____
   4. Diet: maternal
      a. premature births
      b. low birth weight
      c. poorly developed nervous system
   5. Emotional Stress
      a. Mother's increased production of adrenaline diverts blood supply to vital

                organs
         b.   limited research shows low birth weight in infants
         c.   help during labor with labor coach
                (1)   less anxiety
                (2)   shorter labor
      6.   Need for Reasonable Care During Pregnancy
         a._____

VII.   Parental Planning
      A.   Recommendations of the World Health Organization
          1.   _____
          2.   _____
          3.   _____
          4.   _____
          5.   _____

VIII.   Birth, 270 days, or Approximately 9 months
      A.   The Three Stages of Labor after lightening
          1.   Stage One: averages 13 hours
            a.   increase in MMP causes amniotic sac to rupture
            b.   uterine contractions begin 10 -20 minutes apart
            c.   10 to 15% require special equipment for delivery
          2.   Stage Two: average 90 minutes
            a.   cervix dilates
            b.   baby moves down birth canal
                (1)   levels of adrenaline and noradrenaline (catecholamines) increase in fetus
                (2)   adrenaline aids in opening lungs, drying bronchi, facilitates breathing air
                (3)   noradrenaline slows heartbeat, lessens demand for oxygen
            c.   mother uses abdominal muscles to help
                (1)   birthing bar
            d.   position of baby at birth
                (1)   97% _____
                (2)   2.4% _____
            e.   anoxia - oxygen deprivation
                (1)   placenta detaches prematurely
                (2)   _____
                (3)   _____
                (4)   _____
            f.   Cesarean section--surgical opening of the abdomen to deliver infant
                (1)   used less frequently than in past
                (2)   new techniques allow for normal subsequent deliveries
            g.   Birth of infant ends stage 2
          3.   Stage Three
            a.   placenta, etc. expelled
            b.   episiotomy stitched, other after care

IX.   Multiple Births: Twins, Triplets, Quadruplets, etc.

A.   Identical twins--zygote splits or fissions into two identical zygotes

B.   Fraternal twins--two separate eggs fertilized at once

       1.   no more alike than other brothers and sisters

       2.   superfecundity _____

X.   Assessments of Neonates

    A.   APGAR Assessment Scale

       1.   Administered _____

       2.   Measures

               _____

       3.   Indicates overall condition of baby or need for medical assistance

       4.   Good predictor of later neurological or muscular problems

    B.   Brazelton Neonatal Behavioral Assessment Scale

       1.   Scores on 27, nine point behavioral scales, reflexes, response to touch and voices

       2.   More difficult and time consuming than APGAR but gives more detail re: kinds of infant needs

XI.   Premature Births: 7% in US, accounts for 65% of newborn deaths

    A.   Carried less than 37 weeks

    B.   Weight less than 5 ☐ lbs

    C.   "Small for gestational age", full term, less than 5 ☐ lbs

    D.   Underweight infants 40 times more likely to die in first month

       1.   Respiratory problems

       2.   Poor reflexes

       3.   More susceptible to infection

       4.   Later problems in small percentage of premature infants

           a.   learning difficulties

           b.   lower I.Q.

           c.   hearing, vision impairment

           d.   physical awkwardness

       5.   Mothers less responsive to premature infants

           a.   compare to full term inaccurately, unfavorably

           b.   Premature infants who show inconsistent sleep-wake states most likely to develop problems

           c.   gentle touching and handling in incubators aids in 47% faster weight gain

       6.   Prevention of premature deliveries

           a.   drugs to relax uterus and postpone labor

           b.   at risk mothers screened and watched for immediate intercession

       7.   Full term - low weight infant. High infant morality rate correlation

AT ISSUE: Infant Mortality

Notice the advantages of a comprehensive prenatal care program. You outline this one.

E.   Breast feeding: preferred more over last 20 years
    1.   Mothers of premature infants produce milk higher in protein and fat
    2.   Human milk offers wide range of host resistant factors
        a.   Higher levels of amino acids - taurine and cystine
        b.   _____
        c.   _____
        d.   _____
    3.   Fewer food allergies, coughs, respiratory problems, diarrhea
    4.   Contains additional chemicals to nourish the brain
    5.   Offers protection through
        a.   mucin ,_____
        b.   retinoic acid _____
        c.   glycoprotein _____
        d.   kappa-casein _____
        e.   interluken 10 _____

APPLICATION: A Brave New World   *Outline this one too! There are a few surprises!*

■ ■ ■ ■

NAMES TO REMEMBER

Fernand Lamaze

Grantly Dick-Read

World Health Organization

U.S. Collaborative Perinatal Project

T. B. Brazelton

Virginia Apgar

Evelyn Thoman

Howard and Georgeanna Jones

Ronald Ericsson

D.B. Jelliffe

E.F.P. Jelliffe

■ ■ ■ ■

TERMS AND CONCEPTS

The Lamaze Method

childbirth

conception

fallopian tubes

endometriosis

period of the ovum

zygote

blastocyst

trophoblast

uterine epithelium

period of the embryo

differentiation

cellular specialization

immunoglobulins

umbilical cord

placenta

"baby is forming"
"dampening"
spontaneous abortion
the period of the fetus
fetus
gestation period
teratogens
placenta previa
fetal alcohol syndrome
pathogens
toxoplasmosis
rubella
cytomegalovirus
slow virus
AIDS
herpes
anoxia
birth
lightening
labor and stages of labor
ultrahigh-frequency sound scans

birthing bar
catecholamines
cesarean section
breech birth
shoulder presentation
premature infant
APGAR assessment
Brazelton Neonatal Behavioral Assessment Scale
neonate
infant mortality
premature infants
multiple births
identical twins
fraternal Twins
superfecundity
the breast feeding issue
in-vitro fertilization
GIFT
gender preselection
artificial womb

■ ■ ■ ■

GUIDED REVIEW

1. Learning the specific techniques of relaxation, breathing properly, and control of muscular responses, characterizes the _lamaze_ method of childbirth.

2. When the father's sperm and the mother's ova unite, the new codes can result in _diversification_ giving the species a better chance of surviving the _natural selection_ process.

3. Conception usually takes place in the _fallopian tubes_ where a reaction occurs immediately to prevent additional _sperm_ from entering the _ova_.

4. Assuming both parents are healthy, one variable, the woman's _age_ is most influential. The chances of becoming pregnant are best for women between _26_ and _30_ years.

5. The reason older women have a more difficult time becoming pregnant is that they often fail to _ovulate_ due to lower _hormone_ levels.

6.   A fertilized ovum, or ___Zygote___ takes 3 or 4 days to reach the ___uterus___, where it attaches itself. The process takes ___2___ ___weeks___ to complete.

7.   The period of the Embryo lasts from ___two___ ___weeks___ after fertilization to the ___8th___ ___week___ when ___ossification___ begins to occur.

8.   Upon implantation, the trophoblast signals the mother's immune system that a ___baby___ is forming in order to prevent the mother's ___antibodies___ from attacking the embryo.

9.   Not all of mother's antibodies are a threat to the embryo. Some, the ___immunoglobulins___, provide ___disease___ ___resistance___.

10.   When cells develop into skin, blood, and nerve cells etc., cellular ___differentiation___ or ___specialization___ is said to have occurred.

11.   The life support structures called the ___placenta___ and the ___umbilical___ ___cord___ connect the mother and embryo for the purpose of passing in ___nutrients___ and expelling ___waste___.

12.   Approximately ___31___ % of all women experience spontaneous abortion. However, ___96___ % of these women eventually have successful pregnancies.

13.   The period of the ___fetus___ lasts from ___8___ ___weeks___ until birth.

14.   By the end of the seventh month, the fetus will respond to light by ___closing___ its eyes. Ultrahigh-frequency scans may even reveal the fetus sucking its thumb or having the ___hiccups___.

15.   By the eighth month the fetus weighs about ___5___ lbs. Development of the ___brain___ is rapid. However, the ___lungs___ need more time.

16.   ___Teratogens___ are substances capable of causing abnormalities in the fetus. Some examples of these are (try for 5 or 6)
      1. ___nicotine___
      2. ___alcohol___
      3. ___tranquilizers___
      4. ___cocaine___
      5. ___antibiotics___
      6. ___anticonvulsants___

17.   Many disease processes or ___pathogens___ threaten the fetus. Name as many as you can:
      1. ___toxoplasmosis___
      2. ___cytomegalovirus___
      3. ___rubella___
      4. ___herpes___
      5. ___slow viruses___

6. _AIDS_

18. An Rh factor problem will occur if the father's blood is Rh _positive_ and the mother's is Rh _negative_.

19. The Lamaze method recommends that the birthing experience will be made less stressful and labor will be shortened if the mother receives _support_ from her _husband_ or another close friend.

20. Good advice to couples planning to have a family offered by WHO suggests spacing the children at least _two_ _years_ apart.

21. Birth occurs approximately _270_ days or _9_ months after conception, with labor divided into _3_ stages.

22. The second stage of labor may be shortened by the use of a _birthing_ _bar_ to help the mother maintain an upright position. At the end of stage two the baby is _born_.

23. The hormones called _catecholamines_ aid the infant's transition from the womb environment, and through delivery, to the new demands made on its respiratory system.

24. Although most babies are born head first, 2.4% present _breech_ or _rump_ first.

25. If there is danger to the mother or baby using a normal birthing technique, the baby may be taken by _Cesearean section_. If this is done, future deliveries may be accomplished _vaginally_.

26. Identical twins are the result of the _splitting_ of _one_ _zygote_. Fraternal twins are the result of the fertilization of _two_ _seperate_ _ova_.

27. The _APGAR_ test is used to measure five dimensions of the infant's general neurological and muscular condition. The _Brazelton Scale_ measures many more behaviors and is also valuable in determining the special care an infant may require.

28. Premature babies are those who weigh less than _5D_ lbs and who are born less than _37_ weeks after conception, whereas full term babies who are underweight are referred to as _small_ for _gestational stage_.

29. Among other treatment modalities for preemies, gentle touching and handling of a preterm baby for even an extra _45_ _minutes_ a day can result in a surprising _47%_ faster weight gain than those who don't receive this TLC.

30. Although the majority of premature infants have no real problems, some experience later

difficulties including (try for 3 or 4).
1. _learning difficulties_
2. _lower intelligence_
3. _hearing and vision impairment_
4. _physical awkwardness_

31. The high infant mortality rate in the U.S. appears to be mainly due to inadequate _prenatal care_, low _birth_ weight, and lack of _medical support_ for pregnant women.

32. Breast feeding is recommended, when possible, because of the superiority of human milk in offering more _amino acid_, better immunity to _gastrointestinal infections_, and decreased _food allergies_ .

33. In modern clinics, the use of fertility drugs in order to implant more than one healthy zygote has raised the success rate to about _23_ % compared to _30_ % for natural fertilization.

34. In the At Issue section, your author points to a particular problem which contributes to the high infant mortality rate in the U.S. Be prepared to discuss your appraisal of the problems and various solutions.

■ ■ ■ ■

PRACTICE TEST 1

1. The Lamaze birthing method recommends practice with a coach for mothers to learn
    a. relaxation, breathing, and muscle control
    b. self hypnosis and pain control
    c. drug regulation and pain control
    d. how to make an exciting adventure of the delivery

2. Conception normally takes place in the woman's
    a. uterus
    b. fallopian tubes
    c. ovaries
    d. cervix

3. The two week interim after fertilization, when the _____ becomes attached to the uterus, is called _____.
    a. endoderm, the period of the zygote
    b. zygote, the period of the ovum
    c. ovum, the period of the blastocyst
    d. zygote, the period of the embryo

4. The period of the embryo lasts from the end of the second week until _____, which begins during the _____.
    a. ossification or bone formation, 8th week
    b. the establishment of the placenta, 8th week
    c. ossification, 12th week
    d. specialization, 8th week

5. The process of differentiation becomes obvious when the rapidly dividing cells
    a. slowly stop dividing
    b. indicate a genetic defect.
    c. specialize into specific cells such as skin, sensory organs, nerve, muscles, organs.
    d. separate the antibodies of the mother from the embryo.

6. The placenta is remarkable in that it
    a. prevents the mother's antibodies from attacking the embryo.
    b. prevents the mix of blood from the mother to the embryo.
    c. allows certain immunoglobulins to enter the embryo to provide it with some disease resistance.
    d. all of the above.

7. The longest stage of prenatal development is the _____, which lasts _____ months.
    a. period of the fetus, 9
    b. period of embryo, 6
    c. period of the ovum, last 3
    d. period of the fetus, 7

8. Teratogens are substances in the environment that
    a. enhance the health of the baby
    b. cause increased blood flow to the fetus
    c. may cause fetal abnormalities
    d. cause miscarriages only

9. Although most researchers refer to the dangers of smoking by mothers, fathers' smoking
    a. has no effect
    b. can affect his normal sperm production.
    c. creates a smoky environment which can be a hazard to the fetus.
    d. both b and c

10. Fetal Alcohol Syndrome, caused by excessive drinking by the expectant mother, can produce:
    a. babies who are alcohol addicted.
    b. facial, limb, and organ defects, and possible retardation.
    c. blood abnormalities.
    d. no effect; the alcohol is filtered out by the placenta.

11. The rule the text suggests regarding the use of any drug by the mother is to recognize that
    a. whatever feels good to the mother is safe for the fetus.

b.   a safe dose for the mother may be a huge dose for the fetus
c.   a safe dose for the mother is a safe dose for the fetus
d.   any drug will always harm the fetus

12.   The best way to prevent retardation and sensory system defects from toxoplasmosis is to
a.   provide preventive medications
b.   provide vaccination for the children
c.   teach good sanitation methods
d.   teach good nutrition methods

13.   The onset of labor is marked by
a.   uterine contractions.
b.   the amniotic sac rupturing.
c.   baby turns down to the head down position.
d.   lightening.

14.   A baby is referred to as "small for gestational age" when
a.   she weighs less than 5 ☐ lbs.
b.   she is delivered at less than 27 weeks.
c.   she has a low score on the APGAR.
d.   she is full term but weighs less than 5 ☐ lbs.

■ ■ ■ ■

PRACTICE TEST 2

1.   The probability of a woman becoming pregnant, assuming both partners are healthy, is most dependent on
a.   their diet.
b.   the age of the father.
c.   the age of the mother.
d.   the frequency of intercourse.

2.   Once the blastocyst has attached itself to the uterine wall, the outer layer signals the mother's body _____ which triggers her immune system _____
a.   that "a baby is forming", to pass antibodies to the embryo
b.   to develop the uterine epithelium, to begin ossification of the embryo
c.   to develop nurturing connections to the embryo, to prevent immunoglobulins from reaching the embryo
d.   that "a baby is forming", to prevent antibodies from attacking the new embryo

3.   During the first two weeks, the ovum, now called the zygote, journeys to the _____ where it attaches and develops _____ connections from the mother.
a.   fallopian tubes, epithelium

    b.   uterus, gamete
    c.   endoderm, dependent
    d./   uterus, nurturing

4.   The umbilical cord and the placenta provide the connection through which:
    a./   nutrients and wastes pass
    b.   the mother's blood is passed to the embryo
    c.   antibodies from mother are passed to the embryo
    d.   immunoglobulins are prevented from affecting the embryo

5.   Many of the external dangers to the unborn baby can be prevented by a change in the environment and a change in
    a.   just the diet of the mother
    b./   the behaviors of the parents
    c.   the medical community
    d.   bad attitudes

6.   When an expectant mother smokes, the oxygen deprivation to her baby
    a.   can be expressed later in learning and memory deficits
    b.   may affect the ability of baby's lungs to grow and mature
    c.   increases the risk of placenta previa and hemorrhaging
    d./   all of the above

7.   Excessive consumption of alcohol by the expectant mother can result in
    a./   F.A.S. and intellectual defects
    b.   deformation of arms and legs
    c.   significant increase in birth weight
    d.   elevated oxygen levels

8.   Some older, poorer neighborhoods pose a threat of fetal damage through ingestion of heavy metals because of
    a.   crowded conditions.
    b.   poor use of vitamin supplements.
    c./   old plumbing and lead-based paints.
    d.   standing or poor drainage of waste water.

9.   Where a teratogen _____, a pathogen _____.
    a.   advances cellular differentiation; prevents spontaneous abortion
    b./   is a substance which can cause fetal abnormalities; is a disease organism which can cause fetal abnormalities
    c.   is a disease process which can cause fetal abnormalities, is a substance which can cause fetal abnormalities
    d.   is a slow virus which can interrupt some early development, is a chemical which crosses the placental barrier

10.   When the mother's antibodies attack the fetus as a foreign body the reason would most likely be

a.   the mother and the father are Rh negative
b.   the mother and the father are Rh positive
c.   the blood of the mother and the fetus have failed to mix
d.   the father is Rh positive and the mother is Rh negative

11.   Although home births have enjoyed popularity in recent years, careful evaluations should be made beforehand because
a.   the parents should have an MD..
b.   10 to 15% of deliveries require special equipment and help.
c.   midwives are improperly trained to deal with emergencies.
d.   babies should never be born at home.

12.   Premature infants are at risk for survival because they
a.   often have severe respiratory problems.
b.   have underdeveloped skeletal features.
c.   score poorly on the APGAR.
d.   are overly protected by their parents.

13.   In addition to careful monitoring, a successful treatment for incubated premature babies is to provide _____, resulting in _____.
a.   45 minutes of gentle touching per day, a 47% faster weight gain than those not receiving the touching
b.   enriched formula feedings, a 47% faster weight gain than those not receiving the feedings
c.   breast milk to prevent gastrointestinal infections, a 47% faster weight gain than those not receiving the breast milk
d.   additional oxygen and light, a 47% faster weight gain than those not receiving the oxygen and light

14.   Breast feeding is recommended when possible because
a.   breast milk is superior to cow's milk, since it is higher in the amino acids needed in nervous system development.
b.   breast milk kills intestinal parasites not affected by cow's milk.
c.   breast fed babies are less likely to develop food allergies.
d.   all of the above.

ANSWER SECTION

Guided Review

1. Lamaze
2. diversification, natural selection
3. fallopian tubes, sperm, ova
4. age, 26, 30
5. ovulate, hormone
6. zygote, uterus, 2 weeks
7. 2 weeks, 8th week, ossification
8. baby, antibodies
9. immunoglobulins, disease resistance
10. differentiation, specialization
11. placenta, umbilical cord, nutrients, wastes
12. 31%, 96%
13. fetus, 8 weeks
14. closing or shielding, hiccups
15. 5, brain, lungs (respiratory system)
16. teratogens, nicotine, alcohol, tranquilizers, cocaine, antibiotics, anticonvulsants
17. pathogens, toxoplasmosis, cytomegalovirus, rubella, herpes, slow viruses, AIDS
18. positive, negative
19. support, husband
20. 2 years
21. 270, 9, 3
22. birthing bar, born
23. catecholamines
24. breech, rump
25. Cesarean section, normally or vaginally
26. splitting, one zygote, two separate ova
27. APGAR, Brazelton Scale
28. 5 □, 37, small, gestational age
29. 45 minutes, 47%
30. learning difficulties, lower intelligence, hearing and vision impairment, physical awkwardness
31. prenatal care, birth, medical support
32. amino acids, gastrointestinal infections, food allergies
33. 23%, 30%

Practice Test 1

1. a
2. b
3. b
4. a
5. c
6. d
7. d
8. c
9. d
10. b

11.   *b*   13.   *a*
12.   *c*   14.   *d*

Practice Test 2

1   *c*   8.   *c*
2.   *d*   9.   *b*
3.   *d*   10.   *d*
4.   *a*   11.   *b*
5.   *b*   12.   *a*
6.   *d*   13.   *a*
7.   *a*   14.   *d*

CHAPTER FOUR

GROWTH, PLASTICITY, AND INDIVIDUAL DIFFERENCES

■ ■ ■ ■   ◀
                                                                         ◀
LEARNING OBJECTIVES   ◀

You and your friends from Latnem-Poleved, or your study group, have shared the experience of prenatal development and birthing babies. Now, it's time to tell them about the growth and maturation of our infants. Be able to discuss the following issues:

1. Describe how neonates look, their average weight and length, and explain why we think our babies are so beautiful when their heads are too big for their bodies and their skin is often red and wrinkled.
2. Many people still have the idea, as they did a hundred years ago, that babies are both helpless and passive. You'll have to correct this impression by explaining that though we have a long dependency period compared to many animals, our babies are anything but passive. Give them some examples of their sociability and what they can do to engage others in relating to them.
3. Find a way to take them to visit very young infants, where you can show them the reflexes they display. Explain those that are useful even though there are others that are not. You might suggest that some are there that may have been useful in the ancient past.
4. Explain to them the meaning of maturation--you might compare that term with the word "growth" so they can understand the difference. Let them know that growth and maturation are largely controlled by genetics. The example of toilet training the twins will be of help in your discussion. But be sure to explain the meaning of the term "probabilistic epigenesis".
5. Although there are still many who believe motor development follows a genetically determined maturational pattern, new arguments suggest a dynamic and multicausal approach. Be able to explain the work done by Nicholas Bernstein. His position that the body moves in response to the brain and also to gravitational forces, centripetal forces and torque allows such a wide variety of combinations of actions that no brain is big enough to contain so many prewired behaviors.
6. Explain this biodynamic theory of motor development, pointing to the fact that responses that are in keeping with the body's ability and the environment toward results are called attractors. Describe how an infant can go from one attractor to the next, appearing to skip a response which may be more difficult because of the environment or a biological inhibitor. This change is called a "phase shift".

7. A very exciting concept in the dynamic view of motor development is that of the plasticity of the brain. Be able to explain what is meant by plasticity. Describe the flexibility of the infant's solution using Esther Thelen's work with tying babies' legs to a stretchy elastic to make a mobile move.

8. To put the prevailing maturational theories and the new biodynamic theory in an explainable format, describe the discussion in the AT ISSUE section. We find that the brain is active, responsive, inventive, and changes throughout our lives.

9. The Strange Case of The Walking Newborn section is well worth your attention. As you see walking as an attractor, you can also see where environmental factors come into play.

10. If you possibly can, visit a neonatal nursery to see the different activity levels of the individual newborns there. You may find this a perfect opportunity to discuss the Thomas and Chess studies of temperament and the issue of the stability of temperament over time.

11. You'll certainly want to explain what "goodness of fit" means. Do describe the studies of the Masai tribe which illustrate how this "fit" is a part of the child's survival in his/her environment.

12. As you talk together, you may want to explore the advantages and disadvantages there are to being a "difficult" child, or an "easy" child in terms of survival and just plain living in this world.

13. A very important discussion will be that of the interaction of the child's temperament with those of the parents', and how each contribute to the modification of each others' behavior. Do include in your discussion the MacArthur Longitudinal Twin Study. Can it be that genetics influences the final outcome of temperament?

14. Explain what we know about shyness and Kagan's research showing that there is a genetic predisposition toward this trait. Tell them too, about how some resolve their shyness by adulthood. Again remember that the environment may modify these traits.

15. The Application section describes a strong genetic predisposition for the children of the Ache tribe in Paraguay. I am reminded of the teacher who answered a question about which was most important, genetics or environment, with a terse "Yes. Its 100% genetics combined with 100% environment!"

■ ■ ■ ■

CHAPTER OUTLINE

Are you ready to do more on this outline? Read carefully. Remember to leave room for lecture notes.

CHAPTER PREVIEW: Toilet Training Twins. The "experts" learn about maturational forces and biological timetables.

I.   The Neonate: How the Newborn (Neonate) Looks
      Weight and length _____
      Proportionate size of head _____
      Appearance _____
      A.   Infant States-Individual Natural Rhythms; You describe these
            1.   Crying_____
            2.   Waking Activity _____

            3.   Alert Inactivity_____

       4.   Drowsiness _____

       5.   Irregular Sleep _____

       6.   Regular Sleep _____

  B.   A Passive Newborn?

       1.   Research of 60's, 70's surged to show neonates are not passive.

       2.   _____

       3.   _____

       4.   _____

       5.   _____

  C.   The Neonate's Reflexes: Study Table 4.1!

       1.   Reflexes _____

       2.   Some have survival value

            a.   E.g.:_____

       3.   Others may have had value in a more primitive time.

            a.   E.g._____

       4.   Many reflexes disappear with passage of time as higher brain functions develop and learning occurs

II.   Maturation and Dynamic Development. Maturation: a genetically determined biological plan of development relatively independent of experience. This definition must be tempered with the recognition that human development follows a probable path, directed rather than determined by biological heritage. This is the view of probabilistic epigenesis. Note the Chapter Preview.

  A.   Human Growth Also Largely a Function Of Maturation -- See Table 4.2. Summarize this table for your outline

       1.   Rate is rapid after conception, slows down thereafter.

            a.   if rate of growth during first 3 prenatal months continued, individual would

                _____

       2.   Changes in relative size of body parts in ratio as growth continues: example of complex human development

            a.   E.g., head to body length ratio--Figure 4.2

       3.   Individual rates differ from child to child and occurs in spurts- Saltatory growth

       4.   Nutrition effects *You do.*

            _____

  B.   Both Growth and Maturational development follow biological plan which the environment facilitates or inhibits.

III.   Motor development. See Figure 4.3 and remember that babies are individuals with individual rates of development.

  A.   Maturation vs. Dynamic Development

      Motor development once thought of as following a maturational time-table and having a stage-like progression

       1.   Nicholas Bernstein argument for Biodynamic view

            a.   body responds to messages from brain and gravitational and centripetal forces

            b.   motor development emerges as a result of many possible combinations of actions

            c.   brain could not be prewired for so many activities

            d.   motor activities that are in harmony with the environment and the abilities of one's body are called attractors

        e.   dynamic theory addresses the concept of brain flexibility and plasticity rather than a prewired brain

    B.   The Plastic Brain
        1.   Infant's brain ready to change and alter activity based on experience and environment
        2.   Infant explores environment to find effective attractors and actions
        3.   "Infant's brain is based on a flexible system dynamically interacting with the environment that the infant actively explores."

At Issue: Are Two Brains Better Than One?

The debate between maturational and dynamic theories questions how much neural organization is present at birth. The nature/nurture issue revisited. But with something new. *You do this one.*

Two hypothesized systems in the newborn brain
    A.   The Experience-expectant system
        1.   prewired to make sense of common stimuli in the environment
        2.   _____
        3.   _____
        4.   _____
    B.   The Experience-dependent system
        1.   connections acquired more slowly through learning and experience
        2.   _____
        3.   _____
    C.   The Dynamic theory brings new ideas to consider:
        1.   Bernstein's "the degrees of freedom" problem: _____

                _____
        2.   present view of brain compared to older view: _____
                _____

IV.   The Strange Case of the Walking Newborn
        1.   The walking reflex seen first _____ and disappears by _____
        2.   Practicing reflex (with complete support) for four 3 minute sessions a day (total 12 minutes)
            a.   appears to extend length of time of reflex
            b.   encourages voluntary walking to start sooner than expected
                (1)   possible that "reflex" and "volunteer" walking is aspect of same neuromuscular developmental task
            c.   no really long term benefits
        3.   infant's body develops so that walking becomes an easier and easier way to "discover"
        4.   Children walk sooner now than in past
            Note possible environmental contributions
            a.   _____
            b.   _____
            c.   _____
            d.   _____
        5.   Cultural influence shown as children in different countries walk at different ages
        6.   Encouragement of activities beyond maturational ability may be interesting to child, or at least fun for the family, but not necessarily accelerating.

V.   Individual Differences and Temperamental Theories.

Temperament: a relatively consistent, basic disposition inherent in the person that underlies the expression of activity, reactivity, emotionality and sociability.

A.   The New York Longitudinal Study: Alexander Thomas, 1968

     1.   140 children birth through adolescence

     2.   Categorized subjects in terms of "easy" to "difficult" continuums in temperament, through interviews with parents, observational measures

     3.   Six infant personality dimensions: see TABLE 4.3

          a.   _____

          b.   _____

          c.   _____

          d.   _____

          e.   _____

          f.   _____

     4.   Measured at 5 and 10 years

          a.   easy-40%; slow to warm up-15%; difficult-10%; inconsistent-35%

          b.   extremes appear to be stable over 10 year period

          c.   criticisms of Thomas and Chess study

              (1)   _____

              (2)   _____

              (3)   _____

B.   "Goodness of Fit" -- you define _____
_____

     1.   Study of easy and difficult children of the Masai, Africa

          a.   most of "easy" children died _____

          b.   most "difficult" children survived _____

     2.   Problems for "easy" and "difficult" children in Western cultures

          a.   difficult children's behaviors related to serious behavior problems

          b.   greater risk for psychiatric disorders in adolescence

          c.   tend to face more stress, partly a result of own behavior

          d.   easy is preferred by most parents

     3.   Advantage in Western Cultures for "Difficult" and "Easy" children: study of upper and middle class families

          a.   higher IQ scores

          b.   stimulated more, talked to by parent

          c.   not known if lasting but some studies show consistency over time

          d.   easy child may have advantage of ability to attend to tasks and concentrate

C.   Sorting Environmental Influences on Temperament

     1.   Mothers feel less responsive and are less sensitive to difficult babies

     2.   Strife caused by demands result in a cycle of heavy handed discipline by parents and child rebellion - behaviors may continue longer than biological influence

     3.   Description of child temperament may ultimately be result of interaction between temperaments of parents and child - each contributing to the behaviors of the other

     4.   The argument for genetic influence on temperament
MacArthur Longitudinal Twin Study: _____

_____

Robert Plomin's conclusions _____

VI. The Search for Innate Components
    A. Constitutional predisposition of activity level can be predicted in 4 to 8 year olds from infant levels.
    B. Identical twin studies show they suffer the same fears twice as often as fraternal twins
    C. Kagan, et. al studies show inhibited and withdrawn 2 year olds have faster more stable heartbeats than outgoing peers.
    This physical condition exists in 8-year-old children, as well, who have a tendency toward timidity. (Twin Shyness and Anxiety Studies)
        1. However! with intervention, one third of all shy children overcame the problem by adulthood.
    D. The interactionist approach that temperament and environmental influences interact and affect one another.

Applications: The Genetics of Behavior
    A. Behavioral Genetics
    B. The Ache of Paraguay
        1. Children well behind U.S. and Africa countries in walking
        2. Catch up in later childhood
        3. Discouraged from wandering away from mother
        4. Although living conditions and mores have changed, children still show delay in motor development
        5. if mother marries outside of tribe, baby will develop motor skills more quickly.
        6. Appears to be naturally selected behavior
    C. Shows interaction between genetics and environment can have powerful and long lasting effects.

Just between us, can you see some of the problems in researching human behavior? No wonder we get bewildered sometimes, when someone wants a simple answer to the question "Why do people do . . . . ?"

■ ■ ■ ■   ◄
                                                                           ◄
                                                                           ◄

NAMES TO REMEMBER

Myrtle McGraw   New York Longitudinal Study
The Ache   Robert Plomin
Nicholas Bernstein   Jerome Kagan and colleagues
Esther Thelen   The Masai
Alexander Thomas   Michelle Lampl
Stella Chess

■ ■ ■ ■

TERMS AND CONCEPTS

neonate
passivity in neonates
competence in neonates
reflexes
moro reflex
babinski reflex
babkin reflex
blink reflex
diving reflex
knee jerk reflex
palmar reflex
rage reflex
rooting reflex
sucking reflex
walking reflex
maturation
probabilistic epigenesis
behavioral genetics
growth
Saltatory growth

attractors
phase shift
brain plasticity
Biodynamic theory
experience-expectant system
experience-dependent system
degree of freedom problem
reflexive and voluntary walking
temperament and temperament theories
The New York Longitudinal Study
stability of temperament
"easy" and "difficult" babies
"slow to warm up" babies
"inconsistent" babies
"goodness of fit"
intensity of reaction
constitutional predisposition
shyness
interactionist approach

■ ■ ■ ■

GUIDED REVIEW

1.   Myrtle McGraw discovered that bladder training a baby before the infant was nuerologically ready _____ was no more successful than waiting to train his twin who was _____27_____ months old, proving that early toilet training was _futile_____ at that time.

2.   The newborn, or _neonate_ has _red_____ and _wrinkled_ skin, weighs between _____6_____ and _____9_____ pounds, and has a disproportionately sized _head_____ which accounts for _____1/4 th_____ of the baby's length.

3.   That some babies have individual _body_____ _rhythms_ explains why they sleep for different periods of time, and exhibit different levels of _activity____.

4.   Infant studies of the '60's and '70's found infants to be _active____, not _passive__ in their social interactions.

5. Neonates' sociability is evident as they will turn in response to _voices_, look intently at the _faces_ of their caregivers, and initiate _reciprocal intrest_ from their caretakers soon after birth.

6. Reflexes are _unlearned behaviors_ in response to certain stimuli. Many, such as _sucking_, _coughing_, and _blinking_ appear to have evolved because of their _usefullness_.

7. Many of the reflexes become weaker as _higher brain functions_ and _learning_ provide the infant his own responses. That these are lost with time is a healthy _nuerological_ development

8. The term maturation, which directs growth and motor development, is defined as a _genetically determined_ biological plan of development, _independent_ of _experience_.

9. That growth and motor development are not solely the function of biology and that they follow a probable path, describes the concept of _probilistic epigenesis_

10. The most rapid rate of physical growth occurs during the first _3_ _months_ after conception, which, if continued, would result in your weighing, at the age of 20, more than the weight of the entire _solar_ _system_.

11. Michelle Lampl found in her studies of growth in infants and toddlers, that, rather than growing in linear fashion, they will sometimes go for weeks without growing and then grow in a sudden spurt. This growth pattern is known as _saltatory growth_.

12. As an example of an environmental influence, proper _nutrition_ plays an important part in the biological plan of growth and motor development.

13. Many developmental psychologists view motor development as following a maturational plan grounded in the child's _genetics_ and _nueral_ development.

14. A new view of motor development called the _biodynamic theory_ theory of Nicholas Bernstein, argues that the infant moves as a response to his brain, and also to _gravitation_ and _centripetal_ forces, as well as _torque_.

15. Dr. Bernstein pointed out that there are so many possible combinations of actions it would be impossible for the brain to hold them all in a _prewired_ context.

16. According to this theory responses which are easy to do and are in harmony with the ability of one's body and the environment are called _attractors_ When a child moves from one productive response to another much more advanced one, bypassing what may be more difficult in her environment, she has moved through a _phase shift_.

17. As we come to appreciate the purposeful, unique and flexible movements of infants as they

actively explore their environment, we can also appreciate the plasticity of the infant brain .

18. To illustrate that the environment can act only as accelerators or decelerators to the genetic maturational plan, list some possible environmental accelerators for walking:
   1. better nutrition
   2. smaller families ; encouragement
   3. carpeting

19. The Application describing the delayed motor development of the children in the Ache of Paraguay, illustrates the field of behavioral genetics and suggests their late walking behavior may have come about through natural selection .

20. This study is a good example of the fact that there is a significant genetic influence on many behaviors, and at the same time the environment is a powerful modifying influence. The basic theme of our nature vs. nurture issue, then, is interaction.

21. Temperament differences are seen almost immediately in newborns. As we discuss temperament and theories of temperament, we should have a working definition of the term. Go for it!: relatively consistent basic dispositions inherent in the person that underlie and modulate the expression of activity, re-

22. The New York longitudinal study, by Thomas , and chess documented differences in infant temperment beginning with birth and continuing to adolescence.

23. Babies labeled easy have regular rhythms for eating and sleeping, and adapt well to new foods and people.

24. Most babies in the New York Longitudinal study were classified as easy at 40%, while 15% were slow to warm and, thank goodness, only 10% were difficult .

25. The suitability of the child's temperament to his/her environment is known as goodness of fit .

26. Children of the Masai tribe, who were rated as difficult by our description, actually survived best because demanding behavior may be necessary for attention in that culture.

27. There is evidence that "difficult" children in the industrialized Western culture may have more behavior problems in childhood, and may be at a greater risk for psychiatric disorders during adolescence.

28. In one study in middle and upper class families, difficult children scored 20 IQ points higher than their matched "easy" peers.

29. Parents who expect an easy baby may respond to their "difficult" baby with heavy handed disipline . The "difficult" child may respond to this treatment by

activity, emotionality, and sociability.

remaining difficult for a long time after biological influences on his temperament have been modified.

30.   Implications that there is a strong genetic predisposition to activity levels are supported by studies which found that the activity levels of children between ___4___ and ___8___ years old can be predicted by their _neonatal_ activity levels.

31.   _Identical_ twins are _twice_ as likely to share the same fears and anxieties as _fraternal_ twins.

32.   Jerome Kagan and his associates are the first to show a clear-cut connection between temperament and _physiology_

33.   As studies of shyness progress, it has been found that ___1/3___ of all shy children _overcame_ their shyness by _adulthood_ .

■ ■ ■ ■

PRACTICE TEST 1

1.   When Myrtle McGraw attempted to toilet train two one-month-old baby boys, she found it was a futile task. No amount of early training could rush
       a.   the predetermined biological plan of development.
       b.   neurological readiness.
       c.   the genetically timed program.
       d.   a and b

2.   Hollywood movies can no longer fool us. A newborn is really wonderfully
       a.   wrinkled, chinless, and has a disproportionately large head.
       b.   smooth, fat, and fully developed.
       c.   pink and always brown eyed.
       d.   tiny, passive and helpless.

3.   Human neonates
       a.   are helpless and passive.
       b.   are capable of social interactions with their parents.
       c.   eat, sleep, wet, and have reflexes.
       d.   are incompetent in every way.

4.   Unlearned behaviors which are the result of nature are called
       a.   talents
       b.   Moro
       c.   reflexes
       d.   useless

5. The rate of physical growth during the first three months after conception
   a. is slow and deliberate.
   b. is so rapid that if continued at that rate, we'd weigh more than the solar system.
   c. accelerates quickly after the first three months.
   d. both b and c.

6. Physical growth and motor development share at least two major factors
   a. They are mainly dependent on maturation; they are favorite topics of conversation and comparison with parents.
   b. They are a matter of nurture; they are a not matter of nature.
   c. They are mainly due to the environment; parents would rather talk about something else.
   d. They are basically innate; environment has little influence.

7. That a person's biological heritage will direct rather than determine his development along a probable path, is the concept of
   a. deterministic epigenesis
   b. maturational epigenesis
   c. probabilistic epigenesis
   d. motor epigenesis

8. Michelle Lampl found that infants and toddlers do not grow in a linear manner. Rather, their growth alternates between nothing measurable to a sudden spurt. This kind of growth is known as
   a. saltatory growth
   b. decelerating growth
   c. accelerating growth
   d. antilinear growth

9. Nicholas Bernstein's theory states that with the myriad of dynamic and changing possibilities of actions infants exhibit, it would be impossible for
   a. the chid to remember each appropriate behavior
   b. the brain to hold all the behaviors in a prewired context
   c. genetics to dictate all of the actions
   d. environmental forces to dictate all of the actions

10. Esther Thelen's work with infants demonstrated that every movement is unique and every solution is flexible to adapt to changes. These abilities demonstrate
    a. the plasticity of the infant brain
    b. complicated environmentally induced connections in the brain
    c. that the stages of infant behaviors are broadly described
    d. the unfolding of the maturational time-table of development

11. Behavioral genetics studies, such as that of the children of the Ache of Paraguay, have found a genetic influence on many behaviors and that
    a. all behaviors stem from the environment
    b. all behaviors are the result of natural selection

c.   all behaviors become stable over time

d.   the environment is a powerful modifying influence

12.   Differences in temperament reported by Thomas and Chess
        a.   are evident at one year and disappear by age five.
        b.   are not evident before 5 and last until adulthood.
        c.   are evident at birth and at least well into adolescence.
        d.   are nothing more than reactivity.

13.   "Easy" children _____ than "difficult" children.
        a.   are more amenable to change and have more regular eating and bowel rhythms
        b.   withdraw from others more and are more intense in their reactions
        c.   are less adaptable and have more intense reactions
        d.   have irregular eating and sleeping habits and are more demanding

14.   The stability over time of "difficult" temperaments may also be the result of
        a.   no constitutional consistency
        b.   natural selection
        c.   tension caused between baby and parents leading to heavy handed discipline by parents
                and rebellion by the child
        d.   parents who indulge the child in overprotection

15.   Jerome Kagan and his colleagues, in studying temperament and physiological functions, found
        a.   no relationship.
        b.   blood pressure correlations.
        c.   a correlation of shyness and red hair
        d.   a clear cut association between temperamental characteristics and heart beat.

■ ■ ■ ■

PRACTICE TEST 2

1.   The neonate's characteristics at birth seldom resemble any family member
        a.   because they are so small.
        b.   because they have flat noses, high foreheads and receding chins. (On the other hand,
                there's Uncle Gomer.)
        c.   since they aren't able to do anything.
        d.   since they can't talk.

2.   When do babies show sociability?
        a.   at 3 weeks
        b.   at 1 week
        c.   within moments of birth.
        d.   after parents teach them to socialize

3. Coughing, sucking, and crying are examples of reflexes in neonates, and apparently exist because of their _____.
   a. survival value
   b. innate sociability
   c. historical value
   d. need to be learned

4. According to the Berstein's biodynamic theory of motor development, when an infant goes from one attractor, bypassing more difficult behaviors, to arrive at a new productive attractor, he is showing
   a. that he is skipping a stage
   b. a phase shift
   c. a prewired behavior
   d. all of the above

5. A child born on the moon would find that hopping is the best method of locomotion. Hopping in this case would be called
   a. an invention
   b. an accommodation
   c. the result of a prewired program
   d. an attractor

6. An important environmental factor affecting maturation is
   a. learning.
   b. social pressure.
   c. nutrition.
   d. both a and b

7. Differences in temperament reported in the New York Longitudinal Study
   a. are the result of environmental factors
   b. are rated on two levels of activity
   c. are referred to in terms of "goodness of fit"
   d. are described in terms of "easy" and "difficult"

8. According to Thomas and Chess, "easy" children differ from "difficult" children in that "easy" ones
   a. are more demanding and are more rhythmic in eating and bowel habits.
   b. love new situations and are more intense.
   c. have less even rhythms for eating and sleeping
   d. enjoy baths, new foods, and being dressed

9. "Goodness of Fit" refers to
   a. how well the child's temperament fits his school mates
   b. how well the child's temperament fits the environment
   c. how the innate features of temperament fit the child's personality
   d. how the child's temperament fit in with his sibling's

10.   "Goodness of Fit" is illustrated in the Masai tribe where researchers found the difficult children survived best because they _____ than their opposite counterparts.
        a.   were less demanding
        b/   were more demanding
        c.   scored 20 points higher on IQ tests
        d.   all of the above

11.   In a study of middle and upper class families, "difficult" children were found to have IQ scores _____ their "easy" peers.
        a.   20 points lower than
        b.   10 points lower than
        c/   20 points higher than
        d.   the same as

12.   There is evidence to indicate "easy" children are better at _____
        a/   attending and concentrating on school tasks
        b.   getting higher grades
        c.   scoring 20 points higher on IQ tests
        d.   all of the above

13.   Kagan and his colleagues found that a 2-year-old child who is inhibited or withdrawn
        a.   is likely to be more susceptible to stress as he gets older
        b.   shows a faster and more stable heartbeat
        c.   reacts by withdrawing in social situations when he gets older
        d/   all of the above

14.   Studies of shyness show
        a.   no applications for future study.
        b.   a genetic predisposition to shyness.
        c.   that, with proper help, one third will overcome it by adulthood.
        d/   both b and c

ANSWER SECTION

Guided Review

1. neurologically ready, 27, futile
2. neonate, red, wrinkled, 6, 9, head, 1/4th
3. body rhythms, activity
4. active, passive
5. voices, faces, reciprocal interest
6. unlearned behaviors, sucking, coughing, blinking, usefulness or survival value
7. higher brain functions, learning. neurological
8. genetically determined, independent, experience
9. probabilistic epigenesis
10. 3 months, solar system
11. saltatory growth
12. nutrition
13. genetics, neural
14. biodynamic theory, gravitational, centripetal, torque
15. prewired
16. attractors, phase shift
17. plasticity, brain
18. better nutrition, smaller families, carpeting, encouragement of parents
19. behavioral genetics, natural selection
20. interaction
21. relatively consistent basic dispositions inherent in the person that underlie and modulate the expression of activity, reactivity, emotionality, and sociability
22. Thomas, Chess, temperament
23. easy
24. easy, slow-to-warm-up, difficult
25. goodness of fit
26. difficult, demanding
27. psychiatric disorders
28. 20, higher
29. heavy-handed discipline, remaining difficult
30. 4, 8, neonatal
31. identical, twice, fraternal
32. physiology
33. one third, overcame, adulthood

Practice Test 1

1. d
2. a
3. b
4. c
5. b
6. a
7. c
8. a

9.	*b*		13.	*a*
10.	*a*		14.	*c*
11.	*d*		15.	*d*
12.	*c*			

<u>*Practice Test 2*</u>

1.	*b*		8.	*d*
2.	*c*		9.	*b*
3.	*a*		10.	*b*
4.	*b*		11.	*c*
5.	*d*		12.	*a*
6.	*c*		13.	*d*
7.	*d*		14.	*d*

CHAPTER FIVE

NEURAL, SENSORY, AND PERCEPTUAL DEVELOPMENT

■■■■

◀
◀
◀
◀

LEARNING OBJECTIVES

Explaining to our new friends how human babies develop will be a challenge to you. This time you'll be telling them about the development of the nervous system, senses, and perception, abilities we take for granted most of the time. After this chapter, I hope you'll be as fascinated as I am every time I read the research.

1. Now that they know a bit about you and how you are able to function, you'll need to explain that the neonate's nervous system is far less mature and capable than yours. You will need to know the purpose and progress of the myelination of axons throughout the nervous system, what that means, and how long it takes.

2. You saw in Chapter Four that the infant brain may have two separate systems, the experience-expectant and the experience-dependent. In addition you saw the biodynamic theory which views the infant's brain as plastic and flexible in that the infant actively explores the environment and discovers attractors to effect desired results. This view sees abilities developing as a result of many possible combinations and factors, rather than as the result of a prewired inherited brain. In this chapter you will see the importance of the maturity and structure of the neonate brain when you compare it to the adult brain.

3. You'll see an additional aspect of brain plasticity expanded to encompass much more than you saw in the last chapter. See how Chapter Five's discussion fits with what you've already discovered. So much new research is offered almost every day, you will want to notice, for example, that the healthy 2 year old's brain has more synaptic connections than an adult's. You'll also want to note the ways a child can be affected by developmental disability. Note the experiences of the authors of the book The *Children of the Creche* and the study of Guatemalan children by Kagan and Klein as well as your author's comments.

4. You've discussed reflexes and canalized behaviors already, so now you'll need to explain how we use the additional principles of habituation and preferences to study these sensory abilities. Explaining that the research we do is basic as we assess the parameters of infant behavior will help

you understand that we don't yet know many of the "why's". We can be reassured that there is presently a large body of research being dedicated to the topics discussed in this chapter. Do be aware of the problems babies present to researchers.

5.   When you read the At Issue section, and later the Application section, you'll be presented with more research to consider when you explain brain function to others. You'll find these parts of the chapter especially useful now and in later discussions.

6.   Explain how we use reflexes to measure visual and auditory capacities of our neonates and what we find out about visual acuity and auditory development. Babies can hear by about the 7th month after conception and can hear well as soon as the fluids clear after birth. Describe how long it takes for full sensitivity to be reached.

7.   The senses of smell and taste may be especially interesting, since they are so adult-like at so early an age. Know some details on how we study these senses. You'll enjoy learning about nasofacial reflexes.

8.   It will be worth the effort to explain the difference between sensation and perception, since much of the rest of the chapter discusses perception.

9.   The perceptual abilities of the infant are fascinating. Many of the constancies follow a line of probable epigenesis and may be grounded in the experience-expectant system.

10.   Describe the visual cliff and the Gibson and Walk experiments with infants and baby animals. Be sure to explain our problems of testing our own babies, and that, as far as we can tell, our infants aren't afraid of drop-offs till about 6 months of age. Do report the other researchers' findings.

11.   This is a good time to remember the concept of maturation, since many of our perceptual abilities are dependent on actual physical maturation of the brain and body.

12.   Pattern and form perception are good examples of maturing abilities, as is biological motion perception. These studies rely on the habituation method.

13.   Cross-modal perception studies are fun to watch. Babies get so impatient when they're allowed to feel something and not see it at the same time! They love having the experiment end so they can play with the toy.

14.   The At Issue and Applications section discuss the effects and overcoming of early adverse experiences. I'm sure these sections will allow many interesting discussions among your group.

■ ■ ■ ■

CHAPTER OUTLINE

Chapter Preview: Dr. Seuss is read to 2 and 3 day olds by Mom and Dad.
Notice both studies reported.

I.   The Nervous System of the Neonate: Brain, spinal cord and peripheral nerves.
    A.   Maturity of the Structure of the Newborn Nervous System
        1.   EEG readings indicate immaturity
            a.   human brain highly complex
            b.   dendrites of neurons underdeveloped
            c.   portions of neurons not yet myelinated
                (1)   myelin provides
                    (a)   _____

(b) _____

(c) _____

(d) _____

    (2)   myelin necessary for certain muscle control

    (3)   lack of or scarring of myelin sheath seen in M.S.

        (a) _____

        (b) _____

        (c)   similar to results of immature brain of infant

  2.   Infant's maturation tied to timetable of neural growth

    (1)   smiling in infants tied to myelination, which occurs at about the same age the world over

    (2)   full myelination achieved at puberty

B.   Brain Plasticity-- Meaning of term _____

_____

  1.   Evidence of plasticity in 5 to 6 year olds seen in injury to language portion of brain on left hemisphere

_____

  2.   synaptic junctions between neurons seen to be greater in animals raised in enriched environments

  3.   Use of electron microscope shows synaptic density reaches peak in humans at about the age of two

  4.   Declines until about age 16 then remains constant until about 72 yrs.

  5.   These facts suggest a neurologically sensitive period for learning and gaining experience

  6.   three ways a child may become permanently disabled by early experience

    a. _____

_____

    b. _____

_____

    c. _____

_____

  7.   Problems in predicting when a disability can be reversed

_____

_____

  8.   successful recovery seen

    a.   Dennis study in Beirut _____

_____

    b.   Kagan and Klein in Guatemala _____

_____

  9.   Contradictory research cites missed chance for attachments or bonds with significant adults results in children's behaviors including;

_____

_____

AT ISSUE; *You'll want to do this one yourself.*

  1.   Griffin and Harlow, 1966, research with rhesus monkeys Isolation effects at 3 months _____

at 6 months _____
_____
_____

significance of timing of isolation _____
_____

2.   Rene Spitz, 1945, findings of children in foundling home
_____

Effects on children's development _____
_____

at two year follow up _____
_____

Spitz' conclusions_____
_____

II.   Methods of Sensory and Experimental Research
   A.   Experimental Designs
      1.   Single-Stimulus procedure
         a.   _____
         b.   _____
      2.   Preference Method Figure 5.8
         a.   _____
         b.   _____
      3.   Habituation Method Figure 5.7
         a.   _____
         b.   _____

How are you doing? Are you finding outlining a time saving method?
   B. Methodological Problems
      1.   Right side preference
      2.   Condition of infant
         a.   alert
         b.   sleepy
         c.   state of health, of course

III.   The Basic Sensory Abilities of the Infant. Research basic and mostly serendipitous
   A.   Vision
      1.   2 weeks old vision 20/800
         a.   researched through measurements of optokinetic nystagmus. This motion
               called _____
               (1)   black vertical stripes made finer and finer
               (2)   pacifier controlled focus of projected pattern
      2.   Sensitive to changes in brightness
      3.   Detection of movement
      4.   Acuity resembles adult range between 6 months and 1 year
         a.   final acuity determined by
               _____
         b.   the falcon! _____

        c.   all senses become more refined and sensitive during

        _____

B.   Audition: measured by infant responses and changes in heart beat
1.   Functional even prior to birth. After birth, once fluid gone can discriminate between duration, and pitch
2.   Audition dominant to sight for first six months
3.   Almost adult level by 6 months, continues to improve well into school years
4.   Neonates especially react to human voices- prefer vowel sounds
5.   Sensitivity can decrease over life time

C.   Olfaction: Measured by stabilimeter
1.   Well developed:
      a.   _____
2.   Nasofacial responses
      a.   _____

D.   Taste Measured by stabilimeter
1.   same four basic tastes as adults
2.   indicated preference for sweet
3.   highly subject to influence of smell
4.   show preference for salty by 4 or 5 years
5.   will accommodate to levels of sweet and salty and want to continue these levels
6.   taste as a protective measure
      a.   _____

E.   Touch, measured by eliciting reflexes
1.   Reflexes _____
      a._____
      b._____
2.   Females more sensitive than males
3.   Studies "confounded" by the many other neural receptors and social component
4.   Temperature changes may be noticed more than visual changes

IV.   Perceptual Abilities of the Infant: How sensation is interpreted. Many perceptual developments are canalized, follow predictable path, probabilistic epigenesis. Grounded in experience-expectant system
A.   Object Constancies
1.   Size Constancy: define

      _____

      a.   appears between 5 1/2 and 7 months
        (1)   Mr. B.
        (2)   Pygmy and the "insects"
2.   Shape Constancy: define

      _____

      a.   habituation format used
      b.   appears as early as _____
3.   Position Constancy: define

      _____

      a.   becomes strong at about _____

B.   Depth Perception

     1.   Gibson and Walk's Visual Cliff apparatus
         a.   baby animals _____
         b.   human babies _____
         c.   limits of testing human babies _____
         d.   Campos, et al., precrawling infants _____
         e.   Rader's conclusions _____
         f.   locomotion may not be necessary for depth perception
     2.   Computer random dot study stimulates overlap depth cue Figure 5.6
         a.   indicates depth perception, size constancy and position constancy develop between (ages) _____

C.   Pattern and Form Perception--Uses Habituation method. Newborns can discriminate triangles, squares, crosses, and circles
     1.   infants especially attracted to faces and face-like patterns
     2.   By 6 or 7 months can distinguish one face from another, but recognize mother at one month!
D.   Biological Motion Perception: Ability to perceive distinct motion of live objects
     1.   may have evolved to help recognize human motion
     2.   by 3 months
E.   Auditory Processes
     1.   We hear in stereo! definition:
     2.   Wertheimer
         a.   neonate turns to sound as if to look for it.
         b.   degree of accuracy of turn increases with age
V.   Sensory and Perceptual Integration:
     A.   Film and Sound Track Method
         1.   as early as 4 to 6 months of age babies prefer object-sound synchrony
     B.   Cross-modal Perception - Habituation method
         1.   6 months recognized object visually from only tactile contact
         2.   7 months showed some innate predisposition for mathematical comprehension
         3.   Much research in this area
Applications: Overcoming Adverse Early Learning Experiences
You will certainly want to do this one, especially since you've read At Issue and the rest of the chapter
     A.   The Therapist Monkeys
         1.   6 month isolates paired with 3 month old "therapists"
         2.   results _____

            _____

     B.   The Skeels Study
         1.   13 children of orphanage sent to Glenwood State School for retarded adult women
         2.   children's average age 19 months, IQ averaged 64, lower than those who remained behind.
         3.   method of "treating" children at Glenwood

            _____

            _____

         4.   results _____

            _____

5.   Follow-up studies   _____

_____

_____

■ ■ ■ ■

NAMES TO REMEMBER

Dr. Seuss
Kalnins and Bruner
Griffin and Harlow
Children of the Creche
Dennis

R. D. Walk
Eleanor Gibson
Michael Wertheimer
Stephen Suomi
The Skeels Study

■ ■ ■ ■

TERMS AND CONCEPTS

neuron
dendrites
axon
synapse
central nervous system
peripheral nervous system
electroencephalogram, EEG
myelin sheath
multiple sclerosis
brain plasticity
electron microscope
critical periods
experimental designs
single-stimulus procedure
preference method
habituation method
visual acuity

optokinetic nystagmus
visual saccade
auditory perception
stabilimeter
nasofacial reflex
sensation
perception
size constancy
shape constancy
position constancy
depth perception
visual cliff
pattern and form perception
biological motion perception
cross-modal perception
infant walkers
locomotion

■ ■ ■ ■

GUiDED REViEW

1. Two or three day old infants recognized their mother's voice indicating recognition from prenatal experience. They came to prefer their father's voice to other men's only after a few _____.

2. Immature brain waves of the neonate reveal that the dendrites of the neurons are undeveloped and the axons are not _____.

3. The myelin sheath acts as an _____ and aids in _____ _____.

4. One illustration of the fact that maturation follows a time table of neural development is that all babies begin to _____ at about the same age.

5. At the University of Chicago, researchers have discovered through the use of an electron microscope, that synaptic _____ reaches its peak at two years of age. Additionally, they found that at 2 years, infants have _____% more _____ _____ than does the average adult.

6. Illustrating the _____ of the infant's brain, it has been found that if the left hemisphere language center is damaged in a child under six years old, portions of the _____ _____ will take over those functions.

7. Synaptic density declines until about _____ years of age, then remains constant through age _____.

8. Three ways a child may be permanently disabled by early experience are:
    1. _____
    2. _____
    3. _____

9. Researchers have observed that institutionally raised children who have not formed attachments or bonds with significant adults will illustrate the following behaviors which differ from home raised peers:
    1. _____
    2. _____
    3. _____

10. Methods to study infants' neural, sensory, and perceptual abilities include the _____ method, _____-_____ method, and _____ method.

11. Researchers are developing computers which strengthen or weaken their circuits based on the experience they encounter. These computers are called _____ _____, and they mimic the human _____-_____ system.

12. When a researcher presents two stimuli to the infant at the same time, notations are made of the time and frequency the baby looks at one of the stimuli. This method is the _____ method.

13. The value of the _____ method is that it lets you know if the infant has recognized a second stimulus as being different from the first.

14. An inexperienced researcher may not know of the neonate's preference to look towards his _____ side. Another problem which was ignored before 1970 involved the state of _____ and _____ of the baby at the time of the study.

15. Most research into infants' sensory abilities is _____ and _____.

16. That the neonate has visual acuity of 20/800 means that he can see a letter well at _____ feet that an adult with 20/20 vision can identify at _____ feet.

17. When a series of vertical stripes is passed before the infant's eyes, an attempt is being made to measure visual acuity through the reflex of _____ _____.

18. Visual acuity will reach the adult range at about _____ to _____ months of age. However, the final individual ability will depend on _____ _____.

19. Hearing ability is evident _____ _____. Findings to this date indicate infants can discriminate sounds of different _____ and _____.

20. The sense of smell is measured by an infant polygraph called a _____, which shows physiological reactions indicating _____ level discriminations.

21. Most researchers agree that infants respond to the four basic tastes. The _____ taste is preferred by newborns and, interestingly, by four or five years of age, the children add a preference for the _____ taste.

22. _____ babies are more sensitive to touch than _____ babies.

23. The way we interpret what our senses tell our brains is called _____.

24. Understanding that objects remain the same size, no matter how near or far away they are, is known as _____ _____.

25. Realizing that a square is a square no matter what at what angle it is viewed, is known as _____ _____, and is seen as early as _____ _____ of age.

26. Recognizing that objects stay in the same place and maintain the same relative distance from each other, is called _____ _____, and is strong by _____ _____ of age.

27.   Baby animals' reactions to the visual cliff indicate their innate _____ _____.

28.   Human babies are not as easily tested, since they have to be old enough to _____.
       Since many of them preferred the shallow side, it may be that _____ _____
       is innate. However, the conclusions are not clear for humans.

29.   Five month olds reacted to the computer screen simulation of "overlap" in such a way as to
       demonstrate _____ _____, _____ _____, and
       _____ _____.

30.   An infant is allowed to touch and handle but not see an object. When the infant shows
       habituation to that object when presented visually, we can say _____ _____
       transfer or perception has occurred.

31.   Using the preference method, matching and mismatching sounds, and moving pictures,
       experimenters have demonstrated that 4 to 6 month olds are capable of _____
       _____.

32.   The ability to recognize the movements of living beings is called _____
       _____ perception.

33.   The studies of sensory and perceptual abilities help us recognize that human babies are
       neurologically organized to make _____ of their _____.

■ ■ ■ ■   ◀
                                                                                           ◀
PRACTICE TEST 1   ◀

1.   Evidence gathered in a study of 2 and 3 day old infants in North Carolina showed that
       a.   they recognize their mother's voice but prefer other voices
       b.   they prefer their mother's voice, indicating recognition from prenatal experience
       c.   they recognize their father's voice
       d.   they never do discriminate between their father's voice and that of a stranger's

2.   The myelination of infants' nervous system appears to be tied to a timetable of neural maturation,
       as shown by
       a.   EEG readings of prenatal brain function
       b.   their weakness and muscle coordination
       c.   certain specific behaviors, like smiling, occur at the same age in every culture
       d.   they have no bladder control

3.   Some parts of the brain's axons are not fully myelinated until
       a.   puberty
       b.   adulthood

c.   6 months
d.   3 to 4 years

4.   An excellent example of plasticity in the very young child occurs when the speech section on the left side of his brain has been damaged beyond repair. In this case we can expect
a.   since speech is prewired in the brain, that part will be gone forever
b.   prewiring in the brain will allow a new section on the left side to take over the speech function
c.   no specialization has taken place yet so another part of the brain will perform speech functions
d.   a part of the tight hemisphere can take over the function of the destroyed language center on the left

5.   Synaptic connections between neurons in the human brain peaks at about _____ of age, then declines until _____ of age.
a.   5 years, 72 years
b.   2 years, 16 years
c.   1 year, 2 years
d.   4 years, 16 years

6.   In the preference method for the study of infants, reactions are measured as they
a.   look for equal periods of time at two different stimuli
b.   show discrimination between two different stimuli
c.   are presented two stimuli and show more interest in one than the other
d.   both b and c

7.   Problems in experimenting with newborns include
a.   their preference to look to their right
b.   their level of alertness at testing time
c.   the effect of the baby's state of health
d.   all of the above

8.   Research into the sensory abilities of infants is
a.   mostly theoretical and manipulative
b.   mostly basic and serendipitous
c.   mostly applied and single subject
d.   mostly explanatory and descriptive

9.   Visual acuity in infants is measured by
a.   using a pacifier device which focuses a projected picture
b.   the stabilimeter
c.   noting visual saccade or optokinetic nystagmus in response to black lines on a white background
d.   both a and c

10.   Visual acuity of 20/20 is achieved by

    a.   12 to 13 years of age
    b.   17 to 18 years of age
    c.   may never be achieved
    d.   myelination of the axons

11.   Audition tests show
    a.   that hearing ability decreases after 18 months
    b.   newborns appear especially reactive to human voices
    c.   that hearing is underdeveloped in the newborn
    d.   startle reflexes when exposed to low-pitched sounds

12.   The newborn's well developed sense of smell is shown in its responses to pleasant and unpleasant odors. These reactions are called
    a.   increased pacifier activity
    b.   olfactory discrimination
    c.   nasofacial reflexes
    d.   olfactory reflexes

13.   Size constancy
    a.   is the understanding that objects shrink as they get farther away
    b.   is the understanding that objects retain their original size no matter how near or far they are
    c.   needs both eyes to perceive
    d.   cannot be perceived by both eyes

14.   The perception of position constancy is not firm until between 10 and 15 months of age, suggesting that this perception is dependent on the infant's ability to
    a.   understand language
    b.   achieve cross-modal transfer
    c.   acquire crawling and walking experience
    d.   achieve depth perception

15.   The visual cliff apparatus designed by Gibson and Walk, showed
    a.   that small animals and babies reacted identically in avoiding the shallow side
    b.   that only the babies avoided the deep side
    c.   baby animals avoided the deep side but research with humans is not as clear as with animals
    d.   the majority of babies crossed to the deep side

16.   Researchers of cross-modal transfer are currently investigating whether the test used may predict
    a.   early muscular coordination
    b.   later intellectual and cognitive development
    c.   later sensory integration
    d.   future reactivity to sensory stimulation

■ ■ ■ ■

PRACTICE TEST 2

1.   That the 2 and 3 day old infants in the North Carolina study recognized mother's voice but not father's, indicates that
  a.   male voices are not as unique as females voices
  b.   they had been hearing mother's voice in-utero for the last month or two
  c.   they had learned to recognize mother's voice in the 2 days after birth
  d.   fathers should have read to them before birth

2.   EEG tracings in the newborn show that neurons in the brain are
  a.   fully mature and in need of experience
  b.   small and not functional
  c.   immature and not yet myelinated
  d.   maturing in a haphazard way

3.   The white fatty substance that grows around the axons of neurons in the nervous system
  a.   is the myelin sheath
  b.   provides insulation, nourishment, and nerve conductions
  c.   develops as a result of a rigid timetable
  d.   all of the above

4.   Infants at the age of 2 years have fully _____ % more synaptic connections than adults. As this may account for the plasticity and flexibility seen in the infant's learning abilities it may also indicate that this time is a/an _____ .
  a.   50%, neurologically sensitive period
  b   75%, experientially sensitive period
  c.   50%, language sensitive period
  d.   75%, time to learn foreign languages

5.   In the habituation method for studying the neonate's abilities,
  a.   the infant develops the habit of looking in one direction
  b.   the infant gets excited about the first stimuli and bored with the second
  c.   the infant reacts noticeably to a second stimuli after he's become bored with the first
  d.   the infant falls asleep

6.   The physical condition of the infant at testing time
  a.   has no real effect on the results
  b.   has been considered an important issue since 1970
  c.   is taken for granted to be excellent
  d.   ZZZZZZZZZZZZZZ-z-z-z-z-z-z-z-z-z-z-z-z-z-z-z.....z

7.   The optokinetic nystagmus measurements for visual acuity involve
  a.   a stabilimeter
  b.   measurements of the way the eyes jump and skitter across the lines on a paper

c.   measurements of the way the eyes move smoothly over the lines on a paper
d.   measurements of how the head turns to see the lines across a paper

8.   Hearing in the six month old infant
a.   is almost as sensitive as adults
b.   is more acute in males
c.   is not as sensitive as adults
d.   decreases from 6 months on

9.   Newborns' olfactory sense
a.   is as keen as adults'
b.   is better than adults'
c.   is not as developed as adults'
d.   shows a preference for sweets

10.   Perception
a.   is the same as sensation
b.   is the way sensory information is passed on to the brain
c.   is the way we interpret sensory information
d.   is the chemical activity in the neurons as they sense the environment

11.   Shape constancy
a.   is seen through the habituation method as early as 12 weeks
b.   changes as the child gets older than 1 year
c.   does not occur until the child is older than 1 year
d.   none of the above

12.   The shape, size and position constancies appear to develop or be well canalized
a.   to aid the development of the senses
b.   to aid early voluntary walking
c.   to aid in understanding the world and how to function in it
d.   all of the above

13.   Although research is not as clear with humans as with animals, depth perception
a.   may be wholly learned from experience
b.   may be present as early as 3 weeks, according to the looming method
c.   may be an easily canalized behavior
d.   any of these depending on your "nature vs. nurture" point of view

14.   Biological motion perception helps infants to discriminate the unique movement of
a.   living organisms
b.   threatening people
c.   threatening animals
d.   birds and animals

15. It appears that although adversity does happen to some infants, according to the Skeels study, early intervention can aid
    a. in increasing prosocial behavior
    b. in increasing self esteem
    c. in decreasing antisocial behavior
    d. in increasing IQ points significantly

ANSWER SECTION

<u>*Guided Review*</u>
1.   *weeks*
2.   *myelinated*
3.   *insulator, nerve conduction*
4.   *smile*
5.   *density, 50, synaptic connections*
6.   *plasticity, right hemisphere*
7.   *16 years, 72*
8.   1.   *irreparable physical damage to a function on which a later development will depend*
        2.   *a critical period that passes without the child's obtaining the necessary experiences or stimulation*
        3.   *a situation where the child is kept from ever obtaining the learning necessary for proper development*
9.   1.   *seek more attention*
        2.   *more restless and disobedient*
        3.   *are unpopular*
10.   *preference, single stimulus, habituation*
11.   *neural networks, experience-expectant*
12.   *preference*
13.   *habituation*
14.   *right, alertness, health*
15.   *basic, serendipitous*
16.   *20, 800*
17.   *optokinetic nystagmus or visual saccade*
18.   *6, 12, genetic inheritance*
19.   *before birth, loudness, pitch*
20.   *stabilimeter, adult*
21.   *sweet, salty*
22   *female, male*
23   *perception*
24.   *size constancy*
25.   *shape constancy, 12 weeks*
26.   *position constancy, 10-15 months*
27.   *depth perception*
28.   *crawl, depth*
29.   *depth perception, size constancy, position constancy*
30.   *cross-modal perception*
31.   *sensory integration*
32.   *biological motion*
33.   *sense, world*

Practice Test 1
Are you reading the questions carefully?

1.	b	9.	d
2.	c	10.	c
3.	a	11.	b
4.	d	12.	c
5.	b	13.	b
6.	d	14.	c
7.	d	15.	c
8.	b	16.	b

Practice Test 2
Are you reading the choices carefully?

1.	b	9.	a
2.	c	10.	c
3.	d	11.	a
4.	a	12.	c
5.	c	13.	d
6.	b	14.	a
7.	b	15.	d
8.	a		

CHAPTER SIX

INFANT SOCIAL AND EMOTIONAL DEVELOPMENT

■ ■ ■ ■

LEARNING OBJECTIVES

If you studied psychology a few years ago, you'll find some changes in the theories of attachment. In this chapter, you will see the new research which has necessitated a re-thinking of the older approaches and the recognition of new findings leading to new perspectives. You and your study group, or your friends from Poleved, will enjoy the descriptions of the studies of emotions and social attachments as you prepare for your class.

1. In the Chapter Preview you see infants respond to approving or disapproving statements made in three language plus the familiar English and English nonsense syllables. The infants ignored either kind of statements when made in adult-to-adult intonations, but did respond to adult-to-baby sing-song tones. It appears that infants are more sensitive to the tones of our voices, approving or prohibitive, than to the meanings of the words themselves.

2. Although you should understand the psychoanalytic and social learning theories of attachment, you'll want to discuss more carefully the work of Harry Harlow and others described here. They have discovered there is much more to the attachment of child and mother than the satisfaction of primary needs.

3. Do understand and be able to discuss the intraorganismic perspective which sees attachment based on the biological organization of infants. Is the infant neurologically and biologically predisposed to form attachment to caregivers?

4. It is not surprising that someone, in this case ethologist Konrad Lorenz, would investigate D. A. Spalding's work on the following response. You will want to explain the ethological view and know what Lorenz meant by "imprinting" during critical periods.

5. You should be able to explain the work of John Bowlby and his intraorganismic perspective. According to this view, attachment is based on a wide range of behaviors, which, in an evolutionary sense, are designed to make parents and babies intrinsically attractive to each other, and to make attachment a major mode of interaction. Be sure to describe the "internal working model" of relationships between the child and her caregivers.

6.   Tell them what you think of the discussions pro and con regarding mother-infant bonding. See the At Issue to get some of the conflicting views of the researchers.

7.   The work of Mary Ainsworth will be important to describe, especially since she observed attachment from the attachment-exploration balance and the secure-base phenomenon. Do describe the three kinds of attachment Ainsworth defined and the importance of her studies in terms of stability over time. Be sure to explain her methods and the conclusions she reached.

8.   When you add that Michael Lamb and others have included the influences of family stability, you will have a new quality to discuss in the issues of attachment. You will certainly want to include L. Alan Sroufe's investigations of personal competence and peer approval as children get older.

9.   When you are asked about what roles the father plays in attachment and socialization of our babies, you'll want to be ready to talk about the changes that have come about, and the way they interact with their children.

10.   Can you imagine what we'd be like if we had no emotions? What purpose do emotions serve?

11.   Stanley Greenspan has developed six stages of social-emotional development and shows how important it is to understand how emotions tie in with other developmental issues. Notice too, the discrete emotions theory, which espouses the presence of all emotions at birth and the connection of the maturational time-table that allows expression of them. Compare this more biologically oriented theory to the older view that infants possess undifferentiated affective states at birth which gain more definition and expression through socialization rather than through physical maturation of the nervous system.

12.   Stranger anxiety has been discussed and debated for some time. Is it the person, the behavior of the stranger, or that the baby has to share parental attention? Have we learned this or is there a genetic program in place? And are the theories presented in your book mutually exclusive? Pay attention to what you know about separation anxiety and stranger anxiety.

13.   Be prepared to describe the "day-care" issues discussed in the Application section of the chapter. Here's where you can express opinions and your own experience.

You can see that your author has given you good theoretical and research information regarding social and emotional development in infants. Now, take the time to observe babies in their homes and at day care centers to see how these studies apply in everyday life. You can have a really exciting experience watching your textbook come to life as you apply what you're learning to your observations. Be sure to keep up with news and journal articles. These issues are hotly debated.

■ ■ ■ ■

CHAPTER OUTLINE

You'll be doing even more of the outline this time. I hope you have found the effort of linking ideas together in this way as helpful for your studying as other students tell me they have.

Chapter Preview: Infants respond to more than language in terms of tone of voice and sensitivity to emotional content of what is said to them.

I.   Social Ties

Early social and emotional attachments between infant and his caregivers.
- A. Early Theories of Attachment
    - 1. Changes in orientation of theories
        - a. Freud - Psychoanalytic theory
        - b. learning theory
        - c. many changes in last 40-50 years
- B. Monkey Love: Harry Harlow 1960's
    - 1. Infant rhesus monkeys and surrogate mothers
        - a. monkeys showed preference for cloth mothers
            - (1) _____
            - (2) _____
            - (3) _____
        - b. attachment occurs with experience
        - c. social and attachment behavior with siblings, others
        - d. continues after biological needs are met

II. The Intraorganismic Perspective

Attachment not only learned but dependent on biological organization and readiness and that parents and infants are predisposed to form attachment to each other.
- A. Based on experience-expectant neurological system
    - 1. Ethology
        - a. imprinting
            - (1) D. A. Spalding 1873 _____
                - (a) the following response
            - (2) Konrad Lorenz 1937 _____
                - (a) imprinting ducklings _____
                - (b) critical period _____
    - 2. No particular sensitive or critical period in humans
        - a. innate attraction- John Bowlby
- B. John Bowlby (The Nature of a Child's Tie to His Mother) began contemporary theory 1958
    - 1. Attachment is a wide range of individual behaviors in the interaction of infant and parents which are intrinsically satisfying to both infant and parent
    - 2. The development of the attachment process
        - a. the purpose of infant's behavior must be considered
        - b. attachment stems from within the infant
        - c. infant's smiles and cries are intrinsically stimulating to parent to promote activation of interaction
        - d. as strong as mating or parental drive
    - 3. The "internal working model"
        - a. memories of relationship forms model
        - b. infant develops expectation of caregiver
        - c. develops expectation of self in relationship
        - d. infant learns to whom to attach
        - e. well organized during last half of first year
    - 4. The quality of attachment depends on the experience and the quality of the internal working model of both mother and infant

At Issue: The Mother-Infant bond--Kennell & Klaus, Chess and Thomas, etc.
You'll want to outline this "At Issue" since opinions and research have found differences. What do you think?

III.   The Dynamics Of Human Attachment

    A.   Mary Ainsworth-- a new way of viewing attachment situations in which child felt either secure or insecure

        1.   attachment-exploration balance

            a.   _____

            b.   _____

        2.   secure-base phenomenon

            a.   _____

            b.   _____

    B.   Ainsworth's studies: Infant behavior in "strange situation"
Table 6.1 will help you here

        1.   secure attachment shown, 67-70%, _____

        2.   anxious/resistant attachment shown, 10-15% _____

        3.   anxious/avoidant attachment shown _____

        4.   fairly stable over time

        5.   can be improved with change in mother's behavior

    C.   Ainsworth studies of mother's treatment of child in home

        1.   Related to accessibility and quality of attachment related to way mother responds to child

        2.   Mother's response to child's cries

            a.   _____

            b.   _____

            c.   _____

        3.   Mother's style of mothering dependent on her own "working models"

            a.   _____

         4.   Lasting effects

            a.   _____

         5.   Child's temperament

            a.   _____

         6.   Cross cultural research

            a.   Israeli Kibbutzim

            b.   Japan

            c.   Northern Germany

            d.   variations within culture more pronounced than variation between cultures

               _____

    D.   Early Attachment and Later Development
Minnesota Preschool Project: L. Alan Sroufe: securely attached infants show more mastery and competence

        1.   Attachment and Social Relationships

            a.   Social Competence and peer approval _____

        2.   Correlational findings

            a.   _____

    E.   Attachment therapy

        1.   2 year program

2. _____
   F.   Attachment and Family Stability: Michael Lamb
        1.   Influence of whole family stability
        2.   Therapy must address whole family
        3.   a third factor? _____

IV.   Father's Role (research ignored fathers prior to 1970)
   A.   Changes in Role due to mother's role changes
        1.   _____
        2.   _____
        3.   Except for nursing, fathers just as capable of primary care, especially with practice
            _____
        4.   Traditional roles still hold strong in some cases and places
        5.   Fathers' play -- example of different interactions
        6.   2 1/2 year olds choose Dad as playmate
   B.   John Bowlby - distinction of "playmate" and "attachment figure"
        1.   Child understands that mother and father behave differently
        2.   How father responds determines infant perception of him as attachment figure
        3.   How father perceives self determines _____
        4.   Attachment during 1st year _____

V.   Social-Emotional Development   *Do leave room for notes*
   A.   Functions of Emotions
        1.   Charles Darwin The Expression of the Emotions in Man and Animals
            a.   motivation _____
            b.   interpersonal communication _____
        2.   Greenspan's six stages: may differ in ages, but same sequence for all. Stages may overlap. Write a brief description of these
            a.   Stage 1: _____
               _____
            b.   Stage 2: _____
               _____
            c.   Stage 3: _____
               _____
            d.   Stage 4: _____
               _____
            e.   Stage 5: _____
               _____
            f.   Stage 6: _____
               _____

VI.   The Development of Emotions, see table 6.5,
   A.   Positive Emotional Expressions: facial musculature fully developed at birth
        1.   10 week old infants can discriminate mothers' emotional facial expressions and respond with corresponding emotions
            a.   debated ----- traditional theory of socialization
            b.   discrete emotion theory _____
        2.   Table 6.5
            a.   timing of emotion expressions

3.   Separation anxiety
    a.   seen as early as 6 months
    b.   peaks at 18 months
    c.   How is this related to stranger anxiety? or is it?

VII. Fear of Strangers- begins at about 6 months, reaches peak at 8 months - not clear in research. See table 6.6

    A.   is child afraid of new person, or their behavior, parent leaving, or being ignored in presence of stranger?
    B.   ethology theory _____
    C.   social learning theory _____
    D.   rarely show fear of children _____

Applications: Is Day Care a Good Idea?

How is it used?

Quality of Day Care. What determines quality?

Common Sense Needed: What do you think?

How do parents chose a good day-care center?

How did it go? Did you find yourself reading the text more carefully to fill in the outline? Good! Does remembering one piece of information lead you to remembering another? You are putting the information you are reading into your memory. That's the whole idea!

■ ■ ■ ■   ◀
                                                                                         ◀
                                                                                         ◀

NAMES TO REMEMBER

Sigmund Freud	Mary Ainsworth
Harry Harlow	L. Alan Sroufe
John Bowlby	Michael Lamb
D. A. Spalding	Joseph Campos
Konrad Lorenz	Charles Darwin
Kennell and Klaus	Stanley Greenspan

■ ■ ■ ■   ◀
                                                                                         ◀
                                                                                         ◀

TERMS AND CONCEPTS

attachment theories	ethological view
surrogate mother	following response
contact comfort	imprinting
the intraorganismic perspective	critical period
internal working model	bonding

attachment-exploration balance
secure attachment
secure-base phenomenon
strange situation
anxious/resistant attachment
anxious/avoidant attachment
metapelet
social competence
attachment therapy
father's role
sex-stereotypes
playmate

attachment figure
functions of emotions
Six stages of social-emotional development
arousal, quiescence
discrete emotion theory
reflex smiling
social smile
laugh
anger
fear
separation anxiety
stranger anxiety

■ ■ ■ ■

GUIDED REVIEW

1.   According to the research reported in the Chapter Preview, young infants respond to vocal
      tone as well as the _emotional_ content of the words said to them rather than the
      meaning.

2.   As the infant and caregivers form social and emotional ties through their interactions,
      attachment mechanisms become a part of their relationship.

3.   Both Sigmund Freud's and social learning theories proposed that the infant's attachment to her
      parent was formed as a result of the _satisfaction_ of _basic_ _needs_ .

4.   Harlow's experiments with the monkeys and surrogate cloth covered wire "mothers" showed that
      the attachment went beyond _contact comfort_ . The soft mother was used as a
      safe _base_ for exploration and comfort when the monkey was
      frightened, even though no food was available from the "mother".

5.   The most accepted theoretical view in recent years has moved toward the _intraorganismic_
      perspective, which declares that the child is _innately_ or _biologically_
      organized to form _attachment_ to caregivers.

6.   The intraorganismic perspective is thought to be based on the _experience-expectant_
      neurological system, suggesting our species would expect attachment to our caregivers to occur.

7.   As an ethologist, Konrad Lorenz further developed the view that certain behaviors involved in
      ducklings' following the first moving object they saw were _imprinted_, that is, stamped into
      their brains just after birth.

8.   Lorenz also found that there was an optimal time, or a _critical period_ when

the environment must offer the opportunity for these behaviors to emerge or they will not occur.

9. John Kennell and Marshall Klaus believe there is a sensitive period following birth for _bonding_ to occur between mother and newborn. However, they revised their opinion when issues such as adoption and cross cultural research recognized many other _fail_ _safe_ routes to attachment.

10. John Bowlby believes _attachment_ is an entire way of interacting, and that these behaviors must be considered for their _continuity_ of _purpose_.

11. Although there is a predisposition for attachment, Bowlby explains that the infant learns to whom to become attached. He views attachment as a developmental system which is completed during the _second_ half of the _first_ year.

12. By 18 months the child's attachment process begins to form an _internal working model_ which allows him to remember the relationship and know what he can expect from caregivers in different situations.

13. Mary Ainsworth measured attachment addressing two concepts. The first, the _attachment exploration_ balance, is the need for attachment and need to explore the environment. The second, the _secure_ - _base_ _phenomenon_ uses the attachment figure (usually Mom) as a base from which to explore.

14. Using the _strange_ _situation_, Ainsworth recorded the kind of behavior exhibited by the child upon the mother's return. These behaviors demonstrated the quality of the child's sense of security and attachment.

15. Three qualities of attachment were noted. Most children showed _secure attachment_ while the others responded with either _anxious resistant attachment_ (10-15%), or _anxious/avoidant attachment_ (20-25%).

16. The quality of attachment, according the Ainsworth and colleagues, was related to the way mothers reacted to their children. Mothers of avoidant children responded _sensitive_ consistently, and were less _less_ to their child's needs, whereas babies who have most consistent access to a sensitive mother were more _securely attached_.

17. Babies whose mothers were the most accessible to them, cried less and required less contact as they grew older than those _less securely attached_. The lesson here, is that babies who were cuddled and attended to promptly _cried less_ and were _more content_.

18. Cross cultural research concerning attachment shows _1½_ times as much or more variation within a culture as variation between cultures.

19. Alan Sroufe's longitudinal research has shown that children described as securely attached at 15 months were socially _more competent_ and well liked by preschool peers at 3

1/2 years of age.

20. Michael Lamb broadened his study to include the effect of a __stable__ __family__ and the stability of __child__ __care__ arrangements on later social acceptance.

21. Although fathers are as capable as mothers of primary care, their role in most homes appears to be that of __playmate__. The general agreement of researchers is that attachment to fathers can be as strong as to mothers depending on how __responsive__ the father is to the infant's signals. __ness__

22. Although most mothers agree husbands are helping more, the mother still spends over __four__ times as many hours with the infant than the father.

23. At this point, fathers are preferred by infants as __playmates__, while __mothers__ are preferred as the __primary__ __caregivers__

24. In his book, The Expressions of Emotions in Man and Animals, __Charles__ __Darwin__ expressed his belief that emotions have important survival functions.

25. Two services of emotions reported in his book, were those of __motivation__ and the facilitation of __interpersonal communication__

26. __Stanley__ __Greenspan__ (NIMH) combined his and other's research in his outline of six stages of social-emotional development occurring during the first __four__ years.

27. Complex interactions begin when the child sees herself as the originator of social-emotional expressions. This occurs during stage __four__ and is known as the emergence of an __organized sense__ of __self__.

28. When children can understand the way emotions work and we see that they are attempting self-regulation of emotions and behavior we can say they have reached stage 6: __emotional thinking__, the basis for fantasy, reality, and self esteem.

29. According to early research, infants start emotional growth showing only __arousal__ or __quiescence__

30. The discrete emotions theory differs from previous traditional assumptions in that it espouses that all basic emotions exist at birth and that the infant becomes more capable of expressing them as the __nervous system__ matures.

31. This newer theory still does not explain whether babies actually __feel__ the emotions they display.

32. Stranger anxiety in infants who have limited exposure to strangers begins typically at __six__ months and peaks at __eight__ months.

33.   _Social ___ learning___ theory proposes infants learn that parents will interact with
       the stranger and pay less attention to them.

34.   Children in day-care centers usually prefer caregivers there over strangers, and prefer
       mothers over the day-caregivers.

35.   Due to the variety of standards in day-care facilities, parents are advised to look for one that
       provides _activities_ social _interaction_ nutritious food, good _supervision_ and
       supervision safety

■ ■ ■ ■   ◄
                                                                                 ◄
                                                                                 ◄
PRACTICE TEST 1   ◄

1.   When five month old infants were exposed to adult-to-adult comments they _____ them.
       When the infant heard approving or disapproving statements made in adult-to-child tones, they
       responded by _____ to approving statements, and were visibly _____ by disapproving
       statements.
       a.   ignored, cried, cried
       b.   ignored, smiling, upset
       c.   cried, cried, cried
       d.   smiled, ignored, ignored

2.   In contrast to the conclusions of Freud and the learning theorists, the studies of Harry Harlow
       showed
       a.   that there is more than contact comfort or biological need satisfaction in the attachment of
              rhesus monkeys to the surrogate cloth mother
       b.   that attachments of the baby monkeys were formed early and were long lasting
       c.   neither a nor b
       d.   both a and b

3.   Ethologists like Konrad Lorenz view many behaviors, including attachment, as
       a.   bonding
       b.   performed to achieve contact comfort
       c.   an innate drive
       d.   dependent solely on learning

4.   The intraorganismic perspective views attachment as behaviors which are
       a.   both learned and innately predisposed
       b.   learned by association
       c.   stamped into one's brain
       d.   accidental, and then reinforced

5.   Intraorganismic organization describes the infant as biologically ready

a.   to perform behaviors which are intrinsically satisfying to her parents

b.   to form attachments to her caregivers

c.   to form internal working models of the relationships among herself and her caregivers

d.   all of the above

6.   The issue of bonding, despite disagreement, has been useful because it has

      a.   not promoted changes in child custody disputes

      b.   emphasized that there is no critical period right after birth for bonding to occur

      c.   shown that adoptive parents have no hope of being viewed as attachment figures

      d.   encouraged hospitals to allow close parent-infant contact during the first hours and days after delivery

7.   _____ describes a complex ability of the child over 18 months where he or she develops an appraisal of the quality of her relationship with her parents, called _____.

      a.   Mary Ainsworth; an internal working model

      b.   John Bowlby; an internal working model

      c.   John Bowlby; the secure base phenomenon

      d.   Mary Ainsworth; the secure base phenomenon

8.   Mary Ainsworth explored the behaviors involved in attachment in the two concepts of _____ and _____.

      a.   attachment-exploration balance; secure base phenomenon

      b.   bonding; secure base phenomenon

      c.   human attachment; exploration of environment

      d.   attachment-exploration balance; bonding

9.   The most common attachment shown in the Ainsworth studies was _____, while _____ was the second most frequent.

      a.   the attachment exploration balance; anxious/avoidant attachment

      b.   secure attachment; anxious/resistant attachment

      c.   resistant attachment; anxious/avoidant attachment

      d.   secure attachment; anxious/avoidant attachment

10.   The Ainsworth studies showed that the baby who can trust the adult to respond promptly to his needs _____.

      a.   learns to cry more

      b.   becomes more dependent

      c.   cries less

      d.   is spoiled rotten!

11.   Fathers were ignored in research until the 70's because

      a.   they can't give birth to babies anyway

      b.   they aren't interested in babies

      c.   they are less likely to be primary caregivers in most societies

      d.   they have been found to be incompetent as parents

12. Emotions are so important in _____, that researchers combine them as the study of _____.
    a. forming social bonds and attachment; social-emotional development
    b. communication and motivation; The Expression of the Emotions in Man and Animals
    c. universal innate emotional expression; social-emotional development
    d. separation anxiety and stranger anxiety; memory functions in emotions

13. Charles Darwin viewed emotions as serving two valuable functions:
    a. as motivators of behaviors; to help communicate our feelings to others
    b. to form bonds between parent and child; to develop communications
    c. to adapt to the environment; to develop individuality
    d. for survival; for diversification

14. Stanley Greenspan has proposed a stage approach to the range of social emotional development in small children. Nightmares and imaginative play typically occur during the _____ stage, called _____.
    a. second; falling in love
    b. third; developing intentional communication
    c. fifth; creating emotional ideas
    d. sixth; emotional thinking

15. Fear of strangers develops in infants at about _____ months and peaks at about _____ months.
    a. four; six
    b. six; ten
    c. six; eight
    d. eight; ten

■ ■ ■ ■

PRACTICE TEST 2

1. Changes in attachment theory in the past 30 years show that attachment
   a. is dependent on more than satisfaction of biological needs
   b. can be made to other than parents
   c. can happen even when an infant is mistreated by the caregiver
   d. all of the above

2. That attachment is not only learned but is also a matter of biological organization is the view of
   a. the secondary-drive theorists
   b. those who hold the intraorganismic perspective
   c. the imprinting theorists
   d. those who hold the social referencing perspective

3. The Kennell, Klaus conclusions in their of infant-mother bonding, have been replaced because
   a. skin-to-skin contact at birth is essential to proper bonding
   b. bonding is the single route to attachment
   c. bonding has no relationship to attachment
   d. ✓ their research methodology was flawed, and cultural studies show that mother's affection was not any greater in societies that encouraged early infant-mother body contact than in those that don't

4. John Bowlby began contemporary attachment theory by stating that attachment must be seen as
   a. a few specific behaviors which maintain social attachment
   b. ✓ a wide range of interactive behaviors which initiate and maintain social attachment
   c. behaviors which occur after 18 months of age
   d. behaviors which are performed by the infant alone

5. An important aspect of John Bowlby's "internal working model" is that the child develops an appraisal of the _____ as well as _____ in their relationship.
   a. emotions, behaviors
   b. secure base, expectations
   c. ✓ parent, her/himself
   d. bonding, attachment

6. Mary Ainsworth explored the quality of attachment using a laboratory test she called _____, where infants' reaction to _____ was observed.
   a. ✓ the strange situation, the return of the mother
   b. secure attachment, the mother leaving the room
   c. the strange situation, the entrance of the stranger
   d. attachment-exploration, resistant attachment

7. The kind of attachment shown in the Ainsworth studies appeared to be related to the way the
   a. child responded to the stranger
   b. ✓ mother responded to the child
   c. mother responded to the stranger
   d. child responded to day care

8. L. Alan Sroufe and his colleagues found that preschool children judged securely attached at 15 months demonstrated _____ at 3 1/2 years.
   a. unpredictability
   b. unpopularity
   c. inappropriate reactions
   d. ✓ social competence

9. Stanley Greenspan, in integrating the research of many others, has outlined _____ stages of emotional development.
   a. 4
   b. ✓ 6
   c. 3

d.   12

10.   By Greenspan's stage four the child takes emotional dialogue further and exhibits small social-emotional interactions of stage three. An example would be
a.   to complain of nightmares
b.   to manipulate her father by pouting
c.   to ask to be picked up by tugging on fathers hand and holding her arms up
d.   controlling her anger until she gets to her room

11.   Stanley Greenspan's stages cover the first 4 years of social-emotional development culminating in the beginning of the understanding of the need for _____.
a.   the emergence of an organized sense of self
b.   falling in love
c.   self regulation of emotions and social behavior
d.   creating emotional ties

12.   Traditional beliefs have held that since newborns have the facial musculature developed to make the same emotional faces as adults, their emotions
a.   are equally well developed at birth
b.   become developed and differentiated with socialization
c.   are present at birth and are expressed as the nervous system matures
d.   develop one at a time over the first six months

13.   Newer researchers who believe the discrete emotions theory, propose that newborns' emotions
a.   are equally well developed at birth
b.   become developed and differentiated with socialization
c.   are present at birth and are expressed as the nervous system matures
d.   develop one at a time over the first six months

14.   Children in quality day-care facilities including language, social and intellectual development programs, have
a.   formed closer attachment to day-caregivers than their parents
b.   suffered irreparably from the separation from their mothers
c.   become more emotionally stable than home bound children
d.   fared as well or better than those left with individual baby sitters

15.   The most effective day care center will provide
a.   small group interaction of children close in age
b.   teachers well trained in child development
c.   encouragement for children's development of social, language and intellectual skills
d.   all of the above

ANSWER SECTION

Guided Review

1. tone, emotional
2. attachment
3. satisfaction, basic or biological needs
4. "contact comfort", safe base
5. intraorganismic perspective, innately, biologically, attachments
6. experience-expectant
7. imprinted
8. critical period
9. bonding, "fail safe"
10. attachment, continuity, purpose
11. second, first
12. internal working model
13. attachment-exploration; secure-base phenomenon
14. strange situation
15. secure attachment, anxious/resistant attachment, anxious/avoidant attachment
16. less, sensitive, securely attached
17. less securely attached, cried less, more content
18. 1 1/2
19. more competent
20. stable family, child care
21. playmate, responsive
22. four
23. playmates, mothers, primary caregiver
24. Charles Darwin
25. motivation, interpersonal communication
26. Stanley Greenspan, four
27. four, organized sense, self
28. emotional thinking
29. arousal, quiescence
30. nervous system
31. feel
32. six, eight
33. social learning
34. mothers
35. activities, interaction, supervision, safety

Practice Test 1

1. b
2. d
3. c
4. a

5.	d
6.	d
7.	b
8.	a
9.	d
10.	c

11.	c
12.	a
13.	a
14.	c
15.	c

Practice Test 2

1.	d
2.	b
3.	d
4.	b
5.	c
6.	a
7.	b
8.	d

9.	b
10.	b
11.	c
12.	b
13.	c
14.	d
15.	d

CHAPTER SEVEN

LEARNING

■■■■

LEARNING OBJECTIVES

This chapter is going to be fun to explain to your friends. You not only can tell them about learning, you can show them. This is an ideal time to teach your pet a new trick using behavior modification. While they watch, you choose the behavior you want it to learn, shape the behavior, and reinforce it each step along the way. You can show them how TV and movie characters can act as models for children and adults. Send them out shopping and show them how the choices of products they buy were influenced by advertising. All this and ace-ing the test too!

1. In the Chapter Preview you see toddlers learning how to manipulate certain objects by watching other toddlers perform. The learners even remembered how to play with the objects at home two days after they observed their peer "teachers". There will be more about social learning as we pursue this chapter on Learning.

2. You might want to start by showing your friends birds, fish and other animals just doing what comes naturally. Species-specific behaviors are interesting and part of the fun is looking for the releaser stimulus. A mother bird feeding her chick is a prime example. Look where she holds the worm!

3. Talk about the capacity to learn. It appears to be inherited in order to survive. Remember that psychologists cite a general rule that the more highly evolved the species is, the less its behaviors are directed by genes. Is this why there are such varieties of behaviors and adaptations to our environment?

4. You'd better be able to define what learning is, so there'll be no doubt about what you're discussing, as well as helping you remember a sure fire answer to a sure fire test question.

5. Plan to describe the major kinds of learning addressed in this chapter and how they happen. Start with classical conditioning and Ivan Pavlov. Understanding and having a comfortable relationship with the language of classical conditioning is a must. Know what US, CS, UR, and CR mean. We experience this kind of learning all the time. Notice the importance of contingency detection. Oops! A bell is ringing. Somebody answer the phone!

6. The example of the Watson and Rayner work with Little Albert is an interesting, but sad, example of classical conditioning in humans. Objects similar to the rabbit elicited Albert's fear as well as the

original rabbit, illustrating stimulus generalization. Its probably something like the feeling we get when, after a few painful experiences with the dentist, we get the reminder for another check-up.

7.   Show them how Kenneth Clark demonstrated affective conditioning. Come to think about it, they've probably experienced prejudice themselves as visitors from another planet and it may help them to know how their unusual treatment comes about. Ask them to check into their own thinking about earthlings! Of course you don't stereotype anyone, do you? All teachers are . . . WHAT????

8.   Thorndike's law of effect makes sense, doesn't it? His work laid the groundwork for B. F. Skinner to develop his more elaborate theories. A behaviorist I know once said, in summary of behaviorism, "If it feels good, I'll do it again!"

9.   Be familiar with Skinner's views on instrumental learning and reinforcement. You should know that the behavior must happen first and the reinforcement strengthens that behavior as a consequence of it. See how the behavior "operates" on the environment by insuring a desired result?

10.   Talk about how shaping works. Remember when you taught someone to tie their shoe? You might want to take them to a circus to see the animals perform complicated behaviors.

11.   Social learning is somewhat different from the other ways of learning. It is an interaction between environment and thinking. We all have learned this way even if our models have not been rewarded. Remember the first bad word you brought home? No reinforcement for saying it for sure, but you did learn it anyway! AND you learned where not to say that word again!

12.   Imitation is more than the sincerest form of flattery. The value and status of the model in the view of the learner is important. We do some thinking and deciding about the model and the behavior. Here's a time to remember what is meant by canalized behaviors.

13.   Consider the influence of T.V., newspapers, books and magazines. What do your text author and other researchers say about the influence of media and violent behavior?

14.   Related to the media, address the question of children watching violence on T.V. and their aggressive behavior.

15.   Discuss the use of behavior modification as a tool to help change unproductive or unacceptable behavior.

Remember your first hero, or for that matter, your present hero? How do we decide what's important in terms of possessions, even values? What influenced you? What influences have been important to your friends?

■ ■ ■ ■   ◀
                                                                                            ◀
CHAPTER OUTLINE   ◀

Back to work you go! This chapter has so much information, and it's so well organized, you'll enjoy outlining it. Again, more will be left to you than before. How's your confidence? By now, I'll bet you've noticed the author's questions really do highlight important factors and help you to be alert to test items and usable information. Be careful: don't try to modify anyone's behavior without their wanting to work at it, or you'll lose friends fast!

Chapter Preview: Show and Tell. Toddlers learn from peers how to manipulate objects, and remember what they've learned. Social learning.

I.   Built in Behaviors: Reflexes and Instincts
       A.   Species Specific Behaviors: Fixed-response patterns
              1.   Definition
              2.   Triggered by releaser or sign stimulus
                   a.   example of robin and worm
       B.   Reflexes in Humans
              1.   Reflexes of coughing, crying, blinking, swallowing, sucking, etc.
              2.   Ethologist view of baby behavior as sign stimulus for parental behavior as a feature of attachment.
              3.   Remember the general rule in Psychology
                   a.   e.g.: _____

II.   The Importance of Learning: a relatively permanent change in behavior as a result of prior experience
       A.   Survival value of learning
              1.   Does not rely solely on experience-expectant neurology
              2.   Different experiences allow individually different learning
              3.   Ability to learn allows flexibility and individuality of responses

III.   Three Kinds of Learning According to Behavior Theory
       Learning through association of stimuli--Classical conditioning
       Learning through association of response and its consequence -- Instrumental learning -- Operant Conditioning
       Learning through observation of others--Social learning
       A.   Classical Conditioning--Learning through the Association of Responses and Stimuli
              1.   Ivan Pavlov's experiments: dogs made a connection between the presentation of food and seeing someone open the cupboard where food is kept-- called CONTIGUOUS ASSOCIATION--Two stimuli are associated!
                   a.   Pavlov's experiments: food, an UNCONDITIONED STIMULUS, is presented to the dog who responds (without having had to learn) by salivating, an UNCONDITIONED RESPONSE. All of this is unlearned! *Here comes the learning--*
                   b.   Pavlov now presents a bell, then immediately presents the food, and measures the salivation response of the dog. He repeats this many times. Soon he presents the bell, and now does not present the food, and the dog salivates anyway. "Roverkov" has associated the bell with the food and acts the same way to the bell--now the CONDITIONED STIMULUS--as he did to the food--he salivates at the bell! It's a CONDITIONED RESPONSE now. The bell now predicts the arrival of food--or at least he hopes so--called CONTINGENCY DETECTION. The dog has learned to respond to the bell in a way he never did before. (Did I say "somebody answer the phone"?)

You may not want to write this out in such detail, but try it and see if it helps you keep it straight. Refer to Figure 7.2. Now try this paradigm in a different situation. For example, when the kids hear the music from the ice cream truck, what happens? Or when you look at a picture of your first boy/girl friend? You can see there are several associations linked together in life situations with real people.

              2.   The case of Little Albert. Now that you understand the classical conditioning, diagram the mean thing John Watson and Rosalie Rayner did to Albert.
                      Before conditioning: Use appropriate code--US, CS, UR, CR

Rat _____ response _____

Loud noise _____ response _____

During conditioning: Which is which? Rat, loud noise, fear response, crying

CS _____ followed by presentation of US _____ elicits UR _____

After conditioning:

Rat _____ elicits fear response _____

    a.   stimulus generalization _____

    b.   counter conditioning _____

    c.   extinction _____

    d.   habituation: _____

          (1)   H. B. English's attempt to replicate the Watson-Rayner experiment

               (a)   14 month old girl, loud gong

               (b)   brothers in the home!

    3.   Affective conditioning--a stimulus elicits a response, such as involved in beliefs, emotions, attitudes.

        a.   Kenneth Clark: black doll white doll--racial prejudice

          (1)   1960- "Black is beautiful" _____

              _____

        b.   Nunnally, Duchnowski, Parker--kids, syllables and stick figures

              _____

              _____

        c.   Staats and Staats experiment with college students

              _____

        d.   Bittersweet memory _____

              _____

B.   Instrumental Learning: Learning Through the Association of Responses and Stimuli

    1.   The Law of Effect

        a.   E. L. Thorndike -- any act which produces satisfactory results is likely to be repeated when that situation recurs.

        b.   the cornerstone of instrumental learning

    2.   Operant Conditioning

        a.   B. F. Skinner--operants are voluntary behaviors (responses) which have effects on the environment and which can be made stronger by reinforcing consequences, or weaker by unpleasant consequences.

        b.   unlike classical conditioning where the organism is affected by a stimulus before behaving, the behavior happens first, then the consequence tells it if the behavior has value.

    3.   Reinforcement and Extinction

        a.   resistance to extinction used to measure the strength of the response, that is, how long it takes for the behavior to return to original state (Eg: stop occurring) after reinforcement is withdrawn.

             Can you think of an example here? How long did it take for your dog to stop begging at the table after you stopped giving it goodies while you ate dinner?

        b.   reinforcement-- more than reward! It is any stimulus consequence which strengthens the behavior it follows. We now use the term stimulus consequence since the reinforcement offers information to do that behavior again under similar circumstances.

    c.   Ex post facto deductive system--a deduction made after the fact. The effect on behavior of the stimulus consequence must be observed and able to be recorded to avoid guess work on the part of the experimenter.

    A short review of what you've learned about learning. *Here you go! You do this one. See Figure 7.8 for help.*

    (1)   Unlearned response

_____

_____

    (2)   Classically conditioned response

_____

_____

    (3)   Instrumentally learned Response _____

_____

    (4)   SR+ or SR-

_____

_____

    (5)   stimulus generalization

_____

_____

    (6)   discrimination

_____

_____

    4.   Shaping

        a.   teaching complicated behaviors by reinforcing successive approximations. *Here's where you can explain some of the complicated things we do, like learning a new skill. A good example in animals can be seen at the circus where animals do some pretty fancy tricks, or, closer to home, teaching a 5 year old how to tie her shoe.*

IV.   Conditioning in Early Infancy

    A.   Classical conditioning _____

    B.   Operant conditioning _____

    C.   Learning largely responsible for diversity of observable human behavior

        1.   John Watson: father of behaviorism:

            a.   quote 1 _____

            b.   quote 2 _____

        2.   John Locke: tabula rasa

        3.   Modern researchers

            a.   heredity and genetics underlie learning

V.   Social Learning: remember the Chapter Preview

    A.   Observation and Imitation: Monkey See, Monkey Do

        1.   Albert Bandura, Ross and Ross

            a.   modeling aggression

            b.   imitation of aggression

                 (1)   occurs without reinforcement

            c.   Bandura's description of teaching driving using the principles of

reinforcement!
  2.   may be canalized for survival value
      a.   animals learn through observation, too
B.   Performance versus Acquisition--note the distinction!
  1.   When reinforcement makes a difference

_____

  2.   One can learn a behavior without performing it
At Issue: Imitation in Infancy--Baby See Baby Do?
  1.   Controversial, basic and interesting   *You Do!*

_____
_____
_____
_____
_____
_____
_____
_____

C.   Television and Aggression
  1.   Correlational studies of adolescent students who watch aggressive T.V. shows and
          behave aggressively at work and school.
  2.   Study of 4 and 5 year old boys from a Sunday school
      a.   _____
      b.   _____
  3.   Longitudinal studies _____
  4.   Prevention _____
D.   I think Therefore I'm Complicated
  1.   How we organize and process information modifies our behavior
      a.   _____
  2.   Behavior Modification--see Table 7.1
Applications: Behavior Modification, Table of operant techniques used
  1.   Overcoming fear of Dogs
  2.   Toilet Training in less than a day
  3.   Choosing not to spank!

■ ■ ■ ■

NAMES TO REMEMBER

William Quinn   Staats and Staats
Ivan Pavlov   E. L. Thorndike
John Watson, Rosalie Rayner   B. F. Skinner
Little Albert   John Locke
Kenneth Clark   Albert Bandura
Nunnally, Duchnowski, Parker   Andrew Meltzoff

M. Keith Moore   Richard Foxx
Nathan Azrin

■ ■ ■ ■

TERMS AND CONCEPTS

learning
acquired behaviors
fixed-response patterns
stimulus
releaser
sign stimulus
species-specific behaviors
reflexes
habituation
behavior theory
response
classical conditioning
contiguous association
contingency detection
unconditioned stimulus, US
conditioned stimulus, CS
unconditioned response, UR
conditioned response, CR
reinforcement (in classical conditioning)
Little Albert
stimulus generalization
discrimination
counter conditioning

extinction (in classical conditioning)
affective conditioning
the law of effect
instrumental learning
operant conditioning
operant
extinction
reinforcement (in operant conditioning)
stimulus consequence
ex post facto deductive system
shaping
successive approximations
tabula rasa
social learning
model, modeling
imitation
performance vs. acquisition
aggression
thinking and learning
behaviorism
behavior modification
imitation in infancy

■ ■ ■ ■

GUIDED REVIEW

1. The study of learning is the study of __aquired__ behaviors which come to be a __relatively permanent__ part of our behavioral repertoire as a result of experience.

2. Some unlearned behaviors are __species specific__ or __fixed__

response patterns and are triggered by a _releaser_ or _sign stimulus_.

3. Rather than fixed-response behavior, humans possess only a few simple _reflexes_.

4. Although the culture provides us with what we learn, it appears that the _ability_ to learn is inherited and that it involves _flexible adaption_ to the environment.

5. A simple form of learning, _habituation_ comes about when a stimulus is presented so often the subject no longer _responds_ to it.

6. The three major kinds of learning addressed in this chapter are those proposed by _learning_ theory.

7. The famous proponent of classical conditioning, _Ivan Pavlov_, noted his dogs made a _contiguous association_ between the presentation of the food and the opening of the _food cupboard_.

8. In his experiments, Pavlov paired a US (_food_) which elicited a UR (_salivation_) with a bell which previously had evoked no response from the dogs.

9. After several pairings of the food, the _unconditioned stimulus_ with the bell, the dogs responded to the bell presented alone as if the food had been presented. The bell can now be called the _conditioned stimulus_.

10. With each pairing, the food reinforced the power of the bell to elicit the _salivation response_. Salivation in response to the bell is learned and now can be called the _conditioned response_.

11. The dogs had successfully learned that the bell _predicted_ the arrival of the food. This is known as _contigency detection_. In humans, this ability is illustrated when we see a dark cloud, hear thunder, and know a storm is coming.

12. Little Albert's fear response to a white rat was _classically conditioned_ by presenting the CS (the _white rat_), followed by the US (the _loud noise_).

13. Little Albert experienced _stimulus generalization_ when all white furry objects elicited the same fear response.

14. Although it never happened, Albert's fear of white rats could have disappeared or undergone _extinction_ if a process called _counter-conditioning_ had been used.

15. The conditioning of emotions, beliefs and attitudes through associative experiences is called _affective_ conditioning.

16. Kenneth Clark's "good doll, bad doll" experiment is an example of affective conditioning resulting in __racial__ __predjudice__

17. E. L. Thorndike found that when cats were successful in their escape behavior, they repeated the behavior every time they were put in the puzzle box. His statement that behaviors which have a pleasant result will be repeated is his __law__ __of__ __effect__.

18. In classical conditioning the __stimulus__ elicits the __response__.

19. B. F. Skinner broadened the idea of instrumental conditioning to include any combination of behaviors if they had the same effect on the environment. He called these behaviors __operants__ and the learning process __operant conditioning__

20. The strength of operant responses is measured by their resistance to __extinction.__

21. Rather than reward, Skinner prefers the term __reinforcement__ to describe the consequence which __increases__ the strength of the response it follows.

22. An ex-post-facto deduction system describes a deduction made __after__ the __fact__.

23. A child's cry would be a __reflex__ if it were in response to pain, a __conditioned__ __response__ if it were in response to seeing a fire, or __operantly__ __conditioned__ if it were used to avoid going to bed.

24. To obtain a complicated new behavior the technique of __shaping__ is used.

25. The principle of reinforcing successive approximations toward a final response is known as __shaping__.

26. To John Locke, 19th century philosopher, the mind of the newborn infant is a __tabula rasa__ on which learning through experience will define his behavior.

27. John Watson, in his belief that learning is the major factor in the varieties of human behavior recognized that he may have spoken __beyond__ his __facts__.

28. Today, researchers recognize that learning is not solely responsible for the infant's behavior, and that infants are not __passive recipient__ of their environment

29. The most successful conditioning mode in infants has been __operant__ conditioning.

30. Learning through observation of others' behavior is called __social__ __learning__.

31. Even if a model is not reinforced or is punished for a behavior, the observer can __learn__ the behavior.

32. __Immitation__ of a model's behavior which has been punished is __rare__. However,

evidence that the behavior is learned comes when the learner exhibits the behavior at a later, safer time.

33.   Sunday school boys of 4 and 5 who viewed a film in which an adult was aggressive against a clown, engaged in more _aggressive behaviors_ with the clown and toys in their playroom than those who did not see the film.

34.   Perhaps the best method for helping children remain nonaggressive in the face of violence on television is for parents to help children to _descriminite_ between _reality_ and _make_ - _believe_ and to train children to be _gentle_ and _affectionate._

35.   Although Bandura's social learning theory has its roots in _behaviorism_ it also includes the _complex thinking processes_ which modify our behavior.

36.   A set of procedures for changing human behavior, especially by using behavior therapy and operant conditioning techniques is known as _behavior modification_

■ ■ ■ ■   ◀
                                                                                        ◀
                                                                                        ◀
PRACTICE TEST 1   ◀

1.   The study of learning is the study of _____ behaviors which come to be a _____ part of the behavioral repertoire as a result of prior experience.
      a.   reflex, relatively permanent
      b.   acquired, relatively permanent
      c.   species-specific, relatively permanent
      d.   acquired, somewhat temporary

2.   Human inborn responses are recognized by researchers as
      a.   fixed-pattern responses
      b.   species-specific
      c.   reflexes
      d.   complex reflexes

3.   When an individual is exposed to a stimulus so much that he no longer responds to it, _____ has taken place.
      a.   habituation
      b.   sensitization
      c.   perception
      d.   boredom

4. Pavlov became interested in learning when his dogs would salivate at the sight of someone opening the food cupboard door. This phenomenon of learning is known as _____.
    a.   sensitization
    b.   fixed-pattern response
    c.   contingency detection
    d.   species-specific behavior

5. When the dogs in Pavlov's experiment responded to the bell in the same way they had responded to the food, _____ had occurred.
    a.   reinforcement
    b.   classical conditioning
    c.   sensitization
    d.   an unconditioned response

6. In the unfortunate case of little Albert, _____ was observed when he became equally afraid of all white furry objects.
    a.   habituation
    b.   an unconditioned response
    c.   contingency detection
    d.   stimulus generalization

7. If Watson and Rayner had presented the rat over and over without ever pairing it with the gong again, the fear response most likely would have undergone _____.
    a.   habituation
    b.   extinction
    c.   stimulus generalization
    d.   reinforcement

8. Kenneth Clark's experiment with the children and the black and white dolls, illustrated
    a.   affective conditioning
    b.   prejudice conditioning
    c.   attitude conditioning
    d.   belief conditioning

9. "Any act which, in a given situation produces satisfaction, is likely to be repeated if the same situation occurs again," is a statement of the _____ formulated by _____.
    a.   law of effect, E. L. Thorndike
    b.   law of consequences, E. L. Thorndike
    c.   stimulus-response, Ivan Pavlov
    d.   law of contingency, John Watson

10. One major difference between classical conditioning and instrumental learning is that in classical conditioning _____ are strengthened or weakened, whereas in instrumental learning _____ are strengthened or weakened.
    a.   consequences, stimuli
    b.   stimuli, responses

c.   responses, stimuli
d.   stimuli, consequences

11.   The process of reinforcing successive approximations toward a final response is known as
      _____.
      a.   sub-step reinforcing
      b.   shaping
      c.   successive reinforcement
      d.   stimulus generalization

12.   Crying behavior is
      a.   an unlearned reflex
      b.   a classically conditioned response
      c.   an operantly conditioned response
      d.   potentially any one of the above depending on the circumstances

13.   Albert Bandura's description of teaching a student how to drive a car by using only the principles
      of reinforcement, illustrates the value of
      a.   imitative learning
      b.   trial and error learning
      c.   classical conditioning
      d.   operant conditioning

14.   Imitating another's behavior is a salient feature of _____ and can happen even when the
      other's behavior is _____.
      a.   social learning; reinforced
      b.   social learning; not reinforced
      c.   operant conditioning; reinforced
      d.   operant conditioning; not reinforced

15.   A useful operant technique used in behavior modification removes the child from any reinforcing
      activities for a short time and is called
      a.   a token economy
      b.   punishment
      c.   time-out
      d.   an alternating response effort

■ ■ ■ ■   ◄
                                                                                            ◄
                                                                                            ◄
PRACTICE TEST 2

1.   Unlearned responses in animals are known as _____ and are often _____ to the species.
      a.   releaser stimulated behaviors; unique
      b.   reflex stimulated behaviors; sign stimulus

c./   fixed response patterns; specific
d.   reflexes; fixed response patterns

2.   The ability to learn allows the organism to adapt to the environment in a flexible way rather than with the limitations of _____ or _____.
    a./   reflexes; fixed response patterns
    b.   acquired behaviors; sign stimulus releasers
    c.   instincts; reflex behaviors
    d.   species specific; acquired behaviors

3.   In the famous Pavlov experiments, the bell became the _____ after the dogs associated it with the presentation of the _____.
    a.   unconditioned stimulus, food
    b./   conditioned stimulus, food
    c.   conditioned response, food
    d.   unconditioned response, food

4.   Many learning theorists believe that the bell served as a signal that food would arrive. This _____ is as important as the contiguous association of stimuli.
    a.   conditioned response
    b.   unconditioned stimuli
    c./   contingency detection
    d.   unconditioned response

5.   If we stop the car at the traffic light, a red "Eat at Joe's" sign, and all other red advertising signs, we have shown _____.
    a.   habituation
    b.   contingency detection
    c.   environmental learning
    d./   stimulus generalization

6.   Counterconditioning was at least partly accomplished in the '60's when the prejudicial attitude against blacks was linked with a new association. The learning process involved in this kind of attitude formation is known as _____.
    a./   affective conditioning
    b.   extinction
    c.   habituation
    d.   instrumental learning

7.   Thorndike's Law of effect has become a cornerstone of _____, which says that responses are maintained or changed by what happens _____ the response.
    a.   affective conditioning, after
    b.   instrumental learning, before
    c.   stimulus response learning, after
    d./   instrumental learning, after

8.   B. F. Skinner argued that behaviors or _____, as he preferred to call them, can be made
        stronger if they are followed by a _____ consequence.
        a.   stimuli, reinforcing
        b.   operants, punishing
        c.   operants, reinforcing
        d.   stimuli, punishing

9.   Reinforcement occurs when an event _____ the response that _____ it.
        a.   strengthens, follows
        b.   weakens, follows
        c.   strengthens, preceded
        d.   weakens, preceded

10.   According to social learning theory, children learn many behaviors by
        a.   having someone other than parents reinforce behaviors
        b.   observing someone else's behavior
        c.   trial and error
        d.   classical or operant conditioning

11.   In Bandura's second experiment, children rarely imitated the punished model's aggressive behavior.
        However, if these children were offered reinforcements to behave aggressively, they could and did
        imitate the model. This experiment demonstrated the difference between
        a.   acquisition and performance
        b.   forgetting and memory
        c.   punishment and reinforcement
        d.   classical and operant conditioning

12.   Social Learning theory has its roots in behaviorism, and as Bandura proposes,
        a.   it also includes the way we organize and process information
        b.   it is an interaction between environment and thought
        c.   that to ignore thinking would be like attributing "Shakespeare's literary masterpieces to his
                prior instruction in the mechanics of writing"
        d.   all of the above

13.   That a particular stimulus cannot be considered a reinforcer until its effect on a behavior has been
        observed, is the foundation for formulating a self correcting method for attributing reinforcing
        qualities in a future similar situation. This precaution is known as
        a.   a before the fact deduction
        b.   a trial and error deduction
        c.   an ex-post-facto deduction
        d.   a replicated deduction .

14.   Structuring the environment in such a way that inappropriate responses are more difficult to make,
        or make an appropriate response easier to make is called
        a.   token economy
        b.   punishment

c.   time-out

d.   altering response effort

15.   Using a treatment based on behavior modification, Bandura helped some children overcome a debilitating fear of dogs. He did this using the technique known as

a.   extinction

b.   modeling

c.   response cost

d.   positive reinforcement

ANSWER SECTION

Guided Review

1.   acquired, relatively permanent
2.   species specific, fixed response, releaser, sign stimulus
3.   reflexes
4.   ability, flexible adaptation
5.   habituation, responds
6.   learning
7.   Ivan Pavlov, contiguous association, food cupboard
8.   food, salivation
9.   unconditioned stimulus, conditioned stimulus
10.   salivation response, conditioned response
11.   predicted, contingency detection
12.   classically conditioned, white rat, loud noise
13.   stimulus generalization
14.   extinction, counterconditioning
15.   affective
16.   racial prejudice
17.   "law of effect"
18.   stimulus, response
19.   operants, operant conditioning
20.   extinction
21.   reinforcement, increases
22.   made after, fact
23.   reflex, conditioned response, operantly conditioned
24.   shaping
25.   shaping
26.   tabula rasa
27.   beyond, facts
28.   passive recipients
29.   operant
30.   social learning
31.   learn
32.   imitation, rare
33.   aggressive behaviors
34.   discriminate, reality, make-believe, gentle, affectionate
35.   behaviorism, complex thinking processes
36.   behavior modification

Practice Test 1

1.	b
2.	c
3.	a
4.	c
5.	b
6.	d
7.	b
8.	a
9.	a
10.	b
11.	b
12.	d
13.	a
14.	b
15.	c

Practice Test 2

1.	c
2.	a
3.	b
4.	c
5.	d
6.	a
7.	d
8.	c
9.	c
10.	b
11.	a
12.	d
13.	c
14.	d
15.	b

CHAPTER EIGHT

LANGUAGE DEVELOPMENT

■ ■ ■ ■

◀
◀
◀

LEARNING OBJECTIVES

Have you ever learned another language? Are you aware of the rhythm, phones, and phonemes you've had to learn? Chances are, when you learn a second language, you've been more aware of learning the vocabulary than all the details involving tonality and pacing, accent, etc. Reading this chapter will give you all a better appreciation of language, whether it's your first or second!

1. You should understand how language requires the use of signs and symbols within the structure of the rules of how they are to be arranged. This structure is known as grammar and allows for novel constructions.
2. You'll be able to illustrate some of the novel constructs of language, such as those that make learning English both harder and easier. The same is probably true of other languages. Check it out.
3. It's fun to read about the prelinguistic period where evidence shows mothers and tiny infants do have reciprocal, early communications. It's nice to see scientists admit and prove what moms and dads have known for a long time.
4. Know about the value of "gooing". Adults' developed skulls and oral cavities makes it impossible for us to imitate those sounds exactly, but baby's "goo" sounds are vowel-like and thought of as a real start toward language acquisition.
5. Give your friends a chance to meet an infant who babbles to willing listeners. Infants first expand their ability to produce phones and phonemes, and then narrow their repertoire and develop the rhythm which resembles their own language somewhere between 9 and 14 months of age. Babblers will sound for all the world like they are saying something really important. Be able to explain the maturation factor here and what sounds they may expect at a variety of ages before the first word.
6. Explain the word "infans" and what constitutes the first real word.
7. Be able to tell them about the "three bears rule" as they go through the one-word stage.
8. You'll want to point out to them some of the hand signs. That deaf children "babble" in sign language suggests that language is prewired in our species.
9. Describe the importance of naming things and how the child perceives objects. Knowing that things

have names sets the stage for the acquisition of more words and understanding of language.

10.   Define grammar for them, including both phonology and syntax. They'll observe the one-word sentence, the holophrase. Show how the research suggests that babies have an understanding of syntax even in the one-word stage.

11.   Following the one-word stage comes the two-word stage. Take a good look at Figure 8.2 to see how rapidly the size of the vocabulary grows. It makes a perfect base for a test question!

12.   Be sure to understand the way the first sentences start with telegraphic speech. Do explain the acquisition and functionality of grammatical morphemes and how they are learned. It is important to take the trouble to learn the meanings of the terms you encounter.

13.   In the At Issue section, you'll find a fascinating discussion of the acquisition of language skills as a nurture/nature issue. That children may have an influence in developing new language is a relatively new idea: note the Creole example.

14.   It is fun to demonstrate caretaker speech. Now that you've read about it, I'm sure you'll realize you've used caretaker speech in several situations. Even children will use caretaker speech with younger children, especially if they see their parents do it.

15.   How we organize syntax to express what we mean is going to be more complicated to explain, but offers some interesting ideas. Of course you'll want to use spoonerisms for fun and illustration.

16.   Applications: If you've ever wondered whether reading to very small children will help them, do read about the gains the experimental group of two and three year old children made as a result of being engaged in interactive story reading.

■ ■ ■ ■   ◀
                                                                                 ◀
CHAPTER OUTLINE   ◀

Many of the experimental issues we've looked at so far will be seen in the study of language development. You'll be glad you know how studies are done, the designs of studies, and the theoretical approaches to studying language development. Here you go. You do even more this time. Be sure to leave room for lecture notes.

Chapter Preview: The Genetics of Grammar. A fascinating look at a specific language disorder. The failure to attach tense to verbs was at one time thought to be the result of a hearing problem. However, in further investigations, a particular way of assembling words, known as Specific Language Impairment (SLI) was found. It appears in families at about a 4 to 1 ratio, and is a familial disorder. The genetics of this opens for study the possibility that grammar is prewired. Watch for more studies in this regard.

What is Language? More than simple communication, it is the organization of complex rules defining the structure of signs, symbols and sounds which allows creative means of communicating meaning to another. You'll want to re-word this, I'm sure! Do writers get tongue-tied or type-tied? Now there's some language!

I.   The Prelinguistic Period
       A.   Dialogues between 3 day olds and their mothers
       B.   Crying. (Parents are right after all!)
       C.   The first language-like sounds
              1.   Phonation stage
                     a.   comfort sounds _____
                     b.   age _____

       c.   phones and phonemes
          (1)   definitions _____

          _____
          (2)   examples _____
          _____

  2.   Gooing stage
       a.   difference between infant and adult sounds due to

          _____
       b.   grunting sounds, _____

  3.   Expansion stage of the phonemes and phones
       a.   age _____
       b.   sounds _____
       c.   like sounds of own name, mommy, daddy
       d.   Peter Eimas studies conclude infant's brain is prewired for language recognition, and this is phoneme constancy and is classified as perceptual constancy

  4.   Cononical stage
       a.   age _____
       b.   babbling _____
       c.   language background _____
       d.   recognizing and categorizing variations of sounds from own language

          _____

  5.   Contraction stage
       a.   age _____
       b.   narrowed phonemes _____
       c.   pacing and rhythm, babbling _____
       d.   feedback _____

II.   The Linguistic Period: "Infans" -- infancy ends when the first word is spoken
  A.   First words
      1.   age _____
      2.   related to _____
      3.   The Three Bears Rule
          a.   _____
          b.   _____
          c.   _____
          d.   organize into categories
      4.   Superordinate words _____
      5.   Subordinate words _____
  B.   The One-Word Stage
      1.   "Sign" words _____
      2.   Naming _____
          the importance of naming _____
      3.   Pronunciation _____

      4.   Overextension of meaning _____

        a.   why? _____

- C.   First sentences
  1. One word sentence: The holophrase
  2. Still an understanding of syntax
     - a.   syntax _____
     - b.   phonology _____
     - c.   grammar _____
     - d.   naming _____
  3. Acquisition of vocabulary
     - a.   gender
     - b.   time conversant with parents
       see figure 8.2 _____
- D.   Two-word stage: duos
  1. Between 18-20 months, 1000 new two-word statements per month
  2. Universal phenomenon
  3. Table 8.1
- E.   Telegraphic Speech
  1. From two-word to telegraphic speech
  2. Economical--no function words
  3. Rigid word order to express meaning
- F.   Language and Meaning
  1. Word order active rather than passive
  2. Other languages use other means to convey meaning than word order
- G.   Grammatical Morphemes
  1. See table 8.2 for 14 grammatical morphemes (English) and order in which they develop
  2. Order may develop according to function
- H.   Irregular Words
  1. Overregularization
     - a.   Wugs
     - b.   demonstrates _____
- I.   The Development of Syntactic Skills
  1. Semantic aspects: the understanding of the meaning of words
  2. See Table 8.3
  3. MLU _____

III.   Caretaker speech structure
  1. Description _____
     - a.   simple sentences
     - b.   voice tone
  2. Universal _____
     - a.   baby talk?
     - b.   the nature nurture argument
  3. Benefits _____

At Issue: Children and The Origins of Language
  1. The need for exposure to language
  2. Pidgin English in Hawaii converted to a Creole by children

IV.   The Function of Grammar: how to link words together in syntactic structures to convey meaning. Is there an innate grammar?
    A.   Syntax organized before speaking
        1.   Spoonerisms _____
        2.   Semantic aspect _____
        3.   Organize the sentence: first focus is subject at hand - English

              _____

            a.   active sentences
        4.   Henrietta Lempert
            a.   the active voice
            b.   the passive voice

You do the application--
APPLICATION: Strike When the Iron is Hot!   Motivational factors. Child/parent and interactive reading. How to encourage vocabulary and language skills, as well as a strong interest in reading.

NAMES TO REMEMBER

Peter Eimas	Marta Valdez-Menchaca
Jean Berko	Grover Whitehurst
Goldin-Meadow, Mylander	William A. Spooner
Henrietta Lempert	Herbert Terrace
Noam Chomsky	Marta Valdez-Menchaca

TERMS AND CONCEPTS

language	contraction stage
grammar	tonality, rhythm, pacing
dialogues	infans
gooing	The Three Bears Rule
phonology	one-word stage
phonemes	sign language
phones	naming
phonetic expansion	fast mapping
phoneme constancy	pronunciation
babbling	two-word stage
raspberry	duos
cononical stage	first sentence

syntax   grammatical morphemes
MLU   caretaker speech
phonology   baby talk
holophrase   syntactic skills
the passive voice   functional grammar
acquisition of vocabulary   Spoonerisms
telegraphic speech

■ ■ ■ ■

GUIDED REVIEW

1.   Language differs from simple _____ in that it requires the use of _____ or
       _____ within the structure of _____.

2.   _____ is a structure of rules that determine how various signs or symbols are to be
       arranged to convey linguistic meaning. This structure allows the creation of _____
       _____.

3.   As infants mature and grow older, language development follows a _____ which is
       similar in every culture.

4.   Some researchers believe that the beginning of language occur within _____
       _____ after birth and show in the _____ _____ between the
       infant and mother.

5.   Other researchers declare that language acquisition begins during the _____ stage
       with the first language-like sounds. These unique sounds in the first few months are due mainly
       to differences between infants' and adults' _____ and _____
       _____.

6.   A stage of language acquisition that typically occurs between the ages of 2 and 4 months is the
       _____ _____. During this stage, infants combine quasi-vowels from the
       phonation stage with harder sounds that are the _____ of consonants.

7.   The sounds of language include _____, which are the smallest units of speech that can
       affect meaning, and _____, which are the smallest units which do not affect meaning.

8.   Between four and seven months, infants begin to make new sounds including yelps, squeals, and
       even the raspberry, heralding the _____ stage.

9.   During the _____ stage, the infant will increase babbling and produce
       _____ sequences, such as mamama or dadada. It is especially interesting to note that
       although deaf babies do babble manually, they do not use _____ _____.

10. Baby's babble will also include the tonality, _____, and _____ of their language, sounding for all the world like real words.

11. Somewhere between 10 and 14 months, infants restrict their use of phonemes to those common to their own _____. This occurs during the _____ _____.

12. "Infans", in Greek, means _____ _____, suggesting the end of infancy begins with the _____ _____. Studies show this happens between _____ and _____ months of age.

13. The first basic nouns that children use tend to follow the _____ _____ rule.

14. This rule states that a child will learn basic nouns before she learns _____ or _____ nouns.

15. That children learn basic words first universally, suggests that infants are able to form _____ based on experience-expectant neural processes. Another way to say this is that it's in the child's _____.

16. Superordinate or abstract words tend to be adjectives at first. Finally, children over 5 years will use what Bertrand Russell called _____ words which are not related to _____ _____.

17. During the early part of the one-word stage, the child is just as likely to use _____ _____ as the first spoken words.

18. Names of objects are apparently understood at 13 months when the infant _____ _____ the specific object being named even before they were able to say the word.

19. Naming both requires and helps develop the child's ability to _____ _____ on various objects. Naming is a major step in language _____.

20. Children often _____ a definition of a word by using that word for all similarly shaped, colored or moving objects.

21. When a child rapidly narrows down the correct meaning of a word, usually by learning it in context, he is using _____ _____.

22. A _____ is a one word sentence as spoken by small children who apparently have some notion of syntax.

23. The syntax of language refers to the rules used to put words together to form a _____ _____. Grammar, however, is more properly defined as including both _____ and _____.

24. _____, or two-word combinations, begin between _____ months and

appear to occur throughout the world.

25.   During the two-word stage the child may learn more than _____ new statements every month.

26.   Telegraphic speech is a good way to describe the English speaking child's first _____, since they tend to be short and leave out _____ _____. In addition, even at this stage, infants use grammar within a rigid _____ _____.

27.   Using irregular words, like "goed" and "foots" indicates an _____ in the acquisition of grammar.

28.   Adjusting language to the level of the listener, by using a high pitched voice and shorter, simpler sentences is called _____ _____.

29.   _____ believe that the child is a sign stimulus to increase the rate of caretaker speech from adults, whereas _____ _____ argue that adults are shaped to use caretaker speech because the child attends more closely to the short sentences and higher voice.

30.   An interesting possibility that children are neurologically equipped with an inborn _____ base on which to build language was illustrated when children invented _____ from the pidgin they heard from the adults.

31.   _____ are funny examples of the fact that we organize the syntax of a sentence rather than simply _____ _____ _____.

32.   Children appear to organize their sentences by placing the topic of concern _____ in the sentence.

33.   Lempert's observations found that children understand the passive voice best when the topics were about _____ and _____ objects.

34.   Studies showing the importance of motivation in language acquisition indicate that parents can take advantage of children's motivations to stimulate language and vocabulary skills by:

■ ■ ■ ■

PRACTICE TEST 1

1.   In addition to conveying meaning through the use of symbols, language
    a.   doesn't allow the use of novel creations
    b.   allows the creation of novel constructions within the rules of grammar
    c.   allows the creation of novel constructions through the abandonment of the rules of

grammar
d.　　allows the creation of novel constructions only through the use of English grammar

2.　Evidence of the rudiments of language acquisition are thought by some researchers to begin
  a.　　with vocal dialogues between infant and mother within 72 hours after birth
  b.　　with vocal dialogues between infant and mother within six months after birth
  c.　　with the babbling stage
  d.　　with the production of phones and phonemes

3.　The production of phones and phonemes in the infant begins
  a.　　shortly after birth
  b.　　two to three months after birth
  c.　　at 6 or 7 months of age
  d.　　at the time of the first word

4.　"Pah-hk yoah cah-h" compared to "par-rk yer car-r" is an example of differences in
  a.　　phonemes
  b.　　meanings
  c.　　voices
  d.　　phones

5.　An essential component of phonetic contraction toward imitation of the infant's native language
  is
  a.　　feedback
  b.　　maturational development
  c.　　vocabulary acquisition
  d.　　phonetic extension

6.　Infancy ends when
  a.　　the first sentence is spoken
  b.　　the two-word stage begins
  c.　　phonetic extension begins
  d.　　the first word is spoken

7.　The first words children use are nouns which are categorized according to
  a.　　the dog, cat, and mouse rule
  b.　　the three bears rule
  c.　　the three pigs rule
  d.　　the small, medium and large rule

8.　Even before the one-word stage babies tend to
  a.　　communicate through hand gestures
  b.　　name objects
  c.　　use concrete nouns
  d.　　all of the above

9.   Calling any round shaped object "moon" is an illustration of
        a.   underextension of word meanings
        b.   object naming
        c.   overextension of word meanings
        d.   concrete naming

10.   Even with one word, a child might express a _____, or one-word sentence.
        a.   phonologic
        b.   contraction
        c.   holophrase
        d.   grammar construction

11.   The two-word stage develops in the same way
        a.   universally
        b.   as the three-word stage
        c.   telegraphically
        d.   without syntax

12.   An important feature of telegraphic speech in English speakers is
        a.   loose word order
        b.   grammatical morphemes
        c.   rigid word order
        d.   suffixes

13.   Irregular words such as "goed" and "foots" shows a(n) _____ in the acquisition of general
        rules of grammar
        a.   regression
        b.   advancement
        c.   caretaker speech
        d.   suspension of rules

14.   Characteristics of caretaker speech may be
        a.   essential to gain the attention of the child
        b.   shaped by the attention of the child
        c.   reinforced by the caregiver
        d.   all of the above if you are a learning theorist

15.   Syntax is
        a.   the way we organize the words in a sentence to express meaning
        b.   the same as Spoonerisms
        c.   a rule of grammar
        d.   a passive voice

■ ■ ■ ■

PRACTICE TEST 2

1.   Infants develop language in a sequence
       a.   which is similar among children according to their culture
       b.   which is similar among children the world over
       c.   randomly among children the world over
       d.   only according to what is taught to them

2.   Gooing sounds made by infants under 6 months of age are unique in that
       a.   they are vowel sounds like adults produce
       b.   they are vowel-like but differ from adults because of their immature skull, mouth and
              nervous system
       c.   they are combinations of phones and phonemes
       d.   they don't contain any language sounds

3.   Whereas _____ are the smallest units of speech which affect meaning, _____ are the
       smallest units which do not affect meaning.
       a.   phonemes; phones
       b.   phonemes; gooing
       c.   phones; phonemes
       d.   phones; gooing

4.   During the _____ stage between 4 and 7 months, the child exhibits a growing phonetic
       repertoire resulting in babbling as well as yells, growls and even the raspberry!
       a.   phoneme contraction
       b.   raspberry stage
       c.   maximization stage
       d.   expansion stage

5.   Infants begin to show language preference in their babbling by narrowing their use of phonemes
       and using the pace and rhythm of their native language. This stage, which usually occurs
       between 10 to 14 months, is known as the
       a.   phonetic stage
       b.   cononical stage
       c.   contraction stage
       d.   rhythm acquisition stage

6.   Children's first words are usually spoken by _____ on average, and are usually connected to
       an _____ or _____.
       a.   13.6 months; object, action
       b.   2 years; object, action
       c.   2 years; object, person
       d.   6 months; object, action

7.   Naming may well have its foundation when the infant
      a.   maintains eye contact with a parent
      b.   looks at an object because the parent looks at it
      c.   looks at an object when the parent points to it
      d.   all of the above

8.   Simplifying a word to the point of mispronunciation may be due to
      a.   overextension
      b.   faulty hearing
      c.   immature mouth, palate and vocal development
      d.   none of the above

9.   When children grasp a word's proper and perhaps limited definition, they often do this very quickly. This ability is known as
      a.   underextension
      b.   overextension
      c.   fast mapping
      d.   fast acquisition

10.   During the two-word stage, vocabulary may increase
      a.   by more than 1,000 two-word statements a month
      b.   by 500 holophrases a month
      c.   by 1,000 holophrases a month
      d.   around 200 two word statements a month

11.   First sentences may be described as
      a.   Tarzan talk
      b.   telegraphic speech
      c.   three-word combinations
      d.   loosely ordered

12.   Grammatical morphemes are _____, such as plurals, prepositions, etc., which add additional information. English speaking children rely on _____ before they learn to incorporate morphemes.
      a.   function words; rigid word order
      b.   plural words; loosely ordered sentences
      c.   function words; holophrases
      d.   particle words; three word sentences

13.   Language development is considered universal because
      a.   the child provides a sign stimulus to the parent to engage in various language teaching techniques
      b.   the organization of the brain is such that we are "prewired" for language development
      c.   our survival may depend on our ability to communicate to this degree
      d.   all of the above if you're a nativist

14.   Parents can help pre-reading children develop vocabulary and language skill by
   a.   encouraging the child to describe what is happening in the pictures in the story book they
           are reading together
   b.   not interfering with the child's innate ability to develop language skills
   c.   reinforcing their child's independent reading experiences
   d.   encouraging the child to develop their own Creole language

BONUS: Try reciting the stages in sequential order
If you get them right, you can have a walk-around-the-block-with-a-friend-break!

ANSWER SECTION

<u>Guided Review</u>

1. communication, signs, symbols, grammar
2. grammar, novel constructions
3. sequence
4. 72 hours, vocal dialogues
5. phonation, skulls, oral cavities
6. gooing stage, precursors
7. phonemes, phones
8. expansion
9. cononical, duplicated, cononical syllables
10. rhythm, spacing
11. language, contraction stage
12. without speech, first word, 10, 17
13. three bears
14. subordinate, superordinate
15. categories, nature
16. "dictionary", actual objects
17. hand signals, or sign language
18. looks at
19. focus attention, acquisition
20. overextend
21. fast mapping
22. holophrase
23. meaningful sentence, syntax, phonology
24. duos, 18-20
25. 1000
26. sentences, function words, word order
27. advance
28. caretaker speech
29. nativists, learning theorists
30. grammar, Creole
31. Spoonerisms, link words together
32. first
33. live, animate
34. reading often to their children and asking challenging questions requiring expanded answers from them regarding the activities of the subjects in the readings.

<u>Practice Test 1</u>

1.	b	5.	a
2.	a	6.	d
3.	c	7.	b
4.	d	8.	a

9.   *c*
10.   *c*
11.   *a*
12.   *c*

13.   *b*
14.   *d*
15.   *a*

<u>Practice Test 2</u>
1.   *a*
2.   *b*
3.   *a*
4.   *d*
5.   *c*
6.   *a*
7.   *d*

8.   *c*
9.   *c*
10.   *a*
11.   *b*
12.   *a*
13.   *d*
14.   *a*

<u>BONUS:</u>
1.   *phonation stage*
2.   *gooing stage*
3.   *expansion stage*
4.   *cononical stage*
5.   *contraction stage*
6.   *one-word stage*
7.   *two-word stage*
8.   *telegraphic speech*
9.   *full use of grammatical morphemes, phonology, and syntax*
10.   *ability to express self, continued vocabulary building (some of us aren't there YET!)*

Want more points? Match the stage with the age!!!!

CHAPTER NINE

COGNITIVE DEVELOPMENT I: HISTORICAL FOUNDATIONS

■ ■ ■ ■

◄
◄
◄

LEARNING OBJECTIVES

Here comes a chapter with some new vocabulary for you and your friends. The first time I studied cognitive development, I had to spend some extra time getting used to the terms and concepts presented by cognitive theorists. I was glad I did since my Prof loved test questions asking for definitions or presenting descriptions and asking for the matching terms. The best part of learning about these early, and still useful theories is how they will compare with even newer ideas and, at the same time, you can compare these ideas with what you can observe in the children you know.

1. Be able to define cognitive theory so that there is no doubt about the complicated developmental issues you'll see. Where would we be without the ability to think, remember, solve problems, create ideas, and make and test hypotheses?
2. The famous Jean Piaget is a most interesting man to read about. If, by any chance, you are asked to make extra reports, you may want to spend some time looking up information about him. It is important that you understand Piaget's basic philosophy of cognitive development.
3. Do become familiar with the four periods described by Piaget. His epigenetic theory was well developed for his time. His premise that there is a qualitative difference in thinking between children and adults rather than quantitative is the cornerstone of his theory.
4. As you become familiar with Piaget's work, you'll see how his early interest in biology and physiology were an influence on his beliefs. His discussion of adaptation is a prime example. Practice explaining the factors involved here.
5. Take time to understand the sensorimotor period, the first period lasting about two years. It is divided into six sub-stages which not only apply to humans but have been observed in apes, too. The goal of the stage is to understand that objects still exist even though they are out of sight. It's called object permanence. Here's where watching babies you know will be especially interesting, because you can really see these stages.
6. You'll want to know the preoperational abilities. The kinds of reasoning that develop throughout this stage are especially interesting and fun to trace in children. Take special note of the terminology used. There are some simple tests that can be performed with them to illustrate the level of thinking

they have reached. For a time they'll take five pennies instead of one quarter and think they have more!

7.   Egocentrism is a quality of this period which is important to understand, as is horizontal decalage in the next stage. Have I made you curious?

8.   What a difference you'll see when the child reaches the concrete operational stage! Many of the tasks the younger child was incapable of performing are now taken on without difficulty.

9.   And last, comes the period of formal operations in which the child becomes able to hypothesize, test their hypotheses, and reason in a scientific way.

10.   Perhaps the best way to get a handle on each of the stages is to study them with the "compare and contrast" technique. It is easier to trace differences in abilities from stage to stage this way. Later, you may want to use this same technique to compare theories. It works, and helps you remember them.

11.   Be able to explain the difference between Piaget's organismic-structural approach and the behaviorists' mechanistic-functional approach.

12.   Robert Gagne's outline of cognitive development from the "cumulative learning" point of view shows a hierarchy of learning built on experience. Could this point of view ever be integrated with Piaget's?

13.   Discuss the work of researchers such as Baillargeon and Meltzoff who see more in the functions of children's cognitions than Piaget. Be sure to include the arguments against Piaget's theory as well as the strong points.

14.   There is an excellent discussion on telling children they are adopted that is well worth your attention. The same ideas can be applied to telling kids the facts of life or any other complicated concept. Do you think explaining the use of street drugs and other social problems might be handled this way, too?

15.   The Application: Why children stop believing in Santa Claus will give you the basis for a discussion with your friends from Poleved they'll not soon forget! Your study group will enjoy it too!

■ ■ ■ ■   ◀
                                                                                                   ◀
                                                                                                   ◀
CHAPTER OUTLINE   ◀

The new terms in this chapter need careful attention. Do remember to leave room in your outline and lecture notes for the examples your Professor will give you. Learning this chapter well will make the next one even more interesting and will certainly make knowing children more interesting. Hang in there!

Chapter Preview: Mirror, Mirror on the wall. Do I see you? Is it me? The child becomes conscious of himself as an entity apart from others.

I.   Cognition: Internal mental functions
      A.   Includes deciding, remembering, planning, problem solving, and many other intellectual functions.
      B.   James Mark Baldwin _____
II.   Jean Piaget
      A.   Piaget's history
            1.   began as a biologist--a molluskologist!
            2.   child prodigy
            3.   read and was interested in Baldwin's work: adapted terminology

B.   His in depth studies led to great respect and world-wide reading of his work.

C.   Concluded that young children had qualitatively different thought processes when solving problems than older youth and adults

D.   Piaget's Epigenetic theory:

    1.   Cognitive development is the result of the combination of the maturation of the brain and nervous system and of the experiences in the environment which help the individual to adapt.

    2.   There are predictable stages of cognitive development which can be observed during a child's life. These stages are universal. See table 9.1

E.   Some helpful terminology developed by Baldwin, used and augmented by Piaget

    1.   Scheme - the child's basic unit of cognition which allows the infant to organize her world into categories. Eg.:--

    2.   Adaptation: the ability to fit and survive in one's environment. Children adapt in two ways. *You do!*

        a.   Assimilation _____

        b.   Accommodation _____

        c.   Equilibrium-disequilibrium _____

F.   The guidelines for understanding the stages.

    1.   The ages are approximate: infants do not move through the stages by mere virtue of their age

    2.   The order of the stages is firm. A child never skips a stage.

    3.   A child may have cognitive abilities of the stage she is leaving as well as the stage she is entering.

    4.   A child may use strategies of an earlier stage even though she is firmly in the higher stage.

    5.   The stages are universal no matter what the culture.

III.   The Sensorimotor Period (Birth to 2 years)

Feeling more comfortable with the terms? Good! Here's some more for you to do!

GOAL of Sensorimotor Period: Object Permanence: knowing an object exists even out of sight; requires use of symbols or images. Example: Sensorimotor term used because the schemes are related to physical actions in response to what the child senses

example--

A.   Stage 1. Reflex Activity (Birth to 1 Month)

    1.   The refinement of physical reflexes in a systematic way.

    2.   Reflex exercise practice shows accommodation

        a.   examples _____

B.   Stage 2. Self-investigation (about 1-4 months)

    1.   Primary Circular Reactions--discovery of a behavior centered on baby's body which is re-enacted over and over. A time of self investigation.

        a.   examples _____

C.   Stage 3. Coordination and Reaching Out (about 4-8 Months)

    1.   Secondary Circular Reactions --Ready? Here you are with more to do, now that you have Piaget's idea.

        a.   examples _____

    2.   Object permanence begins, however weakly

        a.   examples _____

        3.   John Flavell's observations _____

  D.   Stage 4. Goal-directed Behavior (about 8-12 Months)
        1.   Schemes are now adjusted to _____
            a.   examples _____
        2.   Sequential behavior _____
        3.   Integrates previously separate schemes into one conceptual scheme to single goal directed effort
        4.   Object permanence develops further
            a.   but not quite reached _____

  E.   Stage 5. Experimentation (about 12-18 months)
        1.   Tertiary Circular reactions--active experimental behaviors
            a.   No, Mom, this toddler is not out to drive you nuts! He's just developing a bit of the mad-scientist attitude of "what will happen if I do this ...." Future physicist? Cause and effect relationships.
        2.   Status of object Permanence:
            a.   failure to infer invisible displacements _____

  F.   Stage 6. Problem Solving and Mental Combinations (about 18 -24 months)
        1.   Self awareness
        2.   Combines signs, symbols or images to solve problems
        3.   Can anticipate problem and solution
        4.   May use previous scheme to aid in understanding
        5.   Status of Object Permanence _____

  G.   The stages in Review
        1.   Comparing Samara to our babies! You do this one!
            a.   Stage 1 _____
            b.   Stage 2 _____
            c.   Stage 3 _____
            d.   Stage 4 _____
            e.   Stage 5 _____
            f.   Stage 6 _____
        2.   Sensorimotor period not unique to our species. Emphasizes biological aspects of Piaget's theory.

V.   The Preoperational Period (about 2-7 years)
  A.   Object permanence, use of symbols and internal images mark division between sensorimotor and preoperational stages (there's a test question possibility!)
        1.   Term preoperational means _____
        2.   Two divisions: preconceptual and intuitive stages
            a.   preconceptual stage: (about 2 -4 years)
                (1)   concept definition _____
                (2)   preconceptual child unable to distinguish ---- Sees all similar objects as belonging to same class.
                    (a)   examples: _____
                (3)   two kinds of reasoning
                    (a)   syncretic reasoning: the way preschoolers reason;
                        _____

example _____
     (b)   transductive reasoning: _____
           example _____
           Eg. of this level : animistic thinking ____
           "I have a little shadow that goes in and out with me" a poem
           by Robert Louis Stevenson is a good example

    b.   intuitive stage (about 4-7 years)
        (1)   beliefs based on sensing, feelings or imagination rather than logical thinking
             example: _____
        (2)   not ready for "logical operations"
             example _____
        (3)   Egocentrism: understanding environment from own view
             example _____

VI.   The Period of Concrete Operations (about 7-11 years)
    A.   Use of logical rules: an abrupt and qualitative change
        1.   limited to direct experience
    B.   Identity: marks beginning of concrete operations. Describe this and understand the importance of decentering and conservation ____
        1.   leads to _____
    C.   Reversibility : preoperational children can't imagine doubling back or reversing process
        1.   Examples _____
    D.   Horizontal decalage: See figure 9.2 _____
        1.   Examples _____
    E.   Seriation: Figure 9.3 ordering objects in order of _____
        1.   Example _____
    F.   Classification: sorting objects according to _____
        1.   Example _____
    G.   Numeration: more than counting, understanding classes and subclasses of numbers -- foundation for multiplication and division

VII.   The Period of Formal Operations (11 years through adulthood)
    A.   Can apply logical rules in imaginary situations
    B.   The freedom to hypothesize
        example _____
    C.   Once this stage is reached, the difference between adolescents and adults is merely qualitative

VIII.   Piaget's Influence on American Education
    Teachers are encouraged
    A.   To gear education to _____
        Result _____
    B.   To encourage spontaneous and creative aspects of learning _
        Result _____
    C.   To broaden child's focus _____
        Result _____
    D.   To Encourage children to expand at own level _____
        Result _____

At Issue: An excellent discussion of children's ability to understand complicated ideas at each of Piaget's stages.

IX.   Criticisms of Piaget's organismic-structural approach

    A.   The American Learning Theory Rebuttal

        1.   B. F. Skinner

            a.   mechanistic-functional approach: analogy _____

            b.   "add on" accumulative learning, quantitative, not stage-like

        2.   Robert Gagne

            a.   accumulative learning

            b.   cognitive skills are product of simple prerequisite skills - simple to complex

            c.   example _____ window glass puzzle

    B.   The necessity of defining a good stage theory:

        1.   _____

        2.   _____

        3.   _____

    C.   Experiments challenge the four Piagetian stages

        1.   Renee Baillargeon demonstration of object permanence in younger babies

            a.   experiment _____

        2.   Andrew Meltzoff

            a.   imitation experiment _____

        3.   William Schiff

            a.   stick-in-box _____

    D.   Piaget's stage theory on the descriptive research dimension is masterful, but as an explanatory theory, it is not as clear and is criticized for making premature inductions.

Applications: Why Do Children Stop Believing in Santa Claus (or what have we done to our myth, for goodness sake!)

■ ■ ■ ■

NAMES TO REMEMBER

James Mark Baldwin

Jean Piaget

Sigmund Freud

John H. Flavell

Samara

B. F. Skinner

Robert Gagne

Renee Baillargeon

Andrew Meltzoff

William Schiff

Santa Claus (and perhaps the Easter Bunny!)

■ ■ ■ ■

TERMS AND CONCEPTS

egocentrism
cognitive theory
cognition
epigenetic theory
symbols
logic
mental images
scheme
adaptation
assimilation
accommodation
equilibrium
disequilibrium
sensorimotor period
object permanence
reflex activity
self-investigation
primary circular reactions
coordination and reaching out
secondary circular reactions
goal-directed behavior
experimentation
tertiary circular reactions
mental combinations and problem solving

preoperational period
preconceptual stage
concept
preconcepts
symbolic functions
syncretic reasoning
transductive reasoning
animism
intuitive stage
intuitive thinking
reversibility
the period of concrete operations
logical operations
identity
conservation
horizontal decalage
seriation
classification
numeration
the period of formal operations
hypothesis
organismic-structural approach
mechanistic-functional approach

■ ■ ■ ■

GUIDED REVIEW

1. The chapter preview discusses experiments in which orangutans and chimpanzees are able to recognize _themselves_, thus demonstrating _conscious_ or _self_ awareness. Human children develop this ability between one and two years of age.

2. The focus of cognitive theories is _thinking_ and the way it _develops_.

3. The American psychologist, _James Mark Baldwin_ was a significant influence on _Jean Piaget_, whose early interest was studying the flexibility and adaptation of mollusks to their changing environment.

4. Piaget combined both the influence of _biology_ and _environment_ in his theory.

5. Because humans are genetically similar and also because children share many of the same experiences, Piaget believed that their cognitive development would be fairly _uniform_, and therefore _predictable_.

6. Piaget proposed four major periods of intellectual development in children. They are, in order: _sensorimotor_ _preconceptual_ _concrete operation_, and _formal operations_.

7. Piaget believed that all children will progress through these stages in exactly the _same_ _order_ but not necessarily at the same _age_.

8. Piaget's theory states that children think in _qualitatively_ different ways from adults rather than _quantitatively_ different ways.

9. As the schemes provide an understanding of the environment, the child adapts to her surroundings in two ways; through _assimilation_ and through _accomodation_

10. According to Piaget, the infant begins to build basic units of cognition, called _disequilibrium_ based on the _upward_ understanding he has of things in the environment.

11. Considering all four-legged furry animals as "doggies" is an example of _assimilation_ whereas adjusting one's understanding of four-legged furry creatures to include dogs, cats and squirrels is an example of _accomodation_

12. Piaget believes there is a compelling force which comes about when the child experiences _disequilibrium_ because she cannot understand her environment. By resolving the discomfort, she develops better strategies for accommodating new information and moves _upward_ through the _cognitive_ _stages_.

13. Although the progress of cognitive development is based on an unvarying sequence, a child may enter a new stage showing cognitive aspects of a _higher_ _stage_ as well as a _lower_ _stage_.

14. The first major period of cognitive development, the _sensorimotor period_ is devoted to the attainment of _object permanence_

15. Object permanence is defined as the ability to think internally using _symbols_ and/or _mental_ _images_ to represent objects not present.

16. Of the _six_ stages within the sensorimotor stage, self investigation in the second stage is characterized by repeated acts centered on the infant's own body called _primary circular reactions_

17. In the third stage, the scheme changes to include objects in the environment. These repetitive

movements on objects are known as *secondary circular reactions*

18. First signs of object permanence begin with looking for an object which is *partially hidden*. However, in stage four, the infant will look for an object completely hidden in the place he *most often* found it in the past.

19. In stage five, the child might be called the "experimental scientist" as he learns about *cause* and *effect* relationships.

20. In stage 6, the child is able to use *mental combinations* and therefore can imagine, talk about, and use mental and verbal pictures to *solve problems* Object permanence has developed!

21. Interesting support is given to the biological aspects of Piaget's theory by showing the same stages in *apes*.

22. The major distinction between the sensorimotor period and the preoperational period is the continued use of *symbols* and *internal images*, while the dividing line is marked by internalized thought or *object permanence*.

23. The term preoperational is used because children have not acquired the rules of *logic*.

24. The first of the two stages of the preoperational period, called the *preconceptual* stage, is characterized when the child is *unable* to isolate and distinguish the unique characteristics within a class of objects or events.

25. A concept is the understanding of the *relationship* among objects or properties shared by objects or events in a given group.

26. The preconceptual stage reasoning processes are limited to *syncretic* and *transductive* reasoning.

27. Syncretic reasoning is an immature way of sorting and *classifying objects* This may be due to the fact that the child's understanding of *concepts* is not fully developed.

28. *Transductive* reasoning leads to the child to incorrect conclusions because the child assumes that if two objects are *alike* in one way, they are *alike* in every way.

29. *Animistic thinking* is the belief that some inanimate objects are alive. "The mud puddle is my friend because it likes to make my feet feel good".

30. The last part of the preoperational period is called the *intuitive stage* because children believe what they feel or imagine to be so.

31. A preoperational child is unable to accomplish *reversibility* meaning he cannot reverse a

process to understand that changing the shape of something does not necessarily change the volume.

32.   The occurrence of the period of concrete operations is marked by the ability to use ___rules___ or ___logical___ ___operations___ to form conclusions and solve problems.

33.   The concrete operational child will understand that the amount of material does not change unless something is added or taken away, even though its form may be changed. This understanding describes the ability to apply ___identity___.

34.   Three operations are within the capability of the concrete operations child and show the qualitative leap in cognition at this time. These are ___conservation___ ___decen-___ , and ___reversibility___ ___tration___

35.   A child who, at last, has reached the period of formal operations, can now go beyond their experience and can ___hypothesize___ "what if . ." questions.

36.   In explaining a complicated concept such as adoption to a child, it would be best to explain it ___repeatedly___ as he goes through each of the cognitive stages. In this way he can understand within the capability of each stage, and come to ___fully___ ___understand___ the meaning of adoption.

37.   Piaget's influence on American education is seen when teachers
       1. ___organize class circula to fit child___
       2. _____
       3. _____
       4. _____

38.   Major criticisms of Piaget's ___organismic- structural___ approach have come from American learning theorists, who take a ___mechanistic- functional___ approach.

39.   Robert Gagne's work exemplifies the cumulative learning approach as he describes cognitive skill development as ___building___ on already mastered ___simpler___ ___skills___.

40.   As a description of cognitive development, Piaget's work is ___repeatedly confirmed___. However, his explanations of why cognition develops as he believes is ___not___ ___clearly___ ___defined___.

■ ■ ■ ■

PRACTICE TEST 1

1.   Cognitive development is the study of
       a. ___ the development of internal conscious thinking processes

b.   the development of biological brain maturation
c.   the development of talking skills
d.   the development of physical schemes

2.   Jean Piaget's organismic-structural theory of cognitive development proposes that children
      advance through the periods of intellectual development
      a.   in a rigid time-table for all children
      b.   without skipping any periods, but not necessarily at the same ages
      c.   after the child has accommodated to the environment
      d.   in order to learn symbols and mental images

3.   Adaptation, once purely a biological term, is adapted from Baldwin's work by Piaget and means
      a.   one's ability to interpret the environment
      b.   one's ability to act upon the environment
      c.   one's ability to adjust to the environment
      d.   one's ability to think about the environment

4.   If a little boy sees a mailman and calls him "Daddy", he has demonstrated
      a.   accommodation
      b.   assimilation
      c.   adjustment
      d.   how to embarrass Mom

5.   The force that pushes the child upward through the stages of cognitive development is
      a.   the natural curiosity of the child
      b.   the explanations and teaching of the parents
      c.   the satisfaction felt when the child is in the sensorimotor period
      d.   the disequilibrium felt when the child is unable to understand the environment

6.   The major factor of the sensorimotor period is the
      a.   lack of circular reactions
      b.   lack of object permanence
      c.   lack of memory
      d.   lack of communication

7.   Behaviors which are repeated to recapture a pleasant experience centered on the baby's own body
      are known as
      a.   primary circular reactions
      b.   secondary circular reactions
      c.   tertiary circular reactions
      d.   subcircular reactions

8.   The child's scheme changes in stage six so that he can now
      a.   infer invisible displacements
      b.   reach insightful solutions
      c.   use mental combinations

      d.   all of the above

9.   The major distinction between the sensorimotor period and the preoperational period is
      a.   object permanence
      b.   continued development of the use of mental images and symbols
      c.   use of logical operations
      d.   both a and b

10.   The term preconceptual is used because the child
      a.   has not yet acquired the concept of logical operations and rules
      b.   has not achieved object permanence
      c.   does not have a concept of self
      d.   none of the above

11.   Reasoning at the preconceptual period is limited to
      a.   generalization and discrimination
      b.   language and symbols
      c.   syncretic and transductive
      d.   concepts and ideas

12.   Children in the concrete operational period are limited in their thinking to what they've
      experienced first hand, but during the period of formal operations their thinking can
      a.   not go beyond intuition
      b.   advance to hypotheses beyond their experience
      c.   be limited to monopoly rather than chess
      d.   not understand complicated theories even when explained

13.   Whereas Piaget believed cognitive development came from maturing structures within the
      individual, the learning theorists Watson and Skinner believed it occurred
      a.   from without, by maturation
      b.   from without, by teaching "circus tricks"
      c.   from without, by going through stages
      d.   from without, by "adding on" to the machine

14.   Learning researcher Robert Gagne described the development of complex cognitive skills as
      a.   the ability to memorize rules
      b.   the progress of stage development
      c.   the progression of mastery of elementary skills through complicated skills as a result of
              experience
      d.   all of the above

15.   Both Renee Baillargeon and Andrew Meltzoff found contradictions in Piaget's theory.
      Baillargeon found _____ in 3 1/2 to 5 1/2 month old infants, and Meltzoff discovered that
      infants as young as 9 to 14 months can _____, showing that each behavior occurs
      much earlier than Piaget predicted.
      a.   object permanence, imitate

b.   egocentrism, use animism
c.   syncretic reasoning, use transductive reasoning
d.   assimilation, use accommodation

■ ■ ■ ■   ◀
                                                                        ◀
PRACTICE TEST 2   ◀

1.   Piaget believed that as an infant reacts physically to her environment, she builds her first
        understanding of her surroundings. Piaget called this her
        a.   concept
        b.   routine
        c.   scheme
        d.   cognitive label

2.   When Piaget said children and adults differ qualitatively in cognitive abilities, he meant that
        a.   children actually think differently than adults who have more advanced thought
                processes
        b.   adults have acquired more knowledge than children
        c.   children haven't learned enough language so they lack cognitive abilities
        d.   children don't care enough about learning

3.   Adaptation is accomplished by both _____ and _____.
        a.   assimilation; accommodation
        b.   action; perception
        c.   knowledge; behaviors
        d.   adjustment; accommodation

4.   The acquisition of _____ is essential before the child can solve problems by using
        symbols or mental images.
        a.   primary circular reactions
        b.   secondary circular reactions
        c.   tertiary circular reactions
        d.   object permanence

5.   Repetitive behaviors designed to recapture a pleasant experience centered on objects in the
        environment are known as
        a.   primary circular reactions
        b.   secondary circular reactions
        c.   tertiary circular behaviors
        d.   reflex activity

6.   When a child can abandon the trial-and-error problem solving method, he has accomplished
        a.   object permanence

       b.   the inference of invisible displacements

       c.   the use of mental images, signs and symbols

       d.   all of the above

7.   As the child moves into the preoperational period she becomes capable of

       a.   less use of symbols

       b.   a leap in language development and make-believe play

       c.   understanding complex representations

       d.   conceptual reasoning

8.   The intuitive stage shows examples of the child using her _____ rather than _____.

       a.   rules; imagination

       b.   feelings (or imagination); logic or rules

       c.   animism; syncretic reasoning

       d.   logic; transductive reasoning

9.   John Flavell, William Schiff, and others argue with some of the assumptions of Piaget's stage-bound intellectual functions by conducting experiments which show that

       a.   the children misunderstood the meaning of the questions related to the task

       b.   the children didn't understand the concepts expected at their age

       c.   the children were not able to use symbols and images

       d.   young apes are as intelligent as young human children

10.   Learning theorists see cognitive development as _____ and not necessarily sequential, allowing for _____ and individual differences.

       a.   continuous; diversification

       b.   discontinuous; machine "add ons"

       c.   stage-like; machine "add ons"

       d.   biological; diversification

11.   Which approach to cognitive development takes the machine as its root metaphor?

       a.   the organismic-structural approach

       b.   the mechanistic-functional approach

       c.   the organismic-functional approach

       d.   the mechanistic-structural approach

12.   Renee Baillargeon used habituation to study of 3 1/2 to 5 1/2 month old children to observe

       a.   the possibility of object permanence

       b.   delay of imitation of another's behavior

       c.   early language skills

       d.   memory

13.   The problem even adults have with the window glass puzzle illustrates

       a.   why we don't sell glass for a living

       b.   that we used a rule of conservation rather than the appropriate rule of finding area by multiplying length times width

c. that we may never make it out of the preoperational stage

d. that like many others we have not progressed past the concrete operational stage

14. Most of the criticisms of Piaget have come about as the result of studies showing that children's behaviors don't always fit neatly into Piaget's stages. Many of the criticisms are directed toward

a. his poor description of cognitive development

b. a lack of up to date revisions

c. his use of the epigenetic view

d/ that he based his explanations on premature inductions

15. To explain such complicated concepts as adoption, parents are advised

a. don't tell the child till they've reached the formal operation stage

b. don't tell them at all

c. tell them early and don't worry, they'll figure it out from there

d/ tell them and retell them at successive stages of cognitive development

ANSWER SECTION

<u>Guided Review</u>

1.   *themselves, conscious, self*
2.   *thinking, develops*
3.   *James Mark Baldwin, Jean Piaget*
4.   *biology, environment*
5.   *uniform, predictable*
6.   *sensorimotor, preconceptual, concrete operations, formal operations*
7.   *same order, age*
8.   *qualitatively, quantitatively*
9.   *assimilation, accommodation*
10.   *schemes, sensorimotor*
11.   *assimilation, accommodation*
12.   *disequilibrium, upward, cognitive stages*
13.   *higher stage, lower stage*
14.   *sensorimotor period, object permanence*
15.   *symbols, mental images*
16.   *six, primary circular reactions*
17.   *secondary circular reactions*
18.   *partially hidden, most often*
19.   *cause, effect*
20.   *mental combinations, solve problems*
21.   *apes*
22.   *symbols, internal or mental images, object permanence*
23.   *logic*
24.   *preconceptual, unable*
25.   *relationship*
26.   *syncretic, transductive*
27.   *classifying objects, concepts*
28.   *transductive, alike, alike*
29.   *animistic thinking*
30.   *intuitive stage*
31.   *reversibility*
32.   *rules, logical operations*
33.   *identity*
34.   *conservation, decentration, and reversibility*
35.   *hypothesize*
36.   *repeatedly, fully understand*
37.   a.   *Organize class curricula to fit the child's current stage of cognitive development*
      b.   *Encourage children to be creative and discover knowledge on their own under less structured teaching methods*
      c.   *Offer elective courses to encourage students to apply their operational abilities to many topics*
      d.   *Rather than push students by allowing them to skip grades, encourage children to expand and move*

through class work at their own level of cognitive development.

38.   *organismic-structural, mechanistic-functional*
39.   *building, simpler skills*
40.   *repeatedly confirmed, not clearly defined*

<u>Practice Test 1</u>

1.	*a*
2.	*b*
3.	*c*
4.	*b*
5.	*d*
6.	*b*
7.	*a*
8.	*a*

9.	*d*
10.	*a*
11.	*c*
12.	*b*
13.	*d*
14.	*c*
15.	*a*

<u>Practice Test 2</u>

1.	*c*
2.	*a*
3.	*a*
4.	*d*
5.	*b*
6.	*d*
7.	*b*
8.	*b*

9.	*a*
10.	*a*
11.	*b*
12.	*a*
13.	*b*
14.	*d*
15.	*d*

CHAPTER TEN

COGNITIVE DEVELOPMENT II: MODERN PERSPECTIVES

■■■■
◀
◀
◀
◀

LEARNING OBJECTIVES

This chapter shows you and the Latnem-Poleveds how cognitive psychology is growing. As a relatively new branch of the discipline, this is a good example of one area which demanded the scientific approach spurred on by the events after World War II. You'll see that the computer has been both a tool and an inspiration to the students of intellectual development, and you'll want to show how some of the technology has developed to further our studies.

1. Chapter Preview: Remembrances of things past. Interestingly, its not so peculiar to have to go back to the setting you thought of something in order to remember what that something was. Researcher Carolyn Rovee-Collier says that the setting where the original thought occurred where all of our senses were contributing to the thought are specific parts of an "attention gate". Those pieces of sensory or contextual information are used as stimuli for memory.

2. Now that you have the theory of Jean Piaget well under control, it's time to see what new theories have to offer. You will need to be able to compare and contrast the new with the old.

3. It is interesting that the change in political climate in Russia has allowed the work of Lev Vygotsky to be shared with the rest of the scientific world. You will be able to explain why his theory is called "social-cognitive". Notice too, his position on how developing language relates to cognitive development. Know what he means and how he uses the concepts of the zone of proximal development and scaffolding. What a shame it is that when he was at his most productive, his culture did not allow Lev Vygotsky to share his findings and work with others in other countries in the world.

4. Pascual-Leone's revision of Piaget's position led to his discussion of the factor of M (Mental Power). Be sure to be able to explain this and that he still was not able to explain language acquisition, and left some unanswered questions regarding the precision of schemes.

5. It is important to know the criticisms of both schools of thought on cognitive development in order to understand where interactionists began in developing their approach. The interactionist approach views early cognitive stages as developing in terms of firm stages, whereas later cognitive development can be explained in less rigid stages or levels.

6.   You no doubt remember the metaphors for Piaget's organismic-structural approach and the learning theorists' mechanistic-functional approach. Now we have another metaphor in the understanding of cognitive development: the computer. Here the selective attention and memory functions are the emphasis. Know of Eleanor Gibson's work with children's ability to attend to distinctive features of objects and situations.

8.   The studies of memory are very crucial right now. As students, we need to know all we can about this significant area of study. We can benefit greatly from learning about the memory strategies we can develop as we grow. Motivation is very important here, for children as well as college students!

9.   A most interesting term, "scripts", has been used as a memory strategy. You may be aware of how scripts can tie into the idea of emotional and motivational influences on learning, as well as the way our lifestyles develop.

10.   Metamemory and metacognition are two terms which give us a concise way to communicate the child's awareness of certain cognitive functions. Do you know to what they refer?

11.   Formal Schooling and the need to know or develop skills are both good examples of scaffolding. Do note that "automatic encoding" is found as an independent memory strategy.

12.   Humans are far more interesting than computers, don't you think? Vygotsky recognized self awareness and deliberate control of thought as uniquely human. Is this an idea to be discussed only in your philosophy class?

13.   Researchers study metacognition by examining strategies used by children and adults to reorganize their thinking and memories. Be aware of the differences in this regard between children and adults.

14.   Remember Piaget's discussion about animism in young children's thinking? In this chapter, you see it is not as common as Piaget thought. Piaget's beliefs about the way children classify objects is also challenged in this chapter. Be able to compare and contrast the newer thinking with Piaget's.

15.   Take a close look at the new theoretical approaches. Some theorists note that rather than think of the child as having immature cognitive abilities, it has been shown that there are positive aspects of this immaturity. They suggest that the egocentrism of immaturity is in a sense a boost so that children are not afraid they can't learn new things. It may be that each level allows time for the child to incorporate certain abilities and attitudes of their abilities. Then, of course, there is the question of whether we should push them to ready them for academic lessons to come.

16.   Luria's work with shouted commands to our children is most interesting. Some very useful advice is found in this application!

Ah, if I'd only known then . . . .

■ ■ ■ ■   ◀
                                                                                          ◀
CHAPTER OUTLiNE   ◀

This chapter gives you the comparison material needed to understand the development of cognitive psychology from Piaget to the present. Do it carefully, have fun with the changes that have come about with the newer views presented, and see if there are ideas you'd like to add.

Chapter Preview: Remembrance of Things Past: Redintegrated memories - The value of the "attention gate" for babies and adults. Is memory "situation" specific?

I.   The Social-Cognitive View of Lev Vygotsky
       Vygotsky's work available now that political situation in Russia allows exchange of information
       and ideas.
       A.   Social-Cognitive view
              1.   Encompasses both Bandura's and Piaget's concepts
              2.   Accentuates the role of _____
                     and _____
              3.   Introduces the zone of proximal development and scaffolding
       B.   Culture, Language and Thought
              1.   People born with ability to attend, perceive and remember
              2.   Culture transforms these abilities into higher cognitive functions through
                     a.   social interaction and teaching _____
                     b.   use of language _____
       C.   Stages of language - thought development
              1.   External speech: _____
              2.   Egocentric speech: _____
              3.   Internal speech: (6 to 7 yrs) _____
       D.   Zone of Proximal Development
              1.   Individual prepared at each stage to respond to environment and people
              2.   Allows experience and culture to shape developing cognitive processes
              3.   Adults and culture provide _____
       E.   Effects on American education
              1.   Emphasis on spoken interaction and direction between child and adult to push
                     child to higher levels than child would achieve otherwise
              2.   Stimulates research into areas of language usage, teaching of cognitive skills: e.g.,
                     teaching critical thinking
II.   After Piaget
       A.   Juan Pascual-Leone revised Piaget's theory (Geneva Group)
              1.   Adaptation through assimilation and accommodation
                     _____
              2.   Distinct cognitive developmental stages
                     _____
              3.   M, Mental power is main factor in cognitive development.
                     M = _____
              4.   Stage advancement depends on _____
              5.   Difficulty in counting schemes, or M's _____
              6.   Some questions are still unanswered _____
III.   All the World's a Stage -- Unless . . . .
       A.   Organismic-structural and mechanistic theories can be integrated
       B.   Stage term demonstrated what is probable, but because of variations the term "Level", is
              used to allow more flexibility
       C.   May be that stages are stronger in younger children, than in older when culture provides
              influence.
       D.   Modern thinking is that cognitive development comes from both from within the learner
              and exposure to the environment
At Issue: A Child's Theory of Mind

There's a useful dynamic theory of cognitive development reminiscent of the dynamic theory of motor development. Notice the ages of the children. Does their understanding of mental activity and so of the world depend entirely on the maturation of the brain? Children appear to test their own theories based on experience.
Outline this one, you'll enjoy it.

IV.   Information Processing: uses model of computer. Useful but not theory yet.
        Metaphor--computer. Artificial intelligence attempt to problem solve using series of cognitive operations. Not yet at level of human brain.
        A.   Selective Attention
                1.   Eleanor Gibson: Important to focus on distinctive features
                        a.   younger children _____
                        b.   older children _____
                                (1)   cognitive advances marked by developing ability to handle relevant information without being sidetracked or overwhelmed
        B.   The Development of Memory: Information Processing view
                1.   Infants encode sensory information into memories beginning at birth
                        a.   Infants show storage abilities of distinctive features of objects at 3 months old
                2.   Memory abilities develop at different rates
                        a.   _____
                        b.   _____
                3.   Memory strategies
                        a.   difference in effectiveness of memory among children of 5, 8, and 11 years, due to memory organization
                4.   Scripts: a hypothesized cognitive structure that encompasses a person's knowledge of the typical events in everyday experience
                        a.   children's scripts limited to experience, so make assumptions
        C.   The Development of Memory Strategies
                1.   Rehearsal: repetition of material
                        a.   not seen in children until _____
                        b.   5 and 6 year olds not likely to use this strategy
                        c.   motivation
                2.   Metamemory
                        a.   between 5 and 10 recognize some effort is needed, but not sure how
                        b.   mature efforts begin _____
                        c.   Michelene Chi experiments _____
                        d.   if younger children given more time, will do better
                        e.   H. A. Simon and Allan Newell, developers of executive computer programs
                3.   Metamemory and culture:
                        a.   the importance of formal schooling
                        b.   _____
                        c.   _____
                4.   Metacognition: conscious effort to control and understand thinking
                        a.   Combined with self awareness makes cognition uniquely human

  b.   self awareness _____

5.   Researchers continue study of how children and adults organize information and recall

  a.   strategies used purposefully by children and adults to reorganize their thinking

    (1)   children _____

    (2)   adults _____

B.   children apply new strategies _____

_____

V.   And the Research Continues ....

A.   Animism not as clear as Piaget believed .

  1.   _____

  2.   Rochelle Gelman _____

    _____

    _____

VI.   New Theoretical Approaches look to the positive aspects of the timing of cognitive development

A.   Perhaps the pace of cognitive development provides benefits which would not occur if the pace were accelerated

  1.   metacognition _____

  2.   value of levels _____

    a.   _____

    b.   _____

Application: Speak Softer, I Can't Understand You, A.R. Luria

Loudness- excitement of loudness makes child act more vigorously

Child confuses the "DON'T do" sentence- the "don't" doesn't negate the "go into the street"--as if "don't" is not heard. See Figure 10.4. Experience with young children supports Luria

■ ■ ■ ■

NAMES TO REMEMBER

Carolyn Rovee-Collier
Lev Vygotsky
Jean Piaget
Juan Pascual-Leone
Eleanor Gibson
Michelene Chi
H. A. Simon
Allan Newell

Geoffrey Saxe
John Flavell
Rochel Gelman
Susan Gelman
Kathleen Kremer
A. R. Luria
Saltz, Campbell, and Skotko

■ ■ ■ ■

TERMS AND CONCEPTS

self-awareness
social-cognitive theory
zone of proximal development
external speech
egocentric speech
internal speech
scaffolding
Geneva school
M
Mental Power
schemes
interactionist reconciliation
probabilistic epigenesis
levels--soft stages
terms in Table 10.1
information processing

selective attention
distinctive features
artificial intelligence
memory
computer memory
strategies
encode
retrieval
storage
rehearsal
scripts
metamemory
memory organization
metacognition
a child's theory of the mind

■ ■ ■ ■

GUIDED REVIEW

1.   Soviet Lev Vygotsky's _social_ - _cultural_ theory combines features of the
      theories of _Bandura_ and _Piaget_ .

2.   Two major themes are seen in Vygotsky's theory. These are the influence of culture as expressed
      in the role of its _language_ and the _zone_ of _proximal_ _development_.

3.   He believes that one is born with elemental cognitive functions that need not be learned. The
      culture hones these abilities to _attend_, _percieve_, and _remember_
      through social interaction, and especially through the teaching and use of _language_ .

4.   Contrary to Piaget, Vygotsky believed that _language_ makes thought possible. He
      illustrates this concept in his three stages of speech as they come to govern behavior. The three
      stages are in order _external speech_, _egocentric speech_, and
      internal speech .

5.   Vygotsky argued that at each stage the child is prepared to respond to his own particular
      environment These responses and experiences in his cultural surroundings, the
      zone of _proximal_ _development_ shape his cognitive processes and his

particular way of thinking about the world.

6.   _Scaffolding_ is Vygotsky's term used to describe the support and encouragement adults and the culture provide as a _structure_ to help promote cognitive development.

7.   Where Piaget encouraged children to _make_ _discoveries_ on their own, Vygotsky encouraged the teaching of the use of _language_ and of _cognitive_ _skills_ .

8.   Pascual-Leone's work on behalf of the Geneva School explained stage theory in terms of the increasing _numbers_ of _schemes_ , or _M's_ , the child is capable of handling in the various stages.

9.   Although Pascual-Leone's use of the concept of M supported Piaget's stage theory, there are still unanswered questions such as how preoperational children can handle the _____ and _____ of language, which would not be expected until the concrete operational stage, or how we can count _____.

10. Modern researchers have demonstrated that "stages" only describe the most probable development, known as _____ _____ and agree to use the term "soft stage" or _____ of cognitive development.

11. Parallels between humans and _____ are of interest to the _____ _____ approach. The _____ serves as a model of understanding such cognitive developments as problem solving, _____, and _____.

12. Attempts to develop problem solving logic for computers began with _____ _____'s work in which he found that the computer made many of the same _____ as humans in an elementary logic problem.

13. One of the ways in which humans are superior to computers is that humans can deal with the large amounts of stimuli found in _____ and _____.

14. A crucial factor in processing the volumes of information with which we are bombarded, is the ability to _____ _____ to relevant features of the environment.

15. _____ _____ is the researcher who has studied the aspect of information processing which deals with the increasing ability to focus attention on the _____ _____ of an object.

16. In our book, the _____ _____ and the _____ _____ _____ are examples of Gibson's point that skills must be developed in order to attend to large amounts of information without being sidetracked or overwhelmed by irrelevant material.

17. There appears to be a general mechanism which _____ the speed at which information is

processed as the child ages. Kail's research includes a mathematical formula showing that these changes occur at the same rate _____ _____ _____.

18. In a limited way, an infant is capable of _____ _____ to sensory information and _____ it into memory for retrieval later.

19. That a three month old infant will forget the color of an object while remembering many of its other features, suggests that the color has been _____ into memory as a _____ _____ along with the other features.

20. One component of memory that may be as well developed in 5 year olds as in adults is the ability to judge _____.

21. Creating a _____ according to one's knowledge of everyday typical events is an effective _____ technique. However, one may tend to fill in forgotten events with _____.

22. As children become older, they develop more formal memory strategies such as _____, which involves repeating the material to be remembered over and over again.

23. Researchers have found that even ___ and __ year olds can rehearse and remember information if they are given _____ _____ to observe the information while they rehearse.

24. Between the ages of 5 and 10, children become increasingly aware that their memory works in ways that require special efforts to use it. This recognition is called _____.

25. Michelene Chi's experiment with 10 year olds and college students in recalling the position of chess men on the board, points to the importance of _____.

26. H. A. Simon developed a way for the computer to reorganize its logic, called _____ _____ which may be similar to _____ _____ in humans.

27. Research shows the development of memory strategies, other than recognition, appears to be related to the demand for them, such as those learned in _____ _____.

28. When 4th graders and adults traded memory organization strategies, the results showed an _____ in the 4th graders' success.

29. Although formal schooling plays a major influence in the developing of memory skills, other factors depend on _____ and the need to know presented in the _____.

30. That humans are capable of control over our thoughts and have the ability to think about thinking is called _____.

31. Piaget argued that preoperational children believed that any moving object was alive, illustrating _____. However, Rochel Gelman et. al. discovered that these children acquired

knowledge quickly about live objects and grouped them according to _____
_____.

32. Gelman believes that the preoperational child's special interest in what causes objects to move is _____.

33. Contrary to Piaget's idea that preoperative children believe that even naturally events were caused by _____, Gelman and Kremer, in questioning 4 year olds, found they knew when _____ were the cause and when they were not.

34. Researchers, looking at the advantages of cognitive immaturity, suggest that children's _____ _____ would suffer if they advanced more rapidly. Perhaps the pace of the levels is adaptive so as not to interfere with _____.

35. If the adaptive view of immature cognitive development is correct, it may point to the advantages of the time spent at each level when certain _____ begin to be established..

36. As described in the Application, Luria's work showed how a child became overexcited and confused by _____ _____. His advice is to use a _____, _____, but _____ voice, and to deliver the commands in a positive way.

■ ■ ■ ■

PRACTICE TEST 1

1. Lev Vygotsky's social-cognitive view encompasses the importance of the influence of
   a. the culture, language, and the zone of proximal development
   b. the functions, adding on, and maturation
   c. memory, stages of development, and logic
   d. understanding, conceptual logic, and maturation

2. Vygotsky argued that as the child goes through the stages of language-thought development
   a. language eventually comes to govern the child's behavior
   b. social speech forces the child to think internally
   c. internal thought forces the development of external speech
   d. egocentric speech reflects egocentric thinking

3. Vygotsky's view of the zone of proximal development refers to
   a. the preparedness of the individual to respond to a particular environment at each cognitive level
   b. the cognitive structures collaborate with the environment to create a particular way of thinking

c.   the readiness of children to attend to selective details of an object

d.   both a and b

4.   Scaffolding can be provided by adults and the culture to

a.   support and nurture cognitive development

b.   support, direct, and shape cognitive development

c.   guide children to accomplish more than they would normally

d.   all of the above

5.   Pascual-Leone developed a theory of cognitive development by revising

a.   social learning theory

b.   Gagne's hierarchy of cognitive skills

c.   Piaget's theory

d.   instrumental conditioning principles

6.   Like Piaget, Pascual-Leone's theory

a.   is based on distinct cognitive stages

b.   uses terms for adaptation in the same way as Piaget

c.   leaves unanswered the inconsistency of the preoperational child's use of the rules and
        logic of grammar

d.   all of these

7.   Pascual-Leone's explanation of mental power or M refers to

a.   the strength of the child's memory

b.   the number of ideas or schemes the child can attend to at once

c.   the advancement of language concepts

d.   sensorimotor activities

8.   The view which takes the best supported ideas of both the Geneva school and the
     mechanistic-functional approach is

a.   the functional-structural reconciliation

b.   the organismic-learning theory

c.   the developmental-logical theory

d.   the interactionist reconciliation

9.   Modern theorists use the term _____ to refer to the fact that stages follow the typical or
     most probable development.

a.   typicalistic development

b.   genetic possibility

c.   probabilistic epigenesis

d.   inflexible epigenesis

10. The general consensus of levels of cognitive development differs from Piaget's stages in that they

a.   are more rigid

b.   are more rigid and depend on the environment

c.   are more flexible and are interrelated with the environment

    d.   are less rigid and are independent of the environment

11.   Selective attention is a crucial ability to acquire in order to
    a.   sense the environment
    b.   process meaningful information
    c.   notice all of the stimuli in the environment
    d.   think about the environment

12.   The discussion of Eleanor Gibson makes us cognizant of the need for students to refine selective attention through the use of techniques such as found in our book:
    a.   learning checks and attention directing questions
    b.   rote memory strategies
    c.   rehearsal
    d.   retrieval

13.   Memory strategies begin to appear at about _____, when the child becomes aware of her memory and that she must make an effort to use it. This awareness is known as _____.
    a.   age 15; script memory
    b.   age 10; rehearsal memory
    c.   age 10; metamemory
    d.   age 12; meta-strategies

14.   Although advances in memory skills are seen mostly because of exposure to formal schooling, Geoffrey Saxe found in his studies of street children
    a.   they had surprisingly good mathematical skills
    b.   they learned mathematics skills in order to survive, as they sold goods in the street for a living
    c.   their unusual social situation provided them with the scaffolding to push them beyond what would normally be expected of children their age
    d.   all of the above

15.   Luria's work with the volume of voice commands to small children has resulted in advice to
    a.   speak louder
    b.   speak softer
    c.   speak in longer sentences
    d.   speak in sign language

■ ■ ■ ■

PRACTICE TEST 2

1.   In direct opposition to Piaget, Vygotsky believed that
    a.   thought makes language possible

b./   language makes thought possible
c.   behavior makes thought possible
d.   thought makes behavior possible

2.   The three levels of speech development proposed by Vygotsky are, in order,
      a./   external speech, egocentric speech, and internal speech
      b.   internal speech, egocentric speech, and external speech
      c.   egocentric speech, external speech and internal speech
      d.   egocentric speech, internal speech and external speech

3.   The kind of speech Vygotsky described as egocentric, is, unlike Piaget's view,
      a./   a way of thinking out loud and increases in proportion to the amount of thinking required
                to solve a problem
      b.   not social in any way and expresses the child's egocentric thought
      c.   not tied into thinking or problem solving but is social in nature
      d.   reinforced by parents who enjoy hearing the way children solve problems

4.   Both the concepts of scaffolding and the zone of proximal development are connected with the
      theory of
      a.   Jean Piaget
      b./   Lev Vygotsky
      c.   B. F. Skinner
      d.   Robert Gagne

5.   Vygotsky encourages educators to
      a.   allow children to discover information on their own
      b./   teach cognitive and language skills to students to encourage them to reach for higher
                forms of thinking than they would do on their own
      c.   build a system of rewards and withdrawal of rewards as a way to encourage children to
                learn
      d.   provide the scaffolding to increase the mental power of M's

6.   Juan Pascual-Leone believes the main force in cognitive development is
      a.   language acquisition
      b.   language understanding
      c./   mental power or M's
      d.   across the board conservation

7.   In the Pascual-Leone theory if a child has an M of 2 she would be able to
      a.   remember 2 M's with rehearsal
      b./   focus attention on 2 schemes for comparison, memory, and other cognitive processes
      c.   attend to 2 objects but not remember them
      d.   develop 2 cognitive skills beyond her age group

8.   The basic premise of the interactionist reconciliation approach is that
      a./   the organism and the environment are interdependent

b.   the organism is independent of the environment
c.   the environment is dependent on the organism
d.   stages are not as important as we thought

9.   Modern theorists prefer the term _____ to portray the probable, typical developmental stages.
      a.   grades
      b.   planes
      c.   levels
      d.   plateaus

10.   Information processing theories use the _____ as a model, provoking interest in new areas of cognitive studies.
      a.   machine
      b.   computer
      c.   organism
      d.   camera

11.   A major goal of information processing researchers and their use of the computer and artificial intelligence
      a.   is to duplicate problem solving methods used by people
      b.   is to duplicate levels of memory used by people
      c.   is to duplicate the ability to recognize and organize vast amounts of sensory information as well as people do
      d.   c is the best answer, but experts are working at the others, too!

12.   Eleanor Gibson's work with selective attention
      a.   found children's cognitive advances are related to their developing abilities to focus on distinctive features of objects
      b.   showed small babies fully capable of attending to distinctive features of objects
      c.   showed that children don't use this technique to aid in memory
      d.   showed small children used this technique to understand their environment

13.   Metacognition is
      a.   the ability to know we must remember important information and so learn a variety of memory techniques
      b.   the ability to think about thought and so learn ways of thinking effectively
      c.   the ability to juggle as many M's as possible
      d.   the ability to attend to the distinctive features of objects in out environment

14.   New researchers suggest that slowly developing metacognition may give the preoperational child some advantages, including
      a.   motivation to try harder to learn and understand more
      b.   each cognitive level may offer a special time when certain abilities are laid down
      c.   a maintenance of self confidence since they don't realize how little they really know
      d.   all of the above

15.   According to the Applications section, shouting negative commands to small children may
       a.   excite them into doing the very thing you don't want
       b.   cause them to forget what you said
       c.   reinforce their responses
       d.   make them do it faster

ANSWER SECTION

<u>Guided Review</u>

1. social-cultural, Bandura, Piaget
2. language, zone, proximal development
3. attend, perceive, remember, language
4. language, external speech, egocentric speech, internal speech
5. environment, zone, proximal development
6. scaffolding, structure
7. make discoveries, language, cognitive skills
8. number, schemes, or M's
9. rules, logic, schemes
10. probabilistic epigenesis, level
11. computers, information processing, computer, attention, memory
12. Allen Newell, errors
13. sights, sounds
14. selectively attend
15. Eleanor Gibson, distinctive features
16. learning checks, attention directing questions
17. increases, across the board
18. selectively attending, encoding
19. encoded, distinctive feature
20. recency
21. script, organizing, assumptions
22. rehearsal
23. 5, 10, more time
24. metamemory
25. experience
26. executive programs, cognitive restructuring
27. formal schooling
28. increase
29. scaffolding, environment
30. metacognition
31. animism, shared characteristics
32. innate
33. people, people
34. self confidence. motivation
35. abilities
36. shouted commands; calm, firm, soft

<u>Practice Test 1</u>

1. a
2. a
3. d
4. d
5. c
6. d

7.	*b*
8.	*d*
9.	*c*
10.	*c*
11.	*b*

12.	*a*
13.	*c*
14.	*d*
15.	*b*

<u>Practice Test 2</u>

1.	*b*
2.	*a*
3.	*a*
4.	*b*
5.	*b*
6.	*c*
7.	*b*
8.	*a*

9.	c
10.	b
11.	d
12.	a
13.	b
14.	d
15.	a

CHAPTER ELEVEN

iNTELLiGENCE AND CREATiViTY

LEARNiNG OBJECTiVES

Well! You're more than half way through. How did mid-terms go? Have you noticed that you have visual and auditory memory and even tactile memory as you remember your own notes? And have you found out what kinds of tests your professor likes to give you? Yes? Good! Keep up the good work! I hope you've formed a study group or have enjoyed the fantasy of the Poleveds from Latnem listening to every word. It's time to study intelligence. We don't just open up a person's head and pour it in, do we?

1. Tell them how intelligence testing began with Alfred Binet and Theodore Simon and the children in Paris.
2. Know what the formulas were then for comparing mental age with chronological age and why L. Wilhelm Stern developed the IQ score.
3. Here's a good one. Define intelligence for the folks!
4. Explain what validity and reliability mean in testing. Explain why IQ tests are valid for predicting success in school.
5. Describe factor load and its implications. Know who developed factor analysis and why he bothered.
6. Know how Thurston, Guilford, Gardner and Spearman viewed intelligence in different ways.
7. Give them an overview of Robert Sternberg's Triarchic Theory of intelligence. Show them the model he believes can be applied to any sociocultural context. Explain his position that intellectual skills can be strengthened through his training program. You will find his books very interesting.
8. Describe the research into the role of heritability on intelligence and the two major methods of studying this. Keep in mind the statement of Richard Weinberg regarding the inheritance of traits.
9. Understand the use of correlation coefficients to compare IQ scores of related and unrelated people as you share Table 11.1. Describe the problems of some of the studies as well as what is not explained by correlational studies.
10. Tell them the approach of Joseph Horn (The Texas Adoption Project) as he came to the conclusion that the timing of the influence of genetics and the environment have not been understood until now.
11. Notice the view of your author on the nature vs nurture issue and his optimistic outlook for future

improvements in intelligence.

12.   Discuss the race-intelligence issue raised by Arthur Jensen. This is a good time to explain cultural and language bias. Ask someone from another country to give you a test about daily activities in their country while they take one you've written about American customs. You'll both have fun, and learn the frustrations inherent in the task.

13.   Talk about the adoption of black children into white families and the testing results. This is a good time to tell them about the Larry P. vs Wilson Riles and PASE vs Hannon court cases.

14.   Describe the efforts toward culture free testing using the K-ABC and Raven Progressive Matrices Test.

15.   Explain the research of Sameroff and Seifer in the Rochester Longitudinal Study and their 10 environmental factors which they feel account for large variances in childrens' IQ scores.

16.   Related to #15, you may want to remember James Flynn's exciting work using the Raven culture free test.

17.   As you compare notes on enriching the child's environment to increase your children's scores, describe the Ypsilanti Project and Carolina Abecedarian Project. Explain these programs and their results. Notice that there are no real guarantees with any specific program but that there is agreement that early intervention can help if it is prepared in relationship to the population of children receiving it and is continued into the school years.

18.   Exchange views on creativity. Try describing it's meaning. Its as hard to do as defining intelligence, isn't it? Refer to what Jackson and Messick have defined as the essential ingredients of creativity.

19.   Explain the difficulties of measuring intelligence over time. They will enjoy hearing about the Terman study and the subsequent success of the "kids".

20.   Discuss some of the conclusions you and other researchers have reached, based on this chapter's topic, and of the effects of heredity and environment on intelligence.

■ ■ ■ ■

CHAPTER OUTLiNE

Now you'll do even more of this outline so you can really test that you have the hang of it. I'll give you hints, but the bulk of the work is up to you. Fill in the details according to what you know of your teacher's testing style so that this will be a good way to review, and for your own knowledge's sake for future courses relevant to this subject. The issues of intelligence and intelligence testing will return in several of the courses you'll take in the future.

Chapter Preview: The Ten Year Prediction. Children tested at 7 months, 1 year and 10 years later show us surprising results. Some abilities can be predicted.

I.   Defining Intelligence
    A.   Early theories emphasize inheritance
        1.   Galton --
            b.   Began testing movement
        2.   Positive Eugenics
    B.   Modern theories look at the interaction between inheritance and environment
    C.   Measuring Intelligence -- IQ tests
        1.   Early 1900's test developments

       a.   Alfred Binet   Theodore Simon
           (1)   Binet's formula _____
           (2)   Simon _____
    2.   L. Wilhelm Stern
       a.   Formula for IQ _____
       b.   compared child's score with _____
    3.   Lewis Terman and Stanford University colleagues revision of original test
       a.   _____
       b.   IQ norms established _____

D.   Test Validity--that it measures what it says it will and Test Reliability--that it does so consistently
    1.   Help! No adequate definition of intelligence!
    2.   IQ Tests do measure _____
    3.   IQ tests don't measure _____
    4.   Uses for Intelligence tests
       a.   Good predictor for _____
       b.   clinical assessment _____

E.   Factor Analysis
    1.   Weight given to specific ability is called factor load
       a.   Examples:
           (1)   Stanford-Binet, verbal skills
           (2)   Wechsler Adult Scale--verbal plus non-verbal including hand-eye coordination
    2.   L. L. Thurstone developed factor analysis
       a.   many kinds of intelligence _____
       b.   his goal _____
    3.   J. P. Guilford 1984
       a.   model of 150 factors
    4.   Howard Gardner 1983
       a.   model of 7 kinds of intelligence
    5.   Charles Spearman 1920's
       a.   one kind of general intelligence: g
       b.   g defined as _____

F.   Robert Sternberg's Triarchic Theory of Intelligence
Beyond IQ (1984) Intelligence Applied (1986)
    1.   Three pronged approach to intelligence: broader approach, can be applied in any sociocultural context
    2.   Information processing approach
       a.   componential intelligence _____
           _____
       b.   contextual intelligence _____
           _____
       c.   experiential intelligence _____
           _____
    3.   Sternberg's definition of intelligence
       _____

4.   Working on new Sternberg Multidimensional Abilities test
II.   Heritability of Intellectual Capacity
    A.   Genetics determine structure of brain and differences in the structure
        1.   Size of brain is not related to intelligence
        2.   Many genes plus the environment determine intelligence
        3.   Richard Weinberg statement _____
    B.   Methods of Study of Behavioral Genetics
        1.   Thomas Bouchard, Minnesota Study of Twins reared Apart
            a.   Twin Design, identical and fraternal twins
                _____

        2.   Adoption design, genetically related, raised apart
                _____

        3.   Use of correlation coefficient to find relationship between related pairs
            a.   E.g.: Twins reared apart Table 11.1
                (1)   problems with twins-reared-apart studies
                (2)   new data indicate more significant genetic influence than old studies
            b.   Texas Adoption Study: Joseph Horn
                (1)   correlation of biological and adoptive mothers _____
                (2)   90% of other variables unaccounted
                (3)   other variables could include
                        _____

                (4)   10 years later, effects of genetics on intelligence will-- with time, while effects of environment will
                        _____

                (5)   your author's assessment now and in the future
                        _____

    C.   IQ and Race
        1.   Arthur Jensen
            a.   IQ score difference in blacks and whites
        2.   Sandra Scarr's adoption study _____
                _____

        3.   Scores of Japanese children compared to American
            a._____
        4.   The influence of schooling
            a.   Effects of: summer vacations, a year off from school
    D.   IQ and School Placement
        1.   Larry P. vs. Wilson Riles
            a.   _____
        2.   PASE vs. Hannon
            a.   _____
        3.   Kaufman Assessment Battery for Children-K-ABC
            a.   correlates well with achievement tests
            b.   culture fair but ....
        4.   Culture Fair testing
            a.   Raven Progressive Matrices Test

          b.   still, no completely culture free IQ test
III.   IQ and Environment
        A.   Rochester Longitudinal study, 1970's, Arnold Sameroff, Ronald Seifer
                  1.   Environmental factors count for 49% of variance of children's IQ's
                  2.   10 environmental factors, each carry 4 to 6 IQ test points
                  3.   Environmental factors vary from one population to another
                            a.   James Flynn _____
                  4.   Why increase in IQ in last generation? _____
                            _____

        B.   The Effects of Environmental Stimulation
                  1.   Project Head Start 1960's
                            a.   Weikart and Schweinhart interim Ypsilanti Project report shows
                                      _____
                            b.   Carolina Abecedarian Project: intensive enrichment for four groups
                                      (1)   _____, _____, _____, _____,
                                      (2)   results: _____
                            c.   programs with high academic emphasis most successful
                                      _____
                            d.   early intervention programs can have lasting effects but no guarantee due
                                      to variance in program and population of children
                            e.   best predictor is high IQ all along
At Issue: Birth Order and Intelligence
        A.   Galton noted disproportionate number of British scientists were first-borns
        B.   characteristics of first-borns
        C.   Zajonc and Markus, model of intellectual climate related to birth order
        D.   large families (Eg: 8th, 9th and 10th children)
        E.   birth order effect very subtle and very small. Best to realize many other factors are at
                  work
IV.   Intellectual Changes Over Time
        A.   Example of early testing: Nancy Bayley's Mental and Motor Scale score at 9 months
                  unrelated to IQ scores at five years.
                  1.   Different skills measured on each test. Zero correlation
                  2.   This and other infant scales not useful for prediction of later IQ scores
                  3.   IQ score consistency not seen until approximately 10 years old
                  4.   Some success when there is common denominator measured in infancy and again
                            in later childhood
                            a.   O'Conner, Cohen and Parmelee auditory discrimination
                                      (1)   finding _____
                            b.   Joseph Fagan, visual habituation test
                                      (1)   finding _____
        B.   Terman study 1921 to present
                  1.   Population studied --
                  2.   1950 follow-up studies
                            a.   _____
                            b.   _____
                            c.   _____

        3.   Present follow-up, Pauline Sears

            a. _____

            b. _____

        4.   "Terman kids" now in their 80's

            a. _____

V.   Creativity: see Figure 11.8

     A.   Definition

        1. _____

        2. _____

        3. _____

     B.   Guilford's opinion on convergent and divergent production

        1.   Convergent production _____

        2.   Divergent production _____

        3.   IQ tests measure convergent production not divergent production on which creativity is based

     C.   How Creativity is Acquired

        1.   Experience _____

        2.   Ideational fluency -- Michael Wallach, 1970

            _____

VI.   Final Thoughts on Individual Differences

Biology is not democratic, some may be better equipped for intellectual tasks with healthy excellent brains and nervous systems, however, intelligence can be dramatically affected by a stimulating environment.

Applications: Reaching Their Full Potential: Mainstreaming Handicapped Children

     A.   Public Law 94-142 must provide least restrictive educational environment to meet handicapped child's needs.

        1.   Type of program most important

        2.   Mainstreaming means to include handicapped children in regular academic classes

        3.   The tragedy of ignorance regarding mental handicaps

            a.   Mindie Crutcher

        4.   example of program for children with Down syndrome,

            a.   Minnesota Project EDGE to prepare children for regular classroom

        5.   Other children accept "special" kids well and develop tolerance, compassion, and understanding

        6.   Handicapped children do better than if had been isolated

■ ■ ■ ■

NAMES TO REMEMBER

Rose and Feldman	Alfred Binet
Dr. Seymour Sarason	Theodore Simon
Sir Francis Galton	Wilhelm Stern

L. L. Thurstone
Robert J. Sternberg
J. P. Guilford
Howard Gardner
Charles Spearman
Richard Weinberg
Lee Willerman
Joseph Horn
The Texas Adoption Project
Zajonc and Markus
Arthur Jensen
Sandra Scarr
Kaufman-ABC Battery
Larry P. vs Wilson Riles
PASE vs Hannon
Raven Progressive Matrices Test
Ypsilanti Project

Carolina Abecedarian Project
D. P. Weikart, Lawrence Schweinhart
Joseph Fagan
Arnold Sameroff and Ronald Seifer
Nancy Bayley
Thomas Bouchard
Minnesota Study of Twins Reared Apart
Louis Terman
Pauline and Robert Sears
Jackson and Messick
Michael Wallach
Robert Plomin
National Institute of Health and Human
Development
Mindie Crutcher
Project EDGE

■ ■ ■ ■

TERMS AND CONCEPTS

intelligence
phrenology
mental age
chronological age
intelligence quotient
valid, validity
reliability
factor load
factor analysis
twin design
adoption design
achievement tests
general intelligence
"g"
heritability
triarchic theory
componential intelligence
contextual intelligence

experiential intelligence
correlations
correlation coefficient
birth order factors
culture bias
educational bias
culture fair tests
language free tests
kibbutz
creativity
novelty
appropriateness
transcendence of constraints
coalescence of meaning
convergent production
divergent production
ideational fluency
mainstreaming

■ ■ ■ ■

GUIDED REVIEW

1. In the Chapter Preview, it was found that 11-year-old children who had the best score in
    __perceptual__ processing speed generally were the ones who had the quickest
    __visual__ __recognition__ memory at 7 months of age.

2. The beginnings of efforts to measure intelligence are credited to Sir __Francis__
    __Galton__, who had founded a movement dealing with __positive__
    __eugenics__.

3. The first intelligence test was developed by Alfred __Binet__ and Theodore
    __Simon__ to determine which children in Paris would benefit from __special__
    __education__.

4. The questions on this first test were framed to compare the child's performance or his
    __mental__ __age__ to that of his __chronological age__.

5. L. Wilhelm Stern developed a formula which yielded __intelligence quotient__ scores
    and which could be used to compare the child with his __school__ __peers__.

6. A test is said to be __valid__ if it measures what it claims to measure. However, although
    IQ tests measure many common skills and abilities used in school, they do not measure all facets
    of __intelligence__ such as __creativity__.

7. IQ tests have been used with good validity in predicting success in __school__ and in
    assessments of __nuerological__ and __perceptual__ deficiencies.

8. A problem with some IQ tests is that they are heavily weighted in measuring only one ability
    such as reading or vocabulary. This weight or emphasis is known as __factor__
    __load__, and to correct the problem, L. L. __Thurstone__ developed a method called
    __factor__ __analysis__.

9. J. P. __Guilford__ and Howard __Gardner__ have broadened the concept of intelligence
    and have proposed there are up to __150__ factors and __7__ broad
    categories respectively, which make up the concept called intelligence.

10. Charles Spearman believed intelligence was made up of only one kind of __general__
    __intelligence__ He used __"g"__ to represent the mental __energy__ a person
    uses on any given task.

11. The three components of intelligence according to Sternberg's theory are __componential__
    intelligence, or book smart; __contextual__ intelligence, or street smart; and __experiential__
    intelligence, or learning from one's mistakes by developing new skills and using them.

12. Sternberg's believes that intelligence is a series of ___skills___ influenced by both heredity and ___learning___. He believes that a ___training___ program can strengthen all three forms of intelligence.

13. In terms of the heritability of intelligence or any other behavior, Richard Weinberg stated that genes do not ___fix___ behavior, rather they establish a wide ___range___ of possible reactions to the experience that environments can provide.

14. Correlation coefficients obtained from early twins reared apart studies do not accurately reflect the heritability of intelligence because of the ___flaws___ found in the methods used.

15. The Texas Adoption Project (Joseph Horn) showed small correlations between the children's IQ scores and their ___biological___ and ___adoptive___ mothers. This study left at least ___90%___ of the variables unexplained.

16. Interestingly, after a 10 year interval, the Texas Project showed that the influence of genetics ___increased___ with age, while the effects of the environment ___decreased___ with age.

17. The court cases of Larry P. vs Wilson Riles and PASE vs Hannon resulted in the ruling that childrens' placement in special education programs must include ___other___ ___factors___ in addition to ___IQ___ test scores.

18. Sandra Scarr's adoption study reputes Jensen idea of white superiority of intelligence over blacks, by showing the young black children who were adopted into white families achieved IQ scores ___close___ to ___white___ averages.

19. The K-ABC test, in its effort to reduce cultural and racial bias, correlates well with ___achievement tests___ and has cut the score gap between blacks and whites by about ___half___ or ___seven___ points.

20. Efforts continue to produce language-free and culture fair tests, as evidenced by the ___Raven___ ___Progressive Matricies___ Test.

21. In conducting the Rochester Longitudinal Study, Sameroff and Seifer found 10 ___environmental___ ___factors___ which could account for about 49% of the ___variance___ among IQ scores.

22. The Carolina Abecedarian Project provided intensive intervention for four different groups of children. The children who had the most beneficial results were in the ___preschool___ group, having results lasting through age ___12___.

23. Although many early intervention programs have shown lasting, positive effects, there is ___no___ ___garuntee___ that every program will be effective with every group of children.

24. Problems of predicting IQ in older children based on scales given them as infants is that these scales ___measure___ ___different abilities___. For example, infant scales usually

measure _motor_ _abilities_, while older children's scales usually measure _verbal_ and _cognotive_ skills.

25. Two infant tests which were useful however, included an _auditory_ _memory_ test, and a _visual_ _habituation_ test, both of which had positive correlations with the _Standford Binet_ IQ test.

26. In 1921, Louis Terman began a longitudinal study of children with impressively _high_ IQ scores. Although comparisons of women were difficult due to the cultural norms of the times, male comparisons to the general populations indicated they joined professions at a rate _considerably higher_ than their more normal peers.

27. Women's achievements in the Terman study indicated they experienced more _satisfaction_ than their peers in their work, married _later_, and had children _later_.

28. Present studies by Pauline and Robert Sears, of the Terman "kids", show them to be _healthier_, _happier_, and _richer_, and with lower incidences of _suicide_, _alcoholism_, and _divorce_.

29. Although defining creativity is difficult, we can get close by applying the four criteria set down by Jackson and Messick:
    1. _novelty_
    2. _appropriateness_
    3. _transcendance of constraints_
    4. _coalescence of meaning_

30. _Guilford_ explains the difficulty of IQ tests to predict creativity by showing that these tests rely on _convergent production_, rather than on _divergent production_, which more accurately reflects creativity.

31. Where convergent production depends on developing _one_ _answer_ to the problem, divergent production is the ability to see _many_ _solutions_ to it.

32. Testing creativity by measuring divergent production uses the concept of _ideational fluency_. For example, you may want to test yours by naming as many uses as you can for the daily paper.

33. To sum up the argument of nature vs. nurture as determinants of intelligence, we can see that the _complex_ _interaction_ between _genetic_ _inheritance_ and _experience_ could be measured at about 50-50.

34. The discussion of birth order comparisons illustrate that rather than dramatic differences, they are _small_ and _subtle_, and should be treated as such.

35. Public Law 94-142 (1972) ensures that the handicapped child will be provided with the _least_ _restrictive_ _educational_ _environment_ possible to meet his/her

needs. This mainstreaming effort has been boosted by Public Law 99-457, which allows for _early_ _intervention_ for preschool aged handicapped children.

BONUS: Interview a teacher in a public school mainstreamed class, and ask about the benefits and difficulties for both the handicapped and "normal" children. Ask the teacher what factors are most needed for successful mainstreaming. Write this up as a reasonably short report and dazzle your Prof with your intelligent approach to the course.

PRACTICE TEST 1

1. A singular problem in discussing intelligence is
   a.   that the definition is very specific
   b.   that IQ tests measure intelligence factors accurately
   c.   that it has not ever been adequately defined
   d.   that it has nothing to do with common sense

2. Early theories of intelligence were based on _____, but recently the _____ has been recognized as making significant contributions.
   a.   environment; inheritance
   b.   phrenology; physiology
   c.   inheritance; environment
   d.   eugenics; inheritance

3. The first intelligence test was developed by Binet and Simon and made comparisons between the child's _____ and her _____.
   a.   mental age; chronological age
   b.   performance; mental age
   c.   ability; performance
   d.   normal IQ's; abnormal IQ's

4. One major threat to the validity of an IQ test when excess weight is given to one ability, is known as
   a.   narrow sampling
   b.   heavy factor loading
   c.   loaded questions
   d.   weighted samples

5. _____ developed a model of intelligence which included ___ factors of intelligence functioning.
   a.   J. P. Guilford; 150
   b.   Howard Gardner; 7 broad categories
   c.   Alfred Binet; several

   d.   both a and b

6.   Sternberg's studies have led him to argue in favor of a broader definition of intelligence which
      includes
      a.   componential intelligence
      b.   contextual intelligence
      c.   experiential intelligence
      d.   all of the above

7.   Robert Sternberg's triarchic theory adds importance to the traditional problem solving skills
      measured on IQ tests by including
      a.   the ability to survive and do well in the context of one's own social and cultural
                environment
      b.   the ability to learn new skills through experience and incorporate them into one's
                repertoire of expertise
      c.   the intellectual climate provided by one's place in the birth order of the children in the
                family
      d.   both a and b

8.   Horn's Texas Adoption Project study showed
      a.   a significant correlation between biological mothers and their adopted children
      b.   a significant contribution from both of the adoptee's fathers
      c.   90% of the variables in the adoptee's IQ scores are not accounted for by comparing scores
                of biological or adoptive parents
      d.   birth order variables account for those not explained biologically

9.   Both the cases of Larry P. vs William Riles and PASE vs Hannon illustrated the need for court
      rulings which finally
      a.   allowed placement of students in "special education" classes based on IQ scores alone
      b.   disallowed placement of students in "special education" classes based on IQ scores alone
      c.   eliminated prejudice against minorities
      d.   mandated culture free testing in schools

10.   The Kaufman Assessment Battery For Children has reduced black-white cultural bias with the
      result
      a.   blacks still score 15 points lower than whites
      b.   the IQ differences between blacks and whites have been cut in half
      c.   blacks score better than whites overall
      d.   the K-ABC test showed no correlation with achievement tests of acquired knowledge

11.   Using intellectual measurement tests to evaluate changes in IQ between infancy and 5-year-olds
      has shown
      a.   that tests of infant motor skills are poor predictors of IQ scores at age 6
      b.   that tests for babies emphasize cognitive skills whereas tests for older children emphasize
                motor skills
      c.   a high correlation between IQ scores at the two ages

    d.   that infant scores have good predictive value

12.   The term correlation coefficient refers to the
    a.   lack of a relationship between two variables
    b.   computation of the measurements of two simultaneously occurring events giving information of their relationship
    c.   odds of one event's occurring before the other
    d.   way to avoid predictions of relationships between events

13.   Creativity is a quality defined by Jackson and Messick as consisting of the four following criteria
    a.   imagination, novelty, transcendence of constraints, coalescence of meaning
    b.   novelty, appropriateness, transcendence of constraints, and coalescence of meaning over time
    c.   novelty, appropriateness, traditionally valued applications, meaning
    d.   imagination, moral rightness, without traditional rules, application to society

14.   Guilford believes creativity is measured best by
    a.   convergent production
    b.   novelty and appropriateness,
    c.   divergent production
    d.   the ability to zero in on a single correct answer

15.   Perhaps the best way to sum up the effects of inheritance vs. environment on intellectual development is to recognize the need for
    a.   the inheritance of an excellent, healthy brain and nervous system
    b.   environmental stimulation at home and school, good nutrition and a healthy emotional climate
    c.   the teaching of creativity
    d.   both a and b

■ ■ ■ ■

PRACTICE TEST 2

1.   The first scientific interest in intelligence can be credited to
    a.   Sigmund Freud's psychosexual stages
    b.   Sir Francis Galton's efforts toward positive eugenics
    c.   Lewis Terman's studies of the gifted
    d.   all of the above

2.   L. Wilhelm Stern's formula, which was based on Binet's comparison of mental age and chronological age,
    a.   allowed the comparison of one child with his peers

    b.   yielded a score he called an intelligence quotient

    c.   is expressed as MA/CA x 100 = IQ

    (d.)   all of the above

3.   IQ tests can be validly used to
    a.   measure the correlation between race and intelligence
    b.   measure the intelligence of immigrants to this country
    (c.)   predict school success
    d.   measure creativity

4.   L. L. Thurstone's experience in the Thomas Edison laboratory led him to conclude
    a.   there is only one kind of intelligence
    (b.)   intelligence in one area doesn't mean intelligence in another
    c.   Edison was a mathematical genius
    d.   both a and b

5.   Robert Sternberg sees intelligence as a series of skills which
    a.   are influenced by heredity
    b.   can be developed and strengthened through training in the environment
    c.   will be measured to predict performance and help individuals identify weakness
    (d.)   all of the above

6.   Sternberg argues that
    (a.)   an important part of intelligence is learning the ins and out and realities of how to do well in their own environment
    b.   it is inappropriate to include learning the angles and politics of one's environment to survive well
    c.   one must realize that the size of the brain is related overall to intelligence
    d.   the series of skills which comprise intelligence are entirely learned in the environment

7.   The heritability of intelligence is studied by researching
    a.   the size of the brain
    (b.)   correlations between the IQ scores of both related and unrelated people
    c.   Mendel's laws of the inheritance of traits
    d.   only twins reared apart

8.   After a 10 year period, researchers in the Texas Adoption Project have found
    a.   the influence of genetics on IQ decreases as the children get older, while the effect of the environment increases
    (b.)   the influence of genetics on IQ increases as the children get older, while the effect of the environment decreases
    c.   the influence of genetics on IQ and the effect of the environment equals out as the subjects get older
    d.   both the influence of genetics on IQ and the effects of the environment increase proportionately as the subjects get older

9.   Regarding the heritability of intelligence and other characteristics, Richard Weinberg stated
      a.   90% of all the variables that account for IQ scores are unaccounted for
      b.   Genes establish a range of possible reactions to the range of possible experiences that
            environments can provide
      c.   intelligence levels depend on the degree to which the brain is myelinated
      d.   inheritance and environment each account for approximately 50% of the difference in
            measured intelligence

10.   Ten year results of the Carolina Abecedarian Project intensive enrichment program showed that
      _____ had the most beneficial results, while with children _____ the program
      was less effective.
      a.   preschool children, who had already started school
      b.   the 5 years to 8 years olds, who had already started school
      c.   preschool children, ages 5 through 8
      d.   children who had already started school, who were preschoolers

11.   IQ scores do not become reliable and correlated with adult scores before the age of
      a.   12 or 13
      b.   9 or 10
      c.   6 or 7
      d.   15 or 16

12.   As the Terman study has progressed from 1921 to the present, we see that the children with
      superior IQ's grew
      a.   to be more prone to suicide, alcoholism and divorce than peers of average intelligence
      b.   less likely to choose professions which paid well
      c.   healthier, richer and happier than their average peers
      d.   less satisfied with their work than their average peers

13.   The results of the Terman study show
      a.   genius is not next to insanity
      b.   staying in school long enough to achieve advanced degrees means more flexibility in
            careers and better pay
      c.   money isn't everything, but it sure beats the alternative!
      d.   (guess what) all of these and more

14.   Although IQ tests do not measure creativity, Michael Wallach has used the concept of _____
      _____ to measure _____.
      a.   ideational fluency; convergent production
      b.   novelty; divergent production
      c.   ideational fluency; divergent production
      d.   divergent production; appropriateness

15.   Mainstreaming handicapped children into regular classrooms according to Public Law 99-457 has
      a.   worked best with children with Down syndrome when they have had some form of early
            intervention and/or ongoing help

b.   offered children in regular classrooms the opportunity to learn compassion, tolerance and understanding, as they come to appreciate the potential of the handicapped students

c.   been successful when supported by the school district, teachers and parents, along with careful selection of the special students

d.   all of these

ANSWER SECTION

<u>*Guided Review*</u>

1.   perceptual, visual recognition
2.   Francis Galton, positive eugenics
3.   Binet, Simon, special education
4.   mental age, chronological age
5.   intelligence quotient, school peers
6.   valid, intelligence, creativity
7.   school, neurological, perceptual
8.   factor load, Thurstone, factor analysis
9.   Guilford, Gardner, 150, 7
10.   general intelligence, "g", energy
11.   componential, contextual, experiential
12.   skills, learning, training
13.   fix or determine, range
14.   faults or flaws
15.   biological, adoptive, 90%
16.   increased, decreased
17.   other factors, IQ or intelligence
18.   close, white
19.   achievement tests, half, 7
20.   Raven Progressive Matrices
21.   environmental factors, variance
22.   preschool, 12
23.   no guarantee
24.   measure different abilities, motor abilities, verbal, cognitive
25.   auditory memory, visual habituation, Stanford Binet
26.   high, considerably higher
27.   satisfaction, later, later
28.   healthier, happier, richer, suicide, alcoholism, divorce
29.   novelty, appropriateness, transcendence of constraints, coalescence of meaning
30.   Guilford, convergent production, divergent production
31.   one answer, many solutions
32.   ideational fluency
33.   complex interaction, genetic inheritance, experience
34.   small, subtle
35.   least restrictive educational environment, early intervention

<u>*Practice Test 1*</u>

1.   c
2.   c
3.   a

4.   b
5.   d
6.   d

7.   *d*
8.   *c*
9.   *b*
10.   *b*
11.   *a*

12.   *b*
13.   *b*
14.   *c*
15.   *d*

<u>Practice Test 2</u>

1.   *b*
2.   *d*
3.   *c*
4.   *b*
5.   *d*
6.   *a*
7.   *b*
8.   *b*

9.   *b*
10.   *a*
11.   *b*
12.   *c*
13.   *d*
14.   *c*
15.   *d*

CHAPTER TWELVE

SOCIALIZATION AND PARENTING

■■■■

◀
◀
◀

LEARNING OBJECTIVES

Here's a chapter that will answer many of the questions asked by your friends. How is it we're so different? What does the environment do, and how, that makes even members of the same family so different from one another? How is it that neighboring countries have such differing values? "Ah! Socialization and the different styles of parenting have much influence here," you say wisely. "Oh? What's socialization?" and " How can parenting styles be different when all one has to do is insure the health and survival of the child to adulthood?" they ask. "Let's have lunch," you say and prepare to answer questions and tell them about the following topics.

1. Explain to them what socialization is and how it begins almost the moment a child is born.
2. Point out that socialization is an inevitable and lifetime process. Give them some examples in your own life, even in the present, as you show how the principles in the chapter are applied.
3. Discuss the problems of studying families except in the descriptive and correlational formats of investigation and how cause and effect relationships are difficult to establish. Describe the role of parents and families as agents of socialization.
4. One aspect of the study involves the importance of the child's own development. Give them some background on that, including a thorough explanation of Sigmund Freud's ideas of personality and the psychosexual stages. Explain the importance of the impact of Freud as the first to attempt a grand theory of development.
5. Contrasting Erik Erikson's modern psychoanalytic theory to Freud's will help them understand how the social processes came to be studied over the life time and how the accent of the study has changed as a result of Freud getting us started.
6. Describe how developmental changes affect the socialization process. Table 12.3 will help you put these concepts together. Understanding the individuality of family behaviors and the patterns which can become continuous over time provides another insight into children's personality development.
7. As we presently study parents and children, we see that regulating children's behavior starts after infancy. Explain how the attempt to teach proper behavior is part of the socialization process and how we encourage the child to develop his own ability to regulate his behavior.

8. Describe Diana Baumrind's work on the two major dimensions of parenting. Explain how that breaks down into four major modes of parenting which will have different and sometimes profound results on children's behavior. You will want to study each of these aspects of parenting, and their possible effects in order to discuss this topic thoroughly.

9. Discipline is an issue which is frequently discussed by parents and non-parents. Describing the three different disciplinary practices used by parents will surely start a lively discussion with more than one disagreement, I'll bet! You'll want to include the children's reactions to these that researchers have found. Remember to say that researchers are not drawing conclusions on the best way to raise children. Parents have to decide that for themselves based, hopefully, on learning as much as they can about this tremendous job!

10. Mother's decisions to work outside of the home may be helped along by the studies of children whose parents both work. (I wouldn't suggest for a minute they don't work inside of the home too, I know better!) Talk about the conditions when the families have the toughest time adjusting to mothers' working.

11. We can't ignore the divorce rates in our country. Tell them about the complexity of the disorganization and the transitions involved in children's adjustments to divorce and separation. The Hetherington study will help here. Do add to that the new work being done in studying remarriage factors.

12. Since we have so many one-parent families, you'll want to talk about how mothers and fathers alone are doing. The four general guidelines to parenting may be especially helpful here.

13. A sad conversation, but necessary, will be when you talk about child neglect and abuse. Be able to describe what both terms mean and the responsibility of citizens who see this happening. Give them some ideas on the treatments which have had some success for the parents as well as the children. See what is being done to prevent child abuse in your area.

14. Pay attention to the At Issue discussion about the adjustments made regarding children who are adopted. This timely discussion addresses some of the problems encountered, as well as the concern for adoptions of children from different ethnic groups and races. The question of open adoptions is also raised.

■ ■ ■ ■

CHAPTER OUTLINE

Here's the even dozen! By now, you have outlined your chapters so well it has become a habit, right? Now we get to another chapter you've heard parents wonder about. How did this kid get like this? Enjoy the information.

Chapter Preview: Three ways to parent -- examples of three major styles of dealing with difficult situations.

I.   Socialization
      A.   How socialization is defined _____
            1.   Culture
            2.   Historical context
            3.   Life long process
            4.   Process is reciprocal

a. parent-child interaction
b. child-parent effects
c. third party interaction
5. Studies of family interactions correlational
B. When socialization begins
1. _____
C. The family as a socialization agent
1. Parents the primary socialization agents
a. parents products of own socialization
2. The tasks of parents and children in the socialization process
a. Parents as teachers: see table 12.1
(1) identification
(2) imitation
(3) adoption of roles

II. Socialization and Developmental Change
A. Developmental theories related to child's level of development
1. Sigmund Freud; Psychoanalytic theory
a. Freud's theory attempted to make explanations about behaviors: A grand theory
(1) free association
(2) dream interpretation
(3) slips of tongue
b. three part personality
(1) id represents _____
(2) ego represents _____
(3) superego represents _____
c. Freud's psychosexual stages you do these, include major outcomes and give examples
(1) _____
(2) _____
(3) _____
(4) _____
(5) _____
2. Erik Erikson; Psychosocial Stages
a. As Erikson differs from Freud
(1) _____
(2) _____
(3) _____
b. The Eight stages of Man according to Erikson; Psychosocial stages. Give examples as you do these
(1) _____
(2) _____
(3) _____
(4) _____
(5) _____
(6) _____

(7) _____

(8) _____

C. Scientific appraisal of psychoanalytic theories

1. Critique of Erikson _____

_____

2. Critiques of Erikson and Freud _____

_____

D. Family behavior patterns

1. Continuity -- within change

a. _____

2. Same family, children differ

a. _____

3. Siblings differ in view of relationship of self to other family members

E. Social Regulation

1. Time to regulate autonomous behavior

a. _____

2. Encouraging autonomy

a. _____

3. The how's of teaching self regulation

a. external pressures _____

b. "baby proofing" _____

III. Aspects of Parenting, Diana Baumrind based on Earl Schaefer's earlier work
Interaction of parental permissiveness and the degree of affection form four fields of parenting dimensions

A. Accepting-Permissive _____

1. Loving and accepting

a. democratic _____

b. rules enforced _____

c. children encouraged to develop independently to large degree

_____

d. qualities seen in children _____

2. Permissive _____

a. tolerant _____

b. punishment rare _____

c. parents avoid restrictions and controls _____

d. can be carried to extremes _____

e   qualities seen in children _____

B. Accepting-Demanding _____

1. Warm and affectionate _____

2. High degree of control _____

a. over protectiveness leads to overdependence __

b. qualities seen in children _____

3. Authoritative parents

a. set strict standards of competence and obedience

b. consistent enforcement of standards

c. qualities seen in children

                        (1)   high self esteem, especially in boys
                        (2)   do well in controlled situations
                d.   judicious and fair controls
                        (1)   parents provide scaffolding and are sensitive to children's successes
                                and failures
                e.   especially productive in teen years
                        (1)   social atmosphere unstable at this time
                                (a)   e.g. teens less likely to use drugs than those of accepting-
                                        permissive parents
                                (b)   become more competent, mature and optimistic
                f.   parents not bossy, are committed to the development of child
        C.   Rejecting-Permissive
                1.   Parents model hostility and aggression
                2.   Environment fosters rebellion, anger and disharmony
                        a.   qualities seen in children
        D.   Rejecting-Demanding
                1.   Authoritarian parent
                        a.   strict rules, unquestioned obedience
                        b.   physical punishment commonly used
                2.   qualities seen in children
                        a.   rejecting, demanding, sullen
                        b.   friendships marked by _____
                        c.   have trouble expressing hostility and tend to turn it inward
                                (1)   self punishment
                                (2)   high suicide rates
        E.   Limitations of studies of outcomes of parenting modes
                1.   Limited to studies of middle class families in industrialized Western cultures
                        a.   cultural effects _____
                        b.   _____
IV.   Disciplinary Practices
        A.   Power Assertion -- punishment, removal of privileges, threat
                1.   Hostility aspect -- potentially abusive
                2.   Used more for boys than girls
        B.   Love Withdrawal -- parent physically withdraws, expresses lack of love
                1.   High degree of compliance _____
                2.   Harmful effects _____
        C.   Induction -- reasoning for rule or punishment, appeals to child's pride and desire to be
                grown up
                1.   Comprehension of own behavior and of perspective of others
                2.   Long term compliance _____
V.   Recommendations for Parenting
        A.   _____
        B.   _____
        C.   _____
        D.   _____
VI.   The Shifting Sands of Parenthood

A.   Many changes in values and social traditions make predictions difficult
        1.   _____
        2.   _____

VII.   Working Mothers -- The statistics tell the story
    A.   Changes in Labor force _____
        1.   statistics _____
    B.   Decisions to work: Why enter the work force _____
    C.   More single mothers _____
    D.   Mothers' feelings about employment
        1.   Education effects _____
        2.   effectiveness as parent _____
        3.   feelings about purpose of working _____
        4.   Influence of father's feelings _____
    E.   How maternal employment effects children National Longitudinal Survey of Youth
        1.   Negative effects _____
                a.   _____
                b.   _____
        2.   Positive effects _____
                a.   value of encouraging child's self-sufficiency
                      (1)   _____
                      (2)   _____
                b.   sex differences in children's reaction
                      (1)   _____
                      (2)   _____

At Issue: You'll want to do this one. This information will give you a good basis for discussions. Perhaps you can interview children who have been adopted and are willing to talk about their experience.

VII.   Divorce and One Parent Families:
    A.   Stats _____
        1.   _____
        2   _____
    B.   Remarriage _____
        1.   _____
        2.   _____
    C.   Child's reactions to divorce -- E. Mavis Hetherington
        1.   _____
        2.   _____
        3.   _____
        4.   _____
    D.   Stresses _____
        1.   Short term effects
                a.   _____
                b.   _____
                c.   _____
                    more as you find them
        2.   Long term effects: Judith Wallerstein
                a.   sex differences _____

   b. sibling effects _____

   c. _____

   d. _____

 E. Single Parents

  1. Social isolation _____

   a. Need for services because of less income etc.

   b. Need for emotional as well as financial support

    _____

Application: Parents Under Stress

 A. The Danger of Child Abuse: You'll want to do much more on this.

  1. Definitions of Child Abuse and Child Neglect

  2. Prevalence of child abuse

  3. Psychological maltreatment

  4. Parents who abuse their children

  5. How children are affected psychologically

  6. Intervention, prevention and treatment

NAMES TO REMEMBER

Sigmund Freud

Erik Erikson

Albert Bandura

Earl Schaefer

Diana Baumrind

E. Mavis Hetherington

National Longitudinal Survey on Youth

Virginia Longitudinal Study

U.S. Advisory Board on Child Abuse and Neglect

TERMS AND CONCEPTS

socialization

socializing agent

identification

imitation

adoption of roles

personality

psychosexual development

psychoanalytic theory

id

ego

superego

pleasure principle

reality principle

oral stage

anal stage

phallic stage

latency stage

genital stage

positive fixation

negative fixation

anal retentive
psychosocial stages
terms of psychosocial conflict
basic trust vs. mistrust
autonomy vs. shame or doubt
initiative vs. guilt
industry vs. inferiority
identity vs. role confusion
intimacy vs. isolation
generativity vs. stagnation
ego integrity vs. despair
family continuity
social regulation
"baby proofing"

permissive-demanding parenting
accepting-rejecting parenting
authoritative parents
authoritarian parents
power assertion
love withdrawal
induction
child abuse
child neglect
psychological maltreatment
sexual abuse
crisis nurseries
Parents Anonymous

■ ■ ■ ■

GUIDED REVIEW

1.   _____ can be defined as the interaction of the child and the culture which fosters the child's development of appropriate _____, _____, and _____.

2.   It is easy to say that socialization begins at _____ and is a _____ process.

3.   Rather than being passive receivers of socialization by parents and the culture, the child actively _____ in the process.

4.   Other important aspects of a child's socialization besides the family are _____, _____, and _____.

5.   Researchers study families and their social systems by using _____ and _____ studies. They concentrate mainly on describing the roles of _____, _____, and _____ in the socialization process.

6.   The table describing the tasks of parents and child in the socialization process shows the job of the parent to be mainly that of _____.

7.   According to learning theorists, children learn from their parents through such processes as _____, _____, _____, and _____.

8.   Where Bandura would say children "imitate" their parents, Freud would call this _____, and anthropologists would refer to the process as _____ of _____.

9. Until fairly recently, the accent in studies of social development has been on _____ theory. An exception to this statement is the work of _____ _____, whose psychoanalytic view and outline of _____ _____ addressed the level of the child's development in relationship to his behavior.

10. According to Sigmund Freud, the personality develops as the child passes through _____ _____, the first three of which focus on the child's body, specifically the _____ _____.

11. Contrasted to the oral stage where Freud says the child's pleasure is found in the activities of the _____, the _____ stage marks the time when the child enjoys new-found control of the _____.

12. The _____ _____ occurs when the child finds greatest pleasure in discovery of the genitals. This is the stage when the child must _____ _____ the same sexed parent.

13. In spite of all the criticisms of Freud, psychology credits him with _____ _____ research into _____.

14. As a student of Freud, Erik Erikson argued for a _____ approach, placing greater emphasis on _____ and _____ influences beyond that of _____.

15. Major differences between Erikson's and Freud's theories include that Erikson's covers the entire _____ and that Erikson believes that setbacks can be _____ at a later time.

16. As the child grows older, family behavior patterns appear to be _____. However, there will most likely be changes in the way these patterns are _____.

17. Children as young as _____ years old will, after pressure from others, show efforts toward _____-_____ of autonomous behaviors, based on their understanding of what behaviors are allowed.

18. Parenting styles are described, by Diana Baumrind, in terms of _____ major dimensions. One shows the degree of permissiveness, called _____-_____, and the other indicates the degree of affection, called the _____-_____ dimension.

19. Of the four fields created by the dimensions, we see a democratic environment in the _____-_____ field; although rules are reinforced, children are encouraged to explore and develop _____.

20. Children raised by overly permissive parents tend to be _____, and have poor _____-_____, whereas children of authoritative parents are more _____, _____, and _____.

21. Of the three disciplinary styles discussed in the text, _____ appeals to the child's desire to understand the reasoning behind discipline and of how their behavior _____ _____.

22. The helpful guidelines in the text for successful parenting, include
     1:
     2:

23. The latest figures show that nearly 1/2 of the working mothers are _____ and have a child under _____ year(s) old, and that _____ of working mothers hold _____ _____ jobs.

24. The National Longitudinal Survey on Youth shows that maternal employment during the infant's first year is _____, however, after the first year data show _____ _____ _____.

25. Birnham's study indicates there is a higher self esteem in professionally employed mothers than among equally educated full time mothers unless their _____ offer _____ _____ and share _____ _____.

26. In terms of gender differences in children's reactions to their mother's employment, daughters both _____ their mothers and see them as _____ _____, whereas, sons appear to _____ the situation.

27. A 1985 census shows the number of single parent families has increased by _____% since 1970. In 1990, _____ of all children under 18 will spend time in a single parent home. Further, of all the _____ who remarry, 50% will divorce for a second time.

28. Joint custody offers both parents the opportunity to share in the responsibilities for raising the children. Additionally, fathers not separated from their children under this arrangement may take a more _____ role, both _____ and _____.

29. Children can respond to divorce with several reactions. Some factors involved include: (name several)
     1. _____
     2. _____
     3. _____

30. Of the many stresses suffered by children associated with the divorce of their parents, name as many as you can.
     1. _____
     2. _____
     3. _____

31. Generally, immediately following divorce, _____ have more difficulty coping than

_____, perhaps because they lose their favored parent, and that the custodial mother becomes more _____ and tend to view them more _____.

32.   The level of _____ has been found to have a profound effect following a divorce.

33.   Wallerstein found that 10 years after their parent's divorce, girls had difficulties with (name two)
      1._____
      2._____

34.   Although child neglect and child abuse are sometimes hard to define, child neglect is thought of less as violent behavior against children and more as _____ to provide adequate _____, shelter, safety, and _____ _____.

35.   The psychological effects of child abuse are various and often include: (name at least two)
      1. _____
      2. _____

36.   Studies indicate the need for community support for single parents such as _____, _____, and _____ _____ services.

■ ■ ■ ■

PRACTICE TEST 1

1.   When an infant is treated by others in a way to transmit cultural values, attitudes, and skills, _____ has begun.
      a.   discipline
      b.   socialization
      c.   morality
      d.   learning

2.   As parents are themselves the products of socialization, their major role is one of
      a.   moral leaders
      b.   disciplinarians
      c.   teachers
      d.   peace keepers

3.   Sigmund Freud believed that children learn through watching and imitating their parents. Freud called this process
      a.   imitation
      b.   adoption of roles
      c.   mirroring
      d.   identification

4.   An early attempt to understand the effect of the child's own personality development on the socialization process was suggested by Sigmund Freud. This came to be known as
        a.   psychosocial development
        b.   psychosexual development
        c.   learning theory
        d.   socialization development

5.   Freud proposed that the child's development into a psychologically healthy adult depended on
        a.   movement through the five psychosexual stages during childhood
        b.   identification with the same sexed parent
        c.   avoiding fixation during the psychosexual stages
        d.   all of the above

6.   A more modern psychoanalyst, Erik Erikson, differed from Freud, by placing importance on
        a.   family, friends, society and the culture
        b.   the entire life span
        c.   the ability to overcome set-backs which may have occurred at any stage
        d.   all of the above

7.   Erikson proposed that the healthy development of people came about as a result of ultimately
        a.   resolving the socially opposing conflicts which faced them at each stage throughout life
        b.   overcoming psychosexual fixations at each stage
        c.   learning to adapt one's roles to the environment
        d.   accepting the discipline of parents under any circumstance

8.   As a general rule, family behavior patterns of interaction show continuity over time. However, what does change is
        a.   the personalities of the family members
        b.   the way the patterns are expressed
        c.   the rules of behavior
        d.   all of the above

9.   Socialization patterns within the family which may explain the differences between siblings include
        a.   different treatment of each child, including favoritism
        b.   sibling effects on one another
        c.   each child's physiological predisposition
        d.   all of the above

10.   Diana Baumrind describes two major dimensions of parenting. The dimension which shows the degree of permissiveness is
        a.   the permissive-demanding dimension
        b.   the accepting-rejecting dimension
        c.   the permissive-authoritarian dimension
        d.   the democratic-independent dimension

11.   Children raised by authoritarian parents tend to be
       a.   independent, friendly, and have a high sense of self-worth
       b.   dependent, polite, and obedient
       c.   withdrawn, quarreling, and self punishing
       d.   rebellious, disobedient, and delinquent

12.   Studies of disciplinary practices illustrated in the Chapter Preview indicate that parents who use induction
       a.   obtain long-term compliance rather than simply stopping some immediate behavior
       b.   will create anxiety over fear of abandonment
       c.   may cause even more problems than physical punishment and still not obtain compliance
       d.   are probably harming their children in the long run

13.   The circumstances under which children would be adversely affected by their mother's working can be generally summed up in the following way:
       a.   the mother enjoys her job and cares more for the money than her parenting tasks
       b.   the mother's encouragement of her children's independence has a reverse effect
       c.   the mother feels guilty about abandoning her children, does not wish to work, and her husband objects to her job
       d.   the mother is too tired after work to spend time with her children.

14.   Children's reactions to divorce include
       a.   anger, fear, shock
       b.   guilt, withdrawal, depression
       c.   a drawing closer of brothers and sisters
       d.   all of the above

15.   Typical effects of child abuse in children are seen in the way
       a.   abused children respond to stress in age-mates with emotional outbursts of anger and/or fear
       b.   abused children see themselves as bad and deserving abuse
       c.   they may become sensitized to anger and more noncompliant to parental requests
       d.   any and all of the above

■ ■ ■ ■

PRACTICE TEST 2

1.   Socialization is a lifelong process in which
       a.   parents are the only socializing agents
       b.   the child is completely passive
       c.   the child and his society have a reciprocal relationship
       d.   the child is socialized only in the formative years

2.   During the second year of life, according to John Flavell, children add a significant cognitive
      dimension to their behavior; that of
      a.   the display of affection
      b.   self-regulation of their behavior
      c.   the ability of total compliance
      d.   identification with the parents

3.   Freud believed the phallic stage presented the opportunity for the child to develop into a healthy
      adult by accomplishing
      a.   satisfaction of sucking and chewing needs
      b.   learning to control elimination or retention by controlling anal muscles
      c.   identification with the same sex parent, thereby developing heterosexuality
      d.   identification with the opposite sexed parent, thereby developing heterosexuality

4.   Erik Erikson's third stage differed from Freud's phallic stage by addressing
      a.   the child's need to learn to trust the environment
      b.   the child's need to develop independence and be self-sufficient to avoid self doubt
      c.   the child's need to feel competent, especially when competing with peers
      d.   the child's need to initiate actions on his own with success and acceptance without being
            made to feel guilty

5.   Erikson might say that the most likely stage to be of interest to parents is their own
      a.   identity vs role confusion
      b.   industry vs inferiority
      c.   generativity vs stagnation
      d.   ego integrity vs despair

6.   Children raised in the rejecting-permissive field environment tend to be
      a.   independent, friendly, and have a high sense of self worth
      b.   dependent, polite, and obedient
      c.   shy, quarrelsome, and self punishing
      d.   rebellious, disobedient, and delinquent

7.   Children raised by authoritative parents tend to be
      a.   independent, friendly, and have a high sense of self worth
      b.   dependent, polite, and obedient
      c.   shy, quarrelsome, and self punishing
      d.   rebellious, disobedient, and delinquent

8.   However useful the data used by Baumrind to develop her two dimensional parenting paradigm,
      we should also consider
      a.   the culture of the child(ren)
      b.   that the data is based on middle-class Western society
      c.   the temperament of the parents and children
      d.   all of the above, and others as well

9. The most helpful guidelines for parenting your author suggests are
    a.   try not to be excessively controlling and encourage children to develop self-confidence
    b.   try not to be extremely permissive; reinforce responsible behavior to encourage self control
    c.   try to maintain a warm loving climate where rules are firm and fair
    d.   all of the above

10. Interestingly, both the majority of mothers who work outside of the home, and those who stay at home
    a.   agree that all mothers should stay at home with their children
    b.   believe it is less socially acceptable for a mother to stay at home
    c.   disagree with the proposal that all mothers should stay home
    d.   disagree with the proposal that all mothers should work outside of the home

11. Even though working mothers spend about _____ less a day with their children, an eight year study has shown that young children are _____ affected by their mother's absence.
    a.   2 hours, not adversely
    b.   2 hours, adversely
    c.   4 hours, adversely
    d.   1 hour, not adversely

12. Single parent homes have increased _____ % over 1970, in spite of the ___% remarriage rate.
    a.   400, 75-80
    b.   250, 50
    c.   200, 35
    d.   300, 90

13. Boys may have a more stressful reaction to divorce than girls because
    a.   they are separated from their fathers
    b.   custodial mothers expect to have difficulty with their sons without fathers control
    c.   custodial mothers tend to view their sons more negatively than daughters after divorce
    d.   all of the above

14. An advantage to joint custody arrangements compared to sole custody is that
    a.   both parents will not argue about important decisions about the children
    b.   separated fathers tend to maintain a higher degree of contact with their children
    c.   children lose the influence of the non-custodial parent
    d.   children don't play one parent against another, nor become caught up in their parents' revenge games

15. The most productive treatment for abusive parents is
    a.   Parents Anonymous or other parent support groups
    b.   crisis nurseries or temporary foster care
    c.   both a and b
    d.   jailing the abusive parent

Bonus: It might be an interesting project to interview several children whose parents have divorced and remarried. Many researchers find the upheaval and transition suffered at the time of these life changes is more traumatic for the children than the kind of custodial arrangements made. You may want to look at some of the statements made by children to compare to the studies you have read in this chapter. Consult with your teacher before you submit these children to a questionnaire or interview, however, as well as their parents, for their permission. Ethical considerations are very important.

ANSWER SECTION

<u>*Guided Review*</u>

1. socialization, skills, attitudes, behavior
2. birth; lifelong
3. reciprocates or participates
4. peers, schools, culture
5. surveys, correlational, parents, children, others
6. teacher
7. associations, rewards, punishments, modeling
8. identification, adoption, roles
9. learning, Sigmund Freud, psychosexual development
10. psychosexual stages, erogenous zones
11. mouth, anal, anus
12. phallic stage, identify with
13. stimulating further, behavior
14. psychosocial, social, cultural, parents
15. lifespan, overcome
16. stable, expressed
17. 2, self-regulation
18. two, permissive-demanding, accepting-rejecting
19. accepting-permissive, independently
20. immature, self-control; competent, mature, optimistic
21. induction, affects others
22.   1.   avoid being excessive demanding or permissive
     2.   maintain a warm, loving home where rules are enforced fairly
23. married, 1 year, 71%, full time
24. detrimental, no adverse effects
25. husbands, intellectual stimulation, caretaking activities
26. admire, role models, resent
27. 400, 1/2, 75-80%
28. active, financially, emotionally
29. anger, fear, guilt, withdrawal, depression
30. disruption of schedules, lessening of parent and adult contact, reduction of the level of household income, moving away from familiar friends and schools
31. boys, girls, strict, negatively
32. income
33.   1.   many were afraid to make a commitment and feared betrayal by men;
     2.   their sexual relationships were of shorter duration than average
34. failure, food, health care
35.   1.   the child comes to see himself as "bad" and deserving of the abuse;
     2.   the child becomes more sensitized to adult anger and becomes disturbed and noncompliant when faced with distress
36. medical, social, day care

<u>*Practice Test 1*</u>

1.	*b*
2.	*c*
3.	*d*
4.	*b*
5.	*d*
6.	*d*
7.	*a*
8.	*b*

9.	*d*
10.	*a*
11.	*c*
12.	*a*
13.	*c*
14.	*d*
15.	*d*

<u>*Practice Test 2*</u>

1.	*c*
2.	*b*
3.	*c*
4.	*d*
5.	*c*
6.	*d*
7.	*a*
8.	*d*

9.	*d*
10.	*b*
11.	*a*
12.	*a*
13.	*d*
14.	*b*
15.	*c*

CHAPTER THIRTEEN

THE DEVELOPMENT OF SEXUALITY AND SEX ROLES

■ ■ ■ ■   ◀
◀
LEARNING OBJECTIVES   ◀

This chapter may hold some surprises for you and your study group. That's what makes these issues fun to learn about and discuss. Share what you learn about sexuality and sex roles, and what effects they have on our current attitudes. I guarantee some interesting interchanges. You will want to know about the studies you find in this chapter, so the following are the key points you should know:

1. You should be clear on the differences between primary and secondary sex characteristics and approximately when they occur.
2. Know where the hormones are produced. You'll want to understand the effects of hormones on both the physical development of sex characteristics and their effects on behavior.
3. Be familiar with the studies of how estrogens and androgens affect the behavior of lower animals, especially aggressive behaviors and sexual activity.
4. You'll need to know about the effects of hormone imbalances on the prenatal development of both boys and girls. For example you can tell your friends about CAH and the resulting disorders.
5. Report the study of the genetic disorder discovered in Santo Domingo. The implications of brain programming by hormones in utero are fascinating. It's of special interest to see the support of the families and community for the children involved.
6. A question will come up in your discussions about hormonal influences on aggressive behaviors. We know the influence is there in animals but how will you explain that in humans the differences in adult males and females is more notable than the difference between boys and girls?
7. Are there differences in various skills in men and women? If so, why? Are there brain differences, or does the culture have an influence? Or is it both?
8. Sexual behaviors and orientation may be shaped by environmental forces. Or are they? Recent studies show brain differences near the hypothalamus. If homosexuality or bisexuality is biological, when, who, how? We have much to learn.
9. What about sex roles? How did you learn about what a girl is expected do and what a boy is expected to do?

10. From the time we make a differentiation between blue and pink booties, we begin to shape sex role behavior. How do mothers and fathers treat their children differently according to sex? In what way do fathers have a vital role in shaping sex role behavior?

11. Understand the major theories of how children come to understand their sex roles and gender identity. Be able to differentiate among these clearly.

12. Review the phallic stage of Sigmund Freud to understand the psychoanalytic view. Be able to talk about the present state of this theory's validity.

13. Albert Bandura's social learning theory is a good contrast to psychoanalytic theory. Tell your friends about the environmental effects reported in this one.

14. The third major view, cognitive theory, requires that the child realizes his or her sex and then behaves accordingly. Know the ages at which children will choose sex-appropriate toys; know which sex they are; and when they possess gender constancy. Explain how my oldest daughter could have said, "Now I am a girl, but when I grow up I want to be a very tall man!" (She had become frustrated about reaching the cookie jar as easily as her older brother. P.S. She grew to be 5'9" and could reach anything!)

15. What do you think about Sandra Bem's theory which combines social learning with cognitive views? You'll need to understand the gender schema concept to explain it to someone.

16. Be ready to respond to the issues discussed in the chapter's Application section. Do we need strong gender role differentiation for the sake of self concept, or would that be limiting the development of our view of our own gender identity?

17. Be sure to review the "terms and names" section for tests!

■ ■ ■ ■

CHAPTER OUTLINE

More and more for you to do, again! This time pay special attention to the vocabulary, the ages of children involved in the studies, the theories, and both biological and cultural implications. Egad! Another great grade on a test!

Chapter Preview: Do you want to play "House" or "Army". Children between 7 and 11 years are aware of sex differences and stereotypical sex-role play.

I. Boys and Girls, Men and Women -- The Role of Biology
    A. Primary and Secondary sexual Characteristics
        1. Primary sexual characteristics.
            a. male _____
            b. female _____
        2. Secondary sexual characteristics
            a. male _____
                (1) time of appearance _____
                (2) reproduction capability lasts _____
            b. female _____
                (1) time of appearance _____
                (2) reproduction capability ends _____

B.   Sex Hormones and Chromosomes
     1.   Hormones, sex glands and adrenal cortex of kidneys
          a.   secretion of hormones into blood stream directed by pituitary, which is controlled by brain
          b.   ratio of both estrogens and androgens determines sexual characteristics
          c.   female: ovaries and adrenal cortex of kidney
              (1)   estrogens _____
              (2)   genetic XX _____
          d.   male: testes and adrenal cortex of kidneys
              (1)   androgens _____
              (2)   genetic XY; testosterone necessary, directs undifferentiated gonad to become male
          e.   Frank Lillie study of freemartins
          f.   CAH: congenital adrenal hyperplasia; adult behavior not affected
          g.   Correlational studies of boys whose mothers were given estrogens
     2.   Is it the hormones that play the biggest part in human behavior or is it learning and culture?
C.   Aggression: Hormones or Culture?
     1.   Research _____
     2.   _____
     3.   _____

At Issue: Do males and females have different "natural" skills or traits? Sex differences in variation in ability: You do this one. Here's a start.

I.   Historical debates
II.   Specific skills
    A.   Spatial Abilities _____

          _____
          _____
          _____

    B.   Mathematical Abilities
III.   Sexual Orientation
      Studies of heterosexual, homosexual and bisexual orientation

      _____
      _____
      _____
      _____

This is rather a large batch of research to cover quickly, but it's a peek at what's happening. At least we can appreciate the complexity of research into these two major categories.

IV.   The Role Of Culture: Environment models what is natural behavior for male and female children
    A.   Acquiring sex roles
        1.   Early influences on sex or gender role typing
           a.   as early as birth
           b.   fathers and mothers treat infants differently
               (1)   mothers _____
              (2)   fathers _____

        (3)   other adults _____

B.   Sex Role acquisition:
     1.   Psychoanalytic approach: Sigmund Freud
        a.   approach viewed as scientifically limited and subjective
     2.   Social learning theory: Albert Bandura
        a.   reinforcement and punishment
        b.   modeling, observational learning, etc.
        c.   other variables
     3.   Cognitive view: Lawrence Kohlberg
        a.   realization of sex guides child to behave accordingly

C.   The Development of Gender Understanding
     1.   although child may recognize own sex, does not understand gender constancy
        a.   a small child elects to play with non-stereotypical toy, but will choose a gender "appropriate" toy for another child
     2.   Gender Constancy
        a.   most by age 7
     3.   child engages in stereotypical behavior before cognition
        a.   e.g. parent reinforces assertive behavior in sons

D.   Toy selection
     1.   Social Learning view
     2.   Cognitivist view

E.   Gender Schema Theory: Cognitive-social learning: Sandra Bem
     1.   _____
     2.   _____
     3.   _____

        SEE TABLE 13.1 for summary of the viewpoints

Applications: Overcoming Stereotypes. Do this one thoughtfully. Do we teach stereotypical behavior and expectations in our children? What do you think? Oh. Should we?

■ ■ ■ ■

NAMES TO REMEMBER

Laura Cummings	Julian Stanley
Cholos	Norman Geschwind
Victoria Burbank	Lee Ellis
Camilla Benbow	M. Ashley Ames
Arnold Berthold	Simon LeVay
Frank Lillie	Sigmund Freud
Julienne Imperato-McGinley	Albert Bandura
Santo Domingo boys	Lawrence Kohlberg
Eleanor Maccoby	Jean Piaget
Carol Jacklin	Sandra Bem
Richard Green	

■ ■ ■ ■

TERMS AND CONCEPTS

primary sexual characteristics
secondary sex characteristics
gonads
ovaries
uterus
vagina
clitoris
testes
scrotum
penis
puberty
ejaculation
menarche
menopause
hormones
estrogens
androgens
testosterone
pituitary
XX chromosomes

XY chromosomes
freemartins
congenital adrenal hyperplasia
CAH
cortisone
castration
sex-related variation in abilities
hypothalamus
anatomical brain differences
cultural forces
sex typing
sex roles
sex role identification
sex typed toys
gender understanding
psychoanalytic theory
social learning theory
cognitive theory
gender constancy
gender-schema theory

■ ■ ■ ■

GUIDED REVIEW

1. _____ sexual characteristics evident at birth include the _____, _____, and _____ in the male, and the _____, _____, and _____ in the female.

2. _____ sexual characteristics emerging at puberty include _____ voices, facial and pubic _____, in males, and _____ hips, developing _____, and _____ hair in females.

3. Puberty begins at the time the male is capable of _____, as he is able to _____ _____. A healthy male retains this ability for _____ _____.

4. The beginning of menstruation, called _____, signals the girl's ability to reproduce, an ability which lasts until _____. Girls' capability appears _____ than boys.

5.   Sex _____ are produced on the sex glands and on the adrenal cortex of the
     _____. Although both sexes produce all hormones, the level of _____ will
     be higher in males and _____ will be higher in females.

6.   Genetically, a female's 23rd chromosomes will contain the _____ pair, while the male's
     will show the _____ pair.

7.   A developing embryo will be a _____ unless the Y chromosome is present to signal
     production of more of the androgen _____, which directs the development of the
     _____ _____.

8.   Girls subjected to abnormal amounts of _____ before birth may show a disorder called
     congenital adrenal hyperplasia, or _____. Studies have shown that these girls usually
     grow into adulthood with a _____ orientation.

9.   The Julienne Imperato-McGinley study of boys whose genetic disorders resulted in
     _____ _____ genitals at birth, found these children had been socialized as
     _____. During puberty, when further hormonal secretions formed _____
     genitals, they has no problems adopting the male role because their _____ had already
     been masculinized in _____.

10. Studies of boys whose mothers received large doses of _____ are _____
     and not yet _____.

11. Further evidence in other experiments suggests that the _____ has a large influence on
     the development of _____ _____ behavior.

12. Studies of hormone caused aggression are _____ because of the difficulty in
     _____ hormone levels in humans. Actually, if there is a predictive value in hormone
     studies in humans, one would have to measure the range of _____ _____
     throughout the day.

13. Castration of human males appears to have _____ effect on their sex drive or
     aggression, most likely because their brains had been _____ _____ before
     birth and therefore activated at puberty.

14. Studies of _____ _____ in skills and traits have most recently concentrated
     on anatomical _____ _____. However, this area of study is still being
     investigated.

15. Sex typing includes the _____, _____, and _____ taught by
     culture as appropriate to one's biological sex.

16. Parents tend to begin to shape _____ _____ in their children
     _____ _____ or even before.

17.   Whereas mothers tend to interact with their infant sons _____, fathers are more likely
       to engage them in _____ _____.

18.   When children played with opposite sex toys, _____ were likely to interfere with their
       _____ s' play.

19.   Parents' approach to socializing children toward sex roles is largely dependent on
       _____ _____ _____ training.

20.   Although _____ are a very important source of _____ _____
       learning, other people and events have strong influences as well.

21.   Three major theories, the _____, _____ _____, and
       _____ theories, explain three perspectives of how children develop their
       understanding of their own sexuality, or _____ _____ identification.

22.   Psychoanalytic theory proposes the child understands and adopts sex role identification by
       identifying with the _____ _____ parent.

23.   A less subjective theory, based on the work of Albert Bandura, shows that children are
       _____ for appropriate sex behaviors, and that children learn through
       _____ parent, peers, media, and society as they _____ sex role behavior.
       This is known as _____ _____ theory.

24.   Lawrence Kohlberg, who developed _____ theory, proposed that children first
       become _____ of their _____, then match their behavior to what they
       perceive society expects.

25.   Children develop gender understanding at about the age of _____ _____ .

26.   About 40% of 3 to 4 year olds can comprehend the anatomical basis of gender distinction, and
       will express this understanding of difference even when their friends wear _____ or
       engage in _____ which could be misleading.

27.   Even though their understanding of the permanence of their sex has not occurred, toddlers of 14
       months most often chose to play with toys designed for _____ _____
       _____.

28.   _____ _____ theory has postulated that parents provide stereotypical toys,
       and also reinforce sex appropriate behavior, such as _____ in boys.

29.   In contradiction to social learning theory, studies have shown that although children knew which
       toys were sex-appropriate, they often _____ choose them for themselves. This finding
       opened the door to the combination of the two approaches, called the
       _____-_____ _____ view.

30.   The combination theory of Sandra Bem, called _____-_____ theory, shows how children reach a point where they integrate, bit by bit, information acquired through social learning into a _____ _____ or _____ in which sex appropriate attitudes and beliefs can develop.

31.   Although one study suggests that gender differences in spatial, verbal and intellectual abilities are less marked than 10 or 20 years ago, researchers now realize that these studies are more _____ than expected and much more will have to be learned.

32.   The roles in the American work force have remained stereotypical with women earning _____ % of what men earn, even in the same occupation.

33.   There is a strong possibility that the toys boys are given reflect technological advances, while girls' toys continue to prepare them for a future in _____ and low _____ jobs.

34.   A disadvantage of limiting men and women to stereotypical "male and female" attitudes and emotions is that while some characteristics of each are valuable to both, many are not productive for _____ _____.

35.   To limit stereotyping and encourage choices for both boys and girls, cultures need to cooperate in structuring a more _____ _____.

■ ■ ■ ■   ◄
                                                                                     ◄
                                                                                     ◄
PRACTICE TEST 1   ◄

1.   In contrast to primary sexual characteristics, secondary sexual characteristics appear at
        a.   birth
        b.   adulthood
        c.   puberty
        d.   infancy

2.   Estrogens and androgens are secreted by both the
        a.   XX and XY chromosomes
        b.   gonads and the adrenal cortex of the kidneys
        c.   testes, ovaries and pituitary
        d.   chromosomes and gonads

3.   The sex of the child is determined by genes on the 23rd pair of chromosomes. If it is a(n) _____, the child will be male.
        a.   XX
        b.   YY
        c.   XY

d.   none of the above

4.   Powerful influences in the adoption of sex roles evident in the cases of the Santo Domingo boys
       and the studies made by Margaret Mead, show that _____ is a very important variable.
       a.   prenatal treatment
       b.   hormone balances
       c.   geographical location
       d.   environmental support

5.   Whether biological influences on gender related behavior are stronger than culture and learning
       is a question which must be answered by
       a.   genetic predisposition
       b.   prenatal influences
       c.   continued research
       d.   environmental influences

6.   Studies in sex related variations in spatial and verbal skills are
       a.   clearly the result of cultural determination
       b.   inconclusive
       c.   clearly the result of physical differences
       d.   clearly the result of prenatal brain programming

7.   The shaping of sex roles may begin
       a.   as early as birth
       b.   as soon as parents treat their boys and girls differently
       c.   as soon as parents describe their boy as strong and husky or their girl as delicate and
               pretty
       d.   all of the above

8.   In the experiment where boys played with toys designed for the opposite sex, _____ were
       more likely to interfere or act disgusted.
       a.   fathers
       b.   mothers
       c.   no difference, both mothers and fathers
       d.   the other children

9.   In explaining how children acquire sexual identity, the theory which says the child must identify
       with the same sexed parent is
       a.   social learning theory
       b.   psychoanalytic theory
       c.   cognitive theory
       d.   gender-schema theory

10.   The _____ theory postulates that recognizing one's own sex as male or female is the first
       prerequisite to sex role identification.
       a.   social learning

b.   psychoanalytic
c.   cognitive
d.   gender-schema

11.   Sandra Bem, who has combined _____ and _____ theories, suggests children's cognitive advances allow an integration of their gender understanding and learned sex role appropriate behaviors. Her theory is called
a.   social learning, cognitive; gender schema theory
b.   social learning, psychoanalytic; gender schema theory
c.   cognitive, psychoanalytic; social cognitive theory
d.   gender-schema, social learning; schema social theory

12.   Before children can acquire gender constancy, they must develop _____ which occurs at about age ____.
a.   gender understanding, 7-10 years
b.   gender understanding, 3-5 years
c.   seriation; 7 years
d.   seriation; 12 years

13.   Researcher into homosexuality has demonstrated the national average for male homosexuality is between _____%, and is apparently _____ based.
a.   4-10%, environmentally
b.   1-4%, psychologically
c.   4-10%, biologically
d.   1-4%, environmentally

14.   That both boys and girls will play more actively with trains and cars and more quietly with dolls and domestic toys, suggests
a.   the choice of toys may determine the child's play behavior more than the child's gender
b.   parents encourage active play in both girls and boys
c.   there are fewer "natural" differences between small boys and girls than we thought
d.   both a and c

■ ■ ■ ■

PRACTiCE TEST 2

1.   Puberty is marked by _____ in males and _____ in females.
a.   the first ejaculation of sperm; menarche
b.   the development of primary sexual characteristics; the production of androgens
c.   the production of estrogens; the production of androgens
d.   the appearance of the sex organs; the appearance of sex organs

2.   Sex hormones which occur in appropriate ratios in males and females are called

a.   estrogens in males; androgens in females
b.   estrogens in females; androgens in males
c.   testosterone in females; androgens in males
d.   XX in females; XY in males

3.   When girls have been exposed to large amounts of androgens before birth, they may be born with partially androgenized genitals. However,
a.   their full complement of female genitals allows completely traditional female behavior
b.   their full complement of male genitalia allows for completely traditional male behavior
c.   their confused genitalia forbid normal sexual behavior for their entire lives
d.   they behave in a more rough and tumble way than traditional girls as children, and, as adults, they act as normal heterosexual women

4.   While girls with CAH are growing toward adulthood, they may be considered
a.   ultra feminine because they are less assertive than their peers
b.   feminine because they are more dependent than boys
c.   Tom boys because they like rough and tumble play
d.   bisexual because they have such a broad spectrum of behaviors

5.   The process by which attitudes, behaviors, and traits appropriate to biological sex are incorporated is called
a.   sex typing
b.   role adoption
c.   cultural reinforcement
d.   sex formation

6.   Fathers tend to play more _____ with their sons, while mothers provide more _____ interactions with their sons than their daughters.
a.   physically; physical
b.   verbally; physical
c.   physically; verbal
d.   none of the above

7.   Fathers treat their boys and girls differently according to their sex. Studies show that _____ also treat boys and girls differently.
a.   teachers
b.   mothers
c.   strangers and peers
d.   all of the above

8.   _____ proposes that children integrate all the different sex-typed behavior they have observed and acquired, then shape their attitudes and sex roles according to what they feel is appropriate for them.
a.   social learning
b.   psychoanalytic
c.   cognitive

(d.)   gender-schema

9.   Kohlberg's cognitive theory of sex constancy does not account for the fact that children of ___
        months know the typical occupations of men and women
        a.   12 months
        b.   18 months
        (c.)   26 months
        d.   36 months

10.   Parents tend to pay more attention to _____ behavior in boys while attending more to
        _____ behavior in girls.
        a.   passive; assertive
        (b.)   assertive; passive
        c.   quiet; noisy
        d.   quiet; active

11.   Differences in assertiveness are not apparent at ___ months. They are, however, reinforced in
        boys by _____ and _____.
        a.   28 months; mothers and peers
        (b.)   14 months; parents and peers
        c.   36 months; fathers and peers
        d.   42 months; fathers and peers

12.   Even though half of American mothers are employed, early play and socialization activities
        a.   may leave them unprepared for the new technological employment opportunities
        b.   may render them as "techno-peasants" according to some feminists
        c.   may prepare them for low paying domestic kinds of jobs
        (d.)   all of the above

13.   When children were placed in an open school setting where sex stereotyping was avoided
        (a.)   the children related in more mixed-sex activities, even when they reached the age of 7
        b.   the children separated into same sex groups and argued frequently with one another
        c.   the children became confused about their own sex roles
        d.   the children brought their own sex stereotypical toys with them from home

14.   To overcome adult sex stereotyping which limits employment and social opportunities, we could
        a.   provide models of both males and females who engage in a wide range of roles and
                behaviors
        b.   structure the environment to encourage more interaction for both boys and girls to share
                ideas and activities
        c.   structure the environment to avoid sex stereotyping which would allow a wide range of
                choices in roles and behaviors
        (d.)   all of the above

ANSWER SECTION

<u>Guided Review</u>

1.   *primary, testes, penis, scrotum, ovaries, vagina, uterus*
2.   *secondary, deepening, hair, widening, breasts, pubic*
3.   *reproduction, ejaculate sperm, his lifetime*
4.   *menarche, menopause, earlier*
5.   *hormones, kidneys; androgens, estrogens*
6.   *XX, XY*
7.   *female, testosterone, male genitals*
8.   *androgens, CAH, heterosexual*
9.   *undeveloped male, girls, male, brains, utero*
10.   *estrogens, correlational, conclusive*
11.   *environment, sex role*
12.   *inconclusive, measuring, hormone fluctuation*
13.   *no, hormone sensitized*
14.   *sex differences, brain differences*
15.   *attitudes, behavior, traits*
16.   *sex or gender roles, at birth*
17.   *verbally, physical activities*
18.   *fathers, son*
19.   *their own cultural*
20.   *parents, sex role*
21.   *psychoanalytic, social learning, cognitive, sex role*
22.   *same sexed*
23.   *reinforced, observing, model, social learning*
24.   *cognitive, aware, gender*
25.   *3 years*
26.   *costumes, activities*
27.   *their own sex*
28.   *social learning, assertiveness*
29.   *didn't, cognitive-social learning*
30.   *gender-schema, cognitive organization, scheme*
31.   *complicated*
32.   *60%*
33.   *domestic, paying*
34.   *either sex*
35.   *open environment*

<u>Practice Test 1</u>

1.	*c*	5.	*c*
2.	*b*	6.	*b*
3.	*c*	7.	*d*
4.	*d*	8.	*a*

9.   *b*
10.   *c*
11.   *a*

<u>Practice Test 2</u>
1.   *a*
2.   *b*
3.   *d*
4.   *c*
5.   *b*
6.   *c*
7.   *d*

12.   *b*
13.   *c*
14.   *d*

8.   *d*
9.   *c*
10.   *b*
11.   *b*
12.   *d*
13.   *a*
14.   *d*

CHAPTER FOURTEEN

PEERS, SCHOOL, AND THE SOCIAL ENVIRONMENT

■■■■

◄
◄
◄

LEARNING OBJECTIVES

This chapter will be fun for you and your friends to talk about. The development of social interactions and play show similarities the world over. In this chapter you'll see the importance of these factors as well as how friends, parents, and school can contribute to the developing child. As television has shrunk the world visually, our concern about our children's viewing habits are addressed as well. Be sure to know the following:

1. Know the definition accepted by researchers for the term peers, and what studies are done to record peer interactions during the first year of life. Watch six month olds as they relate to each other if you can. It's worth the trouble to see how they look each other over and are fascinated by noses, eyes, and mouths! No competition here!

2. See how changes occur between the ages of one and two. Know the stages recorded by some researchers as relationships become more complicated.

3. Be able to explain why children begin to declare their possessions as their own in no uncertain terms. The loud "mine" indicates a change in cognition, rather than the pure selfishness that may be interpreted by onlookers.

4. Know how friendships form and what kinds of friendships children of 3 or 4 years can develop. What behaviors and factors enter into these early relationships?

5. A researcher whose work I read the other day reported play as "the work of childhood." Why do you suppose she said that? Be able to describe the structures of the play of preschoolers.

6. Descriptors of play applied in differing combinations have been suggested in your text. Know these and be able to explain them.

7. Social scientists have their own ideas about play. Explain the exploration-play-application sequence they see as evidence of the function of play in humans and advanced animals.

8. Parten's observation of the kinds of behavior involved in play are fun to observe. Be able to identify them, and know how these behaviors differ according to age.

9. Be able to compare and contrast reality play, fantasy play, and social play. Remember Piaget's concept of object permanence as you do this.

10. Notice how children can play very differently from culture to culture, and how our culture structures play activities.

11. Define friendship. Remember how important your friends were in and out of school? Does what you remember fit with the descriptions of acceptance and peer groups in the text? What kinds of issues are important in acceptance by peers? Rejection? When do children become aware of each other's personality characteristics?

12. The values and rules set by peer groups offer special information and standards for children. Interestingly, each group member develops roles and/or status.

13. Social interactions with brothers and sisters are often as helpful in many ways as peers, especially if they are close to the same age. Is sibling rivalry a given in every family? How can it be reduced?

14. Be able to compare the influence of peers and parents. The parenting style is a strong factor in the power of parental influence.

15. Schools, of course, are a reflection of the culture and pass on values and both positive and negative attitudes to the children. Other adults become important. Remember when you came home with an argument with Mom or Dad based on what your teacher said?

16. The discussion in your text about the differences in schools and how those differences are handled is most important. The influence of well trained and dedicated teachers is essential in every school. Do be aware of the disadvantages of today's lower-economic class children, both in and out of school. Note the differences in academic achievement.

17. A most important issue is the effect of T.V. viewing on family life. Television imparts many influences in advertising, sex and role stereotyping, violence, and even styles of learning which may not transfer well to the school setting. You may be surprised to read of the average time children spend in front of the set, compared to doing other things, like reading (she said, sounding like a teacher!)

18. Perhaps the hardest things to remember about television viewing are the good aspects that can come about through watching well chosen programs. For what it's worth, I join others in recommending parental supervision and that parents watch with their children to help them develop perspective on what they watch. Small children have trouble with what's real and what isn't real on T.V, and older children may be powerfully influenced by the models they see.

■ ■ ■ ■

CHAPTER OUTLINE

You're so good at this now, you really don't need me. But since I love to be needed, and because I'm afraid you won't continue to outline the text, I'll keep on giving you some suggestions. Do leave room for your professor's lecture notes.

Chapter Preview:
The Little Emperors. Studies of only children show that academically and socially they are similar to peers with siblings.

I.   The Development of Peer Relationships: Peers: children of approximately (though not necessarily) the same age who interact at about the same behavioral level.

    A.   The First Year: Early Peer Relationships

        1.   The percentage of infants who have an opportunity to interact with other infants

varies with their families and their culture.

2. Studies of the sequence of the development of peer interaction are also seen in mother-infant interactions showing a developmental trend

3. The Onset of Social Awareness
   a. 3 months _____
   b. 6 months _____
   c. 1 year _____

4. The Effect of Toys
   a. 1 toy for two babies _____
   b. at six months _____

B. The Second year: Emotional and Cognitive Changes
   1. Peer relationship stages
      a. _____
      b. _____
      c. _____
   2. Emotional reactions
      a. second year compared to first _____
         (1) _____
         (2) _____
         (3) _____
   3. Cognitive changes
      a. 20 months compared to 6 months
      b. why the 20 month old would be distressed over loss of a toy
      c. not selfishness but a new awareness of _____
      d. the emergence of personality

C. The Preschool years: between the ages of 2 and 5
   1. Friendships
      a. age 3 or 4 _____
      b. friendship defined _____
      c. age 6 - a more sophisticated understanding
         (1) _____
         (2) _____
      d. time with peers compared to adults
      e. determinants of the formation of friendships
         (1) Gottman,1983. Table 14.1
         (2) Gottman,1983. Table 14.2
   2. Play
      a. play defined: the five descriptors
         (1) intrinsic motivation _____
         (2) positive affect _____
         (3) nonlaterality _____
         (4) means rather than ends _____
         (5) flexibility _____
      b. the why of play - ethologists' point of view
         (1) exploration-play-application
      c. kinds of play (include age relationship in your notes)

(1)   solitary play _____

(2)   onlooker play _____

(3)   parallel play _____

(4)   associative play _____

(5)   cooperative play _____

d.   reality play (include age relationship)

e.   fantasy play

(1)   object permanence necessary _____

(2)   gradual emergence _____

(3)   social fantasy play _____

f.   environmental influences in structuring play

(1)   cultural variations _____

(2)   toy orientation _____

(a)   large-muscle toys _____

(b)   fine-muscle toys _____

(3)   A History of Children's Play: The New Zealand Playground, 1840-1950, Sutton-Smith, 1981.

D.   School Age Children

1.   Peer friendships -- (again, note age relationships)

2.   Peer Acceptance -- Predictions of acceptance

a.   factors _____

b.   effects _____

3.   Peer rejection

a.   factors _____

b.   inappropriate behavior _____

c.   effects _____

4.   Peer neglect

a.   factors _____

b.   effects _____

5.   Prejudice

a.   factors _____

b.   effects _____

6.   Children's preferences

a.   same sex and race _____

b.   physical attractiveness _____

c.   early maturers _____

d.   names _____

7.   Character _____

E.   Siblings

1.   Interactions

2.   Differences

a.   _____

b.   _____

c.   _____

3.   Similarities with peers

4.   Influences on each other

At Issue: Sibling Rivalry: Fact or Fiction   Judy Dunn study

    F.   Peer Groups
         1.   Distinguishing features
             a.   age _____
             b.   conformity _____

    G.   Adult versus Peer Influences
         1.   Importance of peers
         2.   Similarities between peers and families
         3.   Areas of greatest influence
             a.   peers _____
             b.   parents _____
                 (1)   parenting qualities _____
         4.   Parental influences on child's choice of friends
             a.   _____
             b.   _____

II.   The Influence of Schools *(This one's for you)*
    A.   Significant Influences
    B.   "a nation at risk"
    C.   School and Social class Figure 14.3
         1.   Lower socio-economic class students
    D.   Differences in schools
    E.   The successful school
    F.   The teacher
    G.   Parents' influence

III.   The Influence of Television
    A.   What children learn
         1.   Time spent watching T.V.
         2.   Use of T.V.
    B.   Documented influences
         1.   Relationship of time watching and school achievement
         2.   T.V. violence and children's aggression
         3.   Watching and reality comprehension
         4.   Watching and reading comprehension figures
             a.   _____
             b.   _____
         5.   Language usage _____
         6.   The development of imagination
             a.   _____
             b.   _____
         7.   Sex role stereotypes
         8.   Notel, Canada
    C.   Suspected Influences
         1.   Comprehension problems in violence
         2.   Models regarding health and safety
         3.   How viewers can use T.V. wisely
         4.   Anderson study surprises

APPLICATIONS All that Glitters. . . .
    "kidvid" commercials
    Action for Children's Television Organization
    Children under 6 years old fail to understand what appears to be real and what is actually real
    John Flavell's work with 3's and 4's show them to be perfect pawns of advertisers
    What can be done?
    What you can do to prevent the manipulation of your children by T.V. commercials?

■ ■ ■ ■

NAMES TO REMEMBER

Gottman	Sesame Street
Rubin, Fein, and Vandenberg	Notel, Canada
Mildred Parten	Judy Dunn
Brian Sutton-Smith	John Flavell

■ ■ ■ ■

TERMS AND CONCEPTS

peers	cooperative play
object centered stage	reality play
simple interactive stage	fantasy play
complementary interactive stage	social fantasy play
personality	peer groups
friendship	peer acceptance and rejection
play	siblings
exploration-play-application sequence	sibling rivalry
the 5 descriptors of play	successful school
solitary play	school and social class
onlooker play	influence of television
parallel play	appearance vs. reality in television
associative play	

GUiDED REViEW

1.   Children who interact at approximately the same behavioral level, are referred to as
      _____ even they may not be the same age.

2.   Common age-related social behavior may not apply to all infants because his or her
      _____ may not provide opportunities for _____ with _____
      _____.

3.   Infants' social interactions with peers and mothers show a general _____ of
      _____.

4.   The infant at 6 months progresses to real interactions of _____, _____
      toward another infant, and _____ interest in a toy of _____
      _____.

5.   According to some researchers, during the first two years, peer relationships pass through three
      stages. During the first, the _____ _____ stage, infants direct their attention
      mainly to an _____ or _____. During the second, the _____
      _____ stage, 18 month olds respond to each other and prefer _____ play
      rather than _____ play. During the third stage, the _____ _____
      stage, the 2 year old is capable of _____ positive social interaction and
      _____ _____ responses.

6.   A child who showed no unhappiness at 6 months when a peer took a toy away, may show great
      _____ at 20 months. This change occurs because of the child's developing cognitive
      _____ _____.

7.   The developing stability of social behavior seen in the _____ _____
      indicates that the child has achieved self-regulation of behavior and the beginning of the child's
      unique _____.

8.   _____ are defined as "mutual preference for interaction, skill at complementary and
      reciprocal peer play, and shared positive affect". In other words, these early relationships
      demonstrate infants' formation of _____ _____ with each other.

9.   As children grow older, they share knowledge about each other's different _____.
      This allows a closer friendship. By age 7, the average child will have as much social contact with
      _____ as with _____.

10.   Important determinants in the establishment of friendships include peers' ability to
      _____ _____ about themselves, find _____ _____
      activities, and resolve _____. They also share _____ _____

about themselves.

11.   Play, although difficult to define, is described using characteristics which combine in a variety of ways. These descriptors are:

    (1) _____

    (2) _____

    (3) _____

    (4) _____

    (5) _____

12.   Perhaps one reason children play is explained by the ethologists who believe the innate predisposition to play is exemplified by the _____-_____-_____ sequence.

13.   Mildred Parten's 1932 observations of different behaviors in play, indicate that younger children more likely to engage in _____ or _____ play, while older children enjoy _____ and _____ play.

14.   Most recent studies indicate that solitary or parallel play can be an _____ kind of play, often a step toward _____ play.

15.   Once two year olds have achieved _____ _____, fantasy play emerges gradually. A clothes basket may become a space ship to a _____ year old child playing alone, and when he is joined by peers, a game of "good guys in space" may develop, illustrating their growing ability toward _____ _____ play.

16.   Brian Sutton-Smith's epilogue to A History of Child's Play indicates that as children's lives and play have become more _____ for them; the _____ differences have been reduced or eliminated.

17.   Children between the ages of _____ and _____ years form close friendships with _____ sexed and aged peers. However, by grade _____ friends of the _____ _____ may be included.

18.   Peer acceptance or rejection begin with the first meeting where peers with a sense of humor, the ability to _____ in _____, or good _____ _____ will be more often accepted than a child who is initially aggressive.

19.   Initial rejection by peers may also affect the acquisition of _____ _____ so that future acceptance by peers may be less likely.

20.   Although learned prejudice may account for some children's preference for same race friends, research indicates that similar _____ _____ and _____ _____ are more important.

21.   Many factors, such as _____ _____, the child's _____, and

_____ _____ may initiate acceptability. However, continued acceptance appears to be determined by the child's _____.

22. Although most sibling relationships are friendly and playful, they often differ from each other in characteristics because of
     (1) _____
     (2) _____
     (3) _____

23. As members of peer groups grow older, the group structure becomes more _____ and _____; and, when children are uncertain of their position on an issue, they are more likely to _____ to _____ _____.

24. Peer influence is strongest in the following areas:
     (1) _____
     (2) _____
     (3) _____
     (4) _____

25. Other adults and parents strongly influence _____ and _____ choices and _____ _____, especially if they are warm and supportive.

26. By adolescence, the average teen will spend more than _____ as much time with peers as with parents. Attempts by parents to influence peer choices and peer influence may drive the child to a _____ _____ _____.

27. The National Committee on Excellence in Education has declared the United States as a _____ _____ _____. Among others, some supporting statements seen by researchers are
     (1) _____
     (2) _____
     (3) _____
     (4) _____
     (5) _____

28. Although schools pass on many attitudes effecting the child's characteristic approach to education, work and social relationships, broad differences exist among schools independent of the _____ level of the neighborhood.

29. Successful schools share some qualities which set them apart. List as many as you can, before you peek! Your Prof will add a few, I'll bet!

30. Most research into the effectiveness of elementary school teachers indicate that they have two unique responsibilities:
     1. _____
     2. _____

31.   As vital as the teacher's influence is, most research believe that parents are even more important as they serve as a source of _____.

32.   As the text author counts the problems encountered by schools, teachers, and students in lower socio-economic neighborhoods, he points to the need for greater _____ _____ to correct these previously stated problems.

33.   Despite some criticisms of children's programs, such as Sesame Street, children who watch the programs with the _____ _____ of parents or teachers can benefit by learning to discriminate between the good and bad features of the programs. Children especially need help to distinguish _____ from _____-_____.

34.   While television watching may have a positive effect in lower socio-economic areas by _____ _____ levels, the negative aspects include inhibition of _____, the reinforcement of _____ _____ stereotypes, and causing a _____ _____ a of the world.

BONUS: Controlling your own T.V. watching time may be difficult if you are one of the millions "brought up" on T.V. Here's a plan that may help, from one T.V. addict to another.
A.   Take a piece of paper and keep a record (honestly) for one week of every moment of television watching. Keep the list on the set or next to your favorite chair.
B.   As each program ends, rate it with letter grades (A best, F for worst) for the value of information or personal value, and number grades (10 for best, 0 for worst) for entertainment value.
C.   Give the program a star if it was really outstanding, and a lemon if it was a disappointing waste of time.
D.   At the end of the week, plan the next week's viewing according to your ratings. Eliminate all regular programs rating below C or 5 and those with lemons.
E.   Leave the room when these are on and do something else. Study, go for a walk, fix something, call a friend even talk to your family, anything other than be in the room with the tube!
F.   In the second week, watch the programs which received good grades the week before, and rate those in the same way. A-F, 10-0, Stars and Lemons.
G.   Eliminate the programs which received grades lower than C's and 5's again for the next (3rd) week's viewing.
H.   Now you have a manageable time of recreation, without guilt or feeling too deprived, and a feeling of mastery over the television. Try it. You'll love being in control--if you slip, do it again!
I.   Give yourself a star, an A, and a 10, and a reward of your choosing! And save your rating sheet!

■ ■ ■ ■

PRACTICE TEST 1

1.   The best definition of peers considers
       a.   children who are the same age
       b.   children who interact at about the same behavioral level

    c.   children who are brothers and sisters
    d.   children of various ages interacting at various levels of behaviors

2.   Some researchers have observed three stages of interaction during the second year. These are
    a.   the smile and touch stage, the object centered stage, the complementary interactive stage
    b.   the simple interactive stage, the imitation stage, the social play stage
    c.   the emotional stage, the cognitive stage, the complementary stage
    d.   the object centered stage, the simple interactive stage, the complementary interactive stage

3.   Cognitive changes in the second year are evidenced by
    a.   the development of a selfish attitude toward possessions
    b.   the progress in sharing toys with another toddler
    c.   the development of self-awareness and the definition of "my" toys
    d.   both a and c

4.   "Preference for interaction, skill at complementary and reciprocal peer play, and shared positive affect" defines _____.
    a.   complimentary interactive play
    b.   the object-centered stage
    c.   the simple interactive stage
    d.   friendships

5.   By the age of 7, a child will spend _____ time with friends and peers compared to adults.
    a.   twice as much
    b.   about as much
    c.   less
    d.   10 times as much

6.   Some believe play helps children become skilled at manipulating objects, and ethologists argue there is an innate predisposition to engage in play. They call this
    a.   exploration-application-completion
    b.   manipulation-exploration-completion
    c.   exploration-play-application
    d.   exploration-manipulation-play

7.   If your child has pretended she has invented a cure for the common cold and is about to receive the Nobel Prize, she most likely exhibits
    a.   fantasy or social fantasy play
    b.   altruism
    c.   parallel play
    d.   both a and b

8.   As children become older, they rely on peers and friends to
    a.   provide toys and activities which they wouldn't have otherwise
    b.   be models of behaviors and to provide social and moral support
    c.   provide standards of self measurement and ways of providing solitary play

d.   all of the above

9.   Children who are rejected by peers may show
    a.   aggressive and inappropriate behaviors, and even if these are controlled and modified, may still be rejected
    b.   socially acceptable behaviors, but will be rejected later if they display aggressive behaviors
    c.   aggressive and inappropriate behaviors, but will be accepted later if these behaviors are modified and controlled
    d.   behavior inappropriate for their sex

10.   Whereas several aspects of the child are important in initial peer acceptance, the most important attribute in determining continued acceptance appears to be
    a.   sex and race
    b.   sex and physical attractiveness
    c.   the child's character
    e.   social skills and attractiveness

11.   Judy Dunn's study of sibling relationships showed
    a.   mother's behavior on the birth of a new baby is a factor in how the older child responds to the new sibling
    b.   "naughty" behavior on the part of the older sibling was often directed at the mother when she was caring for the new infant
    c.   sibling rivalry is not a natural or necessary aspect of every sibling relationship
    d.   all of the above

12.   Adults, especially parents, have a stronger influence than peers in matters of
    a.   academic choices and political views
    b.   sexual attitudes and behaviors
    c.   challenges to authority
    d.   interpersonal behavior

13.   Schools teach more than the 3 R's. They also teach
    a.   boredom or curiosity
    b.   inappropriate competition or cooperation
    c.   fear or confidence
    d.   all of the above and more

14.   That the National Committee on Excellence in Education sees the United States as a "nation at risk" is supported by research showing
    a.   at least 23 million Americans are functionally illiterate
    b.   80% of high school seniors cannot write a persuasive essay
    c.   67% cannot solve math problems that require more than a few steps
    d.   sadly, all of the above

15.   Children in "Notel", Canada, after two years of T.V. viewing, were seen to have
    a.   poorer reading skills

    b.   an increase in aggressive behaviors

    c.   more stereotyping of sex roles in boys and girls

    d.   all of the above

■ ■ ■ ■

PRACTICE TEST 2

1.   As social behavior becomes more predictable in the second year of life, self regulation and the beginning of _____ emerges.
    a.   the child's unique personality
    b.   the child's unique temperament
    c.   the child's unique cognitive ability
    d.   the child's unique emotional expression

2.   Because it is a complicated concept, play can best be described as having at least some of the following qualities:
    a.   intrinsic motivation, nonlaterality, attachment, absence of conflicts, a good result.
    b.   intrinsic motivation, positive affect, nonlaterality, emphasis on means rather than ends, flexibility
    c.   means/end emphasis, organized toward goal, intrinsically motivated, inflexible
    d.   flexible, educational, fun, follows a pattern

3.   Mildred Parten has defined different kinds of activities in the play situation. She noted that younger children tend to engage more often in
    a.   unoccupied behavior, parallel play
    b.   associated play, cooperative play
    c.   onlooker play, cooperative play
    d.   solitary play, parallel play

4.   The ability to engage in fantasy play depends on
    a.   the development of object permanence
    b.   the development of size and shape constancies
    c.   the development of reality play
    d.   the development of social skills.

5.   Brian Sutton-Smith compared the cultural aspect of play in the 1800's with those in the current century. He noted that
    a.   play was more organized in the 1800's; there is more freedom now
    b.   play is more organized now; there was a lack of structure in the 1800's
    c.   they are completely different in each country he investigated
    d.   there are many more activities for children in this century than in the last

6.   General statements about initial acceptance of a child by her peers include

a.   adherence to current achievement oriented skills

b.   willingness to go along with the group's activities

c.   her possession of social skills and a good sense of humor

d.   having something the peers don't have

7.   Children who are neglected by their peers show

     a.   aggressive and inappropriate behaviors which won't be modified until adulthood

     b.   socially acceptable behaviors at first, but aggressive behaviors if acceptance does not occur later

     c.   shyness until they are accepted

     d.   shyness and loneliness which often continues until adulthood

8.   Peers have stronger influences than parents in matters of personal and group identity, clothes and language fads, and

     a.   career choices

     b.   academic choices

     c.   sexual attitudes and behaviors

     d.   political views

9.   Parental attempts to control peer relationships may cause problems

     a.   since the child may be driven to an even greater peer orientation

     b.   since the child may be deprived of the opportunity to develop adequate social skills and confidence

     c.   both a and b

     d.   since it will cause emotional dependence on parents

10.   Schools termed successful have

     a.   demonstrated superior student achievement in every kind of socio-economic neighborhood

     b.   clearly stated academic goals and a certain degree of structure

     c.   teachers dedicated to instilling positive attitudes as well as high academic standards

     d.   all of the above

11.   Holding a child back to repeat a grade

     a.   will cause the child permanent emotional harm

     b.   will help the child increase self-esteem as he masters previously failed school tasks

     c.   will help the child develop social skills

     d.   all of the above

12.   Teachers can make a lasting impression scholastically as well as in children's attitudes toward learning by

     a.   helping students set their goals

     b.   instilling lasting confidence in the student

     c.   both a and b

     d.   formulating strict rules of behavior determined by the school board

13. Parental influences in educational development are even more important than teachers in that parents
    a.   set and model academic standards for their children
    b.   are a source of encouragement, or discouragement
    c.   enforce or fail to enforce completion of homework and attitudes toward education
    d.   all, of course

14. Heavy viewing of television violence has been clearly associated with
    a.   more reactions against violence by children and adults
    b.   increased aggression in children and adults
    c.   increased aggression in children only
    d.   increased aggression in adults only

15. Regarding television watching, preschoolers especially need parents to
    a.   help them understand what's real and what's pretend
    b.   support appropriate programs by communicating with the networks
    c.   help children understand that "what you see is not always what you get" in advertising
    d.   of course, all of these!

ANSWER SECTION

<u>Guided Review</u>

1.   peers
2.   culture, interaction, other infants
3.   sequence, development
4.   smiling, reaching, harmonious, mutual interest
5.   object-centered, object or toy, simple-interactive, social, solitary, complementary interactive, imitating, appropriate emotional
6.   distress, self awareness
7.   second year, personality
8.   friendships, emotional ties
9.   personalities, peers, adults
10.   exchange information, common ground, conflicts, intimate details
11.   intrinsic motivation, positive affect, nonlaterality, means rather than ends emphasis, and flexibility
12.   exploration-play-application
13.   solitary, onlooker, associative, cooperative
14.   alternate, social
15.   object permanence, three, social fantasy
16.   organized, cultural
17.   7, 9, same, 8, opposite sex
18.   engage, conversation, social skills
19.   social skills
20.   academic levels, social class
21.   physical attractiveness, name, early maturation, character
22.   1. genetic influences; 2. differential treatment by their mothers; 3. that each sibling creates and experiences different family environments
23.   organized, formal, conform, peer influence
24.   1. choice of friends;
      2. challenges to authority;
      3. interpersonal behaviors;
      4. language and clothing fads
25.   academic, political, future aspirations
26.   twice, greater peer orientation
27.   "a nation at risk",
      1.   23 million Americans are functionally illiterate,
      2.   high score test schools have been dropping for the last 26 years
      3.   40% of high school seniors cannot draw inferences from written material,
      4.   80% cannot write a persuasive essay,
      5.   67% cannot solve a math problem that requires more than a few steps
28.   socioeconomic
29.   good dedicated teachers, emphasis on academics, clearly stated goals and requirements, regular homework assigned, and graded, active teaching time with clerical support for teachers, effective evaluations of teachers, proper equipment

30.   1. *to help students set their sights on goals*
        2. *to instill confidence in the student, presently and in the future*
31.   *encouragement or discouragement*
32.   *national attention*
33.   *active participation, real, make-believe*
34.   *raising reading, imagination, sex role, negative view*

Practice Test 1

1.	b		9.	a
2.	d		10.	c
3.	c		11.	d
4.	d		12.	a
5.	b		13.	d
6.	c		14.	d
7.	a		15.	d
8.	b			

Practice Test 2

1.	a		9.	c
2.	b		10.	d
3.	d		11.	b
4.	a		12.	c
5.	b		13.	d
6.	c		14.	b
7.	d		15.	d
8.	c			

CHAPTER FIFTEEN

THE DEVELOPMENT OF MORALITY AND SELF-CONTROL

■ ■ ■ ■

◀
◀
◀

LEARNING OBJECTIVES

How do we know what's right and what's wrong? How do we learn to treat others kindly, or do we know without learning? What does our self concept have to do with self control? Have your friends asked you some of these or similar questions? Now you can answer them with the voice of authority, or at least with some studies to back-up your statements. And if you are raising children, these issues will be of particular interest to you. These are a few of the things you'll need to know:

1. Be able to explain prosocial behavior and contrast it with antisocial behavior. Give examples of prosocial behaviors.
2. Define cooperation and be able to discuss why children move from cooperation to competition so easily. To explain what happens with competition, tell about the experiments of M. C. Madsen. Know what can be done to teach children cooperation.
3. Helping behavior is another prosocial behavior. What two factors are important according to Staub? Relate what happens when emergency intervention is necessary, and the reasons children help or don't help. How might we teach children helping behavior?
4. Be able to differentiate between sympathy and empathy. Know the four developmental stages of empathy as described by Hoffman. Discuss exceptions to Hoffman's theory, too. What are the best ways to teach empathy to younger and older children?
5. What are the problems in studies of the correlation of empathy and the behaviors of children? Why is the child's behavior poorly predicted by the level of his/her empathy?
6. What is meta-emotion and why is the study of it important? Talk about role-taking and the benefit of the child's experience. Explain the way the concept of meta-emotion affects the ability to generate strategies to help others change their emotions.
7. Describe sharing and altruism. Your listeners should know that sharing is not always an altruistic behavior. What kinds of intrinsic motivations are involved in altruism? Who is likely to be altruistic? How can we help children learn to share in an altruistic way?

8.   What is self control? Delaying gratification is something that seems to happen more easily as children get older. How do children manage to resist the temptations of immediate gratifications? Be able to discuss the Mischel and Ebbesen experiment showing the strategies children use to delay, such as negative and positive ideation. How might we help children to learn self-control?

9.   Remember Piaget? You'll see him again in the discussion of moral development. He believed that we must understand the child's scheme and that children progress from one to the other of two moralities, which are extremes on the developmental scale. Talk about his approach and be ready to go on to see how Kohlberg built on Piaget's work to develop his level-stage-approach to moral development. You should be familiar with the three major levels and the two stages within each level. Discover how Kohlberg believes children advance to higher levels. What are the major criticisms of Kohlberg's theory?

10.   Read the Application section carefully. When we learn about aggression we begin to have questions about who, why, and under what circumstances it occurs. How can aggression be reduced in our society?

■ ■ ■ ■   ◀
                                                                                                    ◀
CHAPTER OUTLiNE   ◀

You can see immediately that this is a very "economical" outline. Only major headings are included for you to add information and details. You may want to add additional headings for the sake of clarification and quick study for tests. Now that you have the hang of it, feel free to change this outline to suit yourself. Do remember to fill in definitions of terms as you go.

Chapter Preview: Lead Me Not into Temptation
I.   Prosocial Behavior -- benefits others and society
        A.   Cooperation
                1.   Competition interference
                        a.   boys especially, competition and self esteem
                        b.   M. C. Madsen experiment
                                (1)   _____
                                (2)   urban and rural children _____
                2.   Teaching cooperation to children (Spencer Kagan)
                        a.   "We" and "I" _____
                        b.   modeling _____
                        c.   guidance through the experience _____
                        d.   survival and peace _____
        B.   Helping
                1.   Skills and knowledge
                        a.   Staub's hypothesis
                                (1)   skills, knowledge
                                (2)   empathy
                        b.   teaching children to help
                                (1)   More than imitation, even small child knew goals

                (a)   Seen in children as early as 18 to 30 months

        (2)   willingness

                (a)   grade school children more knowledgeable to help, small children more willing

        (3)   knowledge of how and when to help, older children

                (a)   self awareness necessary

                (b)   knew when they were helping

        (4)   teaching children how to help

                (a)   _____

                (b)   _____

                (c)   _____

  2.   Empathy

      a.   Hoffman's 4 stage hierarchy of development of empathy

        (1)   _____

        (2)   _____

        (3)   _____

        (4)   _____

      b.   difference between Hoffman and Piaget on empathy development look for three or more

        (1)   _____

        (2)   _____

        (3)   _____

        (4)   an exception to Hoffman's theory _____

C.   Empathy and prosocial behavior

  1.   induction

  2.   role-taking behavior

  3.   correlations of empathy with prosocial behaviors

  4.   strategies to develop helping and empathy behaviors

  5.   meta-emotion, definition _____

      a.   Empathy and own experience: How empathy develops

        (1)   understanding what it's like to be in need

        (2)   previous experience affects another's reaction to current situation

        (3)   generate strategies to change emotions

        (4)   induction works best with older children

D.   Sharing and altruism; definitions _____

  1.   Sharing not necessarily altruistic

  2.   Intrinsic motivation:

      a.   internalized self reward

      b.   morality and self concept

      c.   modeling and role playing

      d.   experience

      e.   cultural effects

  3.   Sex bias?

  4.   Biological approach vs. social learning

      a.   _____

      b.   _____

At Issue: Do Preschoolers Show Moral Sensitivity?
> Preschoolers are more morally sensitive than expected.

II.   Self-Control and Delay of Gratification
    A.   Self-control: internalized value and reward systems
        1.   Walter Mischel
            a.   10 year follow up studies
            b.   correlation between this ability and high academic scores as well as tolerance for frustration
        2.   examine own behavior - good kid/dumb kid
        3.   find delay method -_____
    B.   Teaching self-control - Mischel, Ebbesen
        1.   delaying, distraction strategies
            a.   age related progressions _____
            b.   negative and positive ideations _____
            c.   modeling _____
            d.   reasoning and objective arguments _____

III.   The Development of Moral Thought
    A.   Piaget's age-related cognitive approach
        1.   "fixed-law" and "social-contract" extremes on continuum
            a.   current scheme _____
            b.   process of understanding social contract __
            c.   progress through continuum _____
            d.   support for Piaget _____
    B.   Kohlberg's Moral Stage theory
        1.   Three levels, two stages in each
            a.   preconventional _____
            b.   conventional _____
            c.   postconventional _____
                (1)   changes in stage 6 _____
            d.   exposing child to level or two above own, provides incentive to advance to next level
            e.   Heinz' Dilemma
        2.   Criticisms of Kohlberg
            a.   poor correlation with actual behavior _____
            b.   situational forces often dictates behavior _____
            c.   culturally based _____
            d.   ignores emotions _____
    C.   Women and Morality
        1.   Carol Gilligan
            a.   Kohlberg theory male biased
            b.   men and women care and help from different point of view
    D.   Three requirements of conscience development proposed by Grusec and Goodnow:
        1.   _____
        2.   _____
        3.   _____

Application: Controlling Aggression and Violence

A. The theories of aggression
  1. _____
  2. _____
  3. _____
B. Critiques of theories
  1. cultural aspects _____
  2. _____
  3. _____
C. How can aggression be controlled?
  1. _____
  2. _____
  3. _____
  4. _____
  5. _____
  6. _____
  7. _____

■ ■ ■ ■   ◄
                                                           ◄
                                                           ◄
NAMES TO REMEMBER

M. C. Madsen   Walter Mischel
Azrin and Lindsley   Ebbe Ebbesen
Spencer Kagan   Lawrence Kohlberg
Ervin Staub   Carol Gilligan
Martin Hoffman   J. E. Grusec
Jean Piaget   J. J. Goodnow

■ ■ ■ ■   ◄
                                                           ◄
                                                           ◄
TERMS AND CONCEPTS

prosocial behavior   person permanence
antisocial behavior   role taking
cooperation   comprehensive empathy
competition   Piaget stages of cognitive development
"we" and "I"   meta-emotion
helping   sharing
empathy   altruism
Hoffman's stages of empathy development   self-control
distress reaction   delay of gratification

negative ideation   Preconventional level
positive ideation   Conventional level
moral thought, morality   Postconventional level
Piaget's theory of moral development   Heinz' dilemma
"fixed law" morality   "The Prisoner's Dilemma"
"social-contract" morality   aggression
Kohlberg's stages of moral development

■ ■ ■ ■

GUIDED REVIEW

1.   Prosocial behavior, the opposite of antisocial behavior, includes _____,
       _____, and _____.

2.   According to Madsen's studies of cooperation vs. competition, cooperation tends to
       _____ with age, while competition _____ with age, even to the extent that
       success is sacrificed for the sake of saving one's _____-_____.

3.   Cross cultural studies of urban and rural children show that urban children are more
       _____ than rural, and that American children are more _____ regardless of
       their sex and background.

4.   Spencer Kagan suggests teaching the concept of "we" rather than "I" to reduce _____
       and encourage _____ in children.

5.   Modeling _____ _____ may be another way of reducing competition,
       although this must be repeated often for the _____ _____.

6.   Another way to teach cooperation, is to guide the child through first-hand experience, which will
       give her knowledge of _____ prosocial behaviors can help others. Through teaching
       cooperation the child develops a greater sense of _____ _____.

7.   _____ behaviors provide needed services or skills to others.

8.   Staub speaks of two factors important in helping. One is to possess _____ and
       _____ to be effective, and the other is to have _____ with the person in
       need.

9.   While older children are more likely to help others because of their _____
       _____, which facilitates their knowledge of when and how to help, younger children
       also often display a _____ to _____.

10. An important aspect in helping behaviors is to know what kinds of
_____ to use and under what _____ another is liable to need help.

11. Furthering Staub's ideas on empathy, Hoffman contrasts his _____ stages of empathy
development with _____ stages of _____ _____.

12. Hoffman qualifies his comparison to Piaget by pointing out that cognitive advances don't create
empathy, they only _____ its expression, and that empathy may occur at
_____ _____.

13. _____ that is, helping the child understand how helping behaviors lessen a friend's
distress, will work best with _____ children capable of
_____-_____.

14. Role-taking ability, which shows the ability to _____, is not always correlated well
with _____ _____.

15. Factors which must be taken into account include children's focus on their own _____
_____ more than the victim's, and the tendency to react more to children who are
perceived to be _____ to _____.

16. Even high role-takers are more likely to help when an _____ is watching. Perhaps the
helper can also take the role of the _____ _____ and realize that the adult
will be _____ with the child's attempts to help.

17. The understanding and knowledge about emotions is referred to as
_____-_____.

18. Studies of meta-emotion recognize three major factors which lead to this kind of knowledge.
They are:
1._____
2._____
3._____

19. An altruistic act is not motivated by _____ _____, but rather is controlled
by _____ systems of self reward and morality.

20. Altruism is illustrated by the litter experiment with fifth graders who wanted to maintain their
positive _____-_____ of being neat and tidy.

21. One effective way of teaching children to share without receiving external rewards, is
_____ _____. However, _____ and _____ are the
most important factors as children come to appreciate the needs of others and the
_____ of their helping acts.

22. Among the influences on sharing behavior are _____ and the _____ in

which sharing occurs. Other encouragement for children is to ask them to _____ and to think _____ _____.

23.   Rather than being an "unnatural" behavior, altruism may be a _____ easily learned behavior needed for _____

24.   To control one's behaviors through internal value systems rather than through the use of external pressures is called _____-_____. Inherent in this concept is the ability of the child to delay _____ _____.

25.   The children who were the most successful at delaying gratification, invented _____ to help them _____ the _____. The ability to do this followed a developmental, age related _____.

26.   In Piaget's cognitive view of moral thought, _____-_____ morality and _____-_____ morality represent the extremes on the developmental scale through which the child progresses as his _____ changes.

27.   Whereas _____-_____ morality refers to absolute rules which must not be broken, _____-_____ morality refers to agreed upon arrangements which encourage mutual cooperation and mutual gain.

28.   Kohlberg's _____ _____ theory was built on Piaget's work, and addressed the attitudes and beliefs of children which help them distinguish between _____ and _____.

29.   Kohlberg's three levels, the _____, the _____, and the _____, demonstrate the level of cognitive reasoning attained by the individual.

30.   Preschoolers who participated in the Prisoner's Dilemma game tended to consider the feelings of their playmates, and restricted play so the others could _____ _____, too.

31.   These 4 year olds demonstrated that they were operating at Kohlberg's _____ stage, which is known as _____ _____.

32.   Kohlberg's theory has been criticized as being culturally biased in favor of _____ _____ _____ and that it is not valid as a measurement of moral reasoning.

33.   A serious defect in moral development theories is that the data gathered does not correlate well with _____ _____. Is this what parents mean when they say "Do as I say, not as I do!"?

34.   Although anger and aggression, like other emotions, may be easy to learn because of our biological heritage, the behaviors involved depend on our _____ and _____.

35.   Imitating models, knowledge of the _____ of our behavior, and _____ we
         are _____ of effective aggression are all important factors determining aggression.

■ ■ ■ ■   ◀
                                                                                                     ◀
PRACTICE TEST 1   ◀

1.   Prosocial behaviors which benefit others are seen in
         a.   cooperation, helping, and sharing
         b.   competition, delay of gratification, and helping
         c.   sharing, aggression, and helping
         d.   competition, cooperation, and sharing

2.   In his experiment with children and the marble game, M. C. Madsen discovered that
         a.   cooperation declines with age
         b.   competition can become a common response
         c.   both a and b
         d.   competition is always paired with aggression

3.   Kagan's recommendations for teaching cooperation to children include
         a.   creating a "we" rather than "I" atmosphere
         b.   repeated modeling of cooperation will be necessary for younger children
         c.   guiding them through first-hand experiences so they can see the advantages and develop
                 a sense of social responsibility
         d.   all of the above

4.   Staub's and others' work with helping behaviors have led to observations that the following are
         important factor(s) in helping:
         a.   knowing how to help effectively
         b.   having empathy for the person in need
         c.   both a and b
         d.   that younger children are more likely to help than grade school children

5.   When a child can respond appropriately to another's distress because he can imagine himself in
         the other's position, he is in Hoffman's _____ stage.
         a.   first stage, distress reaction
         b.   second stage, person performance
         c.   third stage, role-taking
         d.   fourth stage, comprehensive empathy

6.   Meta-emotion, which is _____, may have a significant effect on the development of
         empathy and helping behaviors.
         a.   the ability to put one's self in the other person's shoes and the ability to change the other's
                 emotions

      b.   one's understanding and knowledge of emotions

      c.   knowledge of emotions and learning to ignore them to complete a task

      d.   to be able to experience what other is going through in their situation

7.   Altruism may be taught to children through

      a.   role playing to give the child experience

      b.   rewarding competitive behaviors

      c.   rewarding cooperative behaviors

      d.   there are no ways of teaching this, you just have to wait until the child is old enough to achieve role-taking understanding

8.   When people of any age can control their own actions despite the external pressures of the immediate situation, they are showing _____ and are relying on internalized value systems.

      a.   role-taking ability

      b.   altruism

      c.   self-control

      d.   morality

9.   Mischel and Ebbesen hypothesized that children were more capable of waiting if they could see their reward; they found

      a.   that they were wrong; the delay strategies children used were the key to delaying gratification.

      b.   that they were correct; seeing the reward helped the children to wait.

      c.   if made no difference; neither seeing the reward or using cognitive strategies helped.

      d.   that using either negative or positive ideation proved equally successful.

10.   Piaget described in his cognitive approach to moral development

      a.   the social processes involved in modeling and induction

      b.   the two principle moralities, fixed law and social contract morally

      c.   the S-R-S approach

      d.   that the person's morality depends on obedience to authority

11.   Lawrence Kohlberg's stage theory is similar in structure to _____ in that _____.

      a.   Hoffman's hierarchy of empathy development; the stages are not quantitatively different

      b.   Piaget's cognitive stages; a child will proceed through the stages and will proceed sequentially, never skipping a stage.

      c.   Hoffman's hierarchy of empathy development; advancement in cognitive development only modifies the expression of empathy rather than creating it.

      d.   Piaget's cognitive stages; there are the same number of stages.

12.   In the Prisoner's Dilemma game four year olds

      a.   were at the expected Preconventional level

      b.   were at the expected Stage 2

      c.   restructured their play allowing others to gain pennies too, which showed more moral sensitivity than would be expected for their age.

    d.   restructured their play allowing others to gain pennies too, which showed less moral sensitivity than would be expected for their age.

13.   Studies of aggression from the ethological point of view argue that aggression is
    a.   a learned response which is reinforced through modeling
    b.   a built in response to specific situations
    c.   an inevitable result of being blocked in an effort to reach a goal
    d.   a result of brain structures and/or different levels of hormones and neurotransmitters

14.   Studies of aggression from the physiological point of view argue that aggression is
    a.   a learned response which is through modeling
    b.   a built in response to specific situations
    c.   an inevitable result of being blocked in an effort to reach a goal
    d.   a result of brain structures and/or different levels of hormones and neurotransmitters

15.   Although our capacity to be emotional is _____, the situation that provokes the emotion depends on _____.
    a.   learned from experience; predetermination
    b.   canalized; innate responses
    c.   innate; learning and experience
    d.   learning and experience: innate predispositions

■ ■ ■ ■

PRACTICE TEST 2

1.   Cooperation, as a prosocial behavior, is seen spontaneously in young children, however in older children _____ is seen to correlate with _____.
    a.   competition; positive self image
    b.   cooperation; positive self image
    c.   competition; negative self image
    d.   cooperation; negative self image

2.   In his cross cultural research, M. C. Madsen found that older children in _____ areas have a more competitive outlook than children in _____ areas.
    a.   rural, urban
    b.   urban, rural
    c.   New Guinea, America
    d.   country, city

3.   Ervin Staub's studies of helping behaviors have suggested that there are two factors involved in helping. One is that the person needs to know how to help; the other is that one must be able
    a.   to sympathize with the person needing help

b.   to have empathy with the person in need
c.   to feel the same need as the other
d.   to allow the other person to help themselves

4.   According to Hoffman, empathy
a.   can be seen in infancy and continues to grow in complexity and expression with time
b.   is not seen until the age of 7
c.   is developed in qualitatively different stages, similar to Piaget's
d.   has been researched for as many years as cognitive theories

5.   Children who have high role-taking ability help other children more often than those who are low in this ability. However,
a.   these measurements of the degree of empathy tend to ignore factors such as focus on one's own distress level, and the likelihood of choosing some one of the same sex and race to help
b.   prosocial behavior does not include empathy
c.   children are more likely to help another if an adult is present and they can take the role of the adult as well
d.   both a and c

6.   Altruism refers to
a.   an act that is motivated by the extrinsic reward that follows
b.   an act that is not motivated by self interest
c.   an act which is illustrated by the solution of dividing the doughnut between two children
d.   sharing

7.   Sharing behaviors may be encouraged in children by
a.   modeling sharing behavior
b.   asking children to share
c.   asking children to think happy thoughts about sharing
d.   all of the above

8.   Walter Mischel's 10 year follow-up study of children who developed strategies to delay gratification even when rewards were visible found that these children
a.   were more intelligent
b.   were more attentive and goal oriented
c.   had, as adolescents, the best academic scores
d.   all of the above

9.   Researchers have found ways to help children learn to delay gratification by
a.   punishing failure to delay
b.   written objective arguments in favor of waiting
c.   showing them strategies to help spend the waiting time
d.   showing them the reward to come

10.   Piaget's theory of moral development is illustrated in his experiment with 5 and 10 year olds in

which
a.   the youngest children responded in terms of the social-contract level because they recognized the intentions of the naughty child
b.   the 10 year olds responded in terms of the social-contract level because they recognized the intentions of the naughty child
c.   both a and b
d.   neither a nor b

11.   Kohlberg's moral dilemma experiment shows a person at the law and order stage is operating in the _____ level, because he believes that _____.
a.   preconventional; the consequence of the decision determines whether its good or bad
b.   postconventional; the end may be good but the end doesn't justify the means
c.   conventional; one must do one's duty to maintain social order
d.   conventional; one should operate within one's conscience in accord with universal principles

12.   Criticisms of Kohlberg's theory have included
a.   it shows cultural and sexual bias
b.   it has poor correlations with actual moral behavior
c.   both a and b
d.   that it does not reflect learning abilities

13.   Studies of aggression from the learning theory point of view, argue that aggression is
a.   a built in response to specifically sensitive situations
b.   a learned response that is reinforced through modeling
c.   an inevitable result of being blocked in an effort to   reach a goal
d.   a result of brain structures and increased levels of hormones and transmitters

14.   The frustration-aggression explanation has been modified to include the fact that frustration can lead to _____, and that those experiencing this can react with _____.
a.   psychological pain and depression; violence and aggression
b.   brain disorders; hallucinations and delusions
c.   schizophrenia; prosocial behaviors
d.   depression; hallucinations

15.   In viewing aggression as a sex-typed behavior, we see that
a.   boys are expected to be more aggressive than girls
b.   the same behavior exhibited by boys and girls is seen to be more aggressive when viewed in girls
c.   learned aggression does not seem to depend on gender but on the child's experience
d.   researchers suggest we should teach both boys and girls how to defuse anger and learn more appropriate behaviors
e.   all of these

ANSWER SECTION

Guided Review
1.   cooperation, helping, sharing
2.   decline, increases, self-esteem
3.   competitive, competitive
4.   competition, cooperation
5.   cooperative behaviors, very young
6.   how, social responsibility
7.   helping
8.   knowledge, skills, empathy
9.   greater knowledge, willingness, help
10.   strategies, circumstances
11.   four, Piaget's, cognitive development
12.   modify, any age
13.   induction, older, role-taking
14.   empathize, prosocial behavior
15.   empathetic distress, similar, themselves
16.   adult, adult observer, pleased
17.   meta-emotion
18.   having experienced the need for empathy in others; understanding that previous experience may affect
      emotions in the present circumstances; the ability to generate strategies to change the present emotions,
      such as comforting a hurt or disappointed child
19.   self interest, internalized
20.   self-image
21.   role playing, age, experience, consequences
22.   modeling, culture, share, happy thoughts
23.   canalized, easily learned, survival
24.   self-control, immediate gratification
25.   strategies, pass, time, pattern or sequence
26.   fixed-law, social-contract, scheme
27.   fixed-law, social-contract
28.   moral stage, right, wrong
29.   preconventional, conventional, postconventional
30.   win pennies
31.   third, interpersonal concordance
32.   Western, white males
33.   moral behavior
34.   socialization, experience
35.   consequences, knowing, capable

Practice Test 1
1.   a   3.   d
2.   c   4.   c

5.	c
6.	b
7.	a
8.	c
9.	a
10.	b

11.	b
12.	c
13.	b
14.	d
15.	c

Practice Test 2

1.	a
2.	b
3.	b
4.	a
5.	d
6.	b
7.	d
8.	d

9.	c
10.	b
11.	c
12.	c
13.	b
14.	a
15.	e

CHAPTER SIXTEEN

CHILD DEVELOPMENT IN OTHER CULTURES

■ ■ ■ ■

◀
◀
◀

LEARNING OBJECTIVES

Learning about children in other cultures can certainly help us to better understand the relationship between nurture and nature, for nowhere will you see the nurture effects so evident. Hopefully, some in your study group can add information from their own experience. While you think about the societies represented here, consider the effects of the environmental differences, as well as the possible heritable influences which should be considered. Now, on to the task of digesting this chapter.

1. Be aware of the reasons we study child development in other cultures. Certainly our behavior is affected by the way we think about and understand our environment and we must remember the control our culture has on the way we think and behave.

2. Be able to tell your friends about the advantages of cross cultural research. Theories developed in one culture may not be useful in another because of limited and different variables. Know the effects of the contextual factors.

3. Factors showing the difficulties involved in cross cultural research are important as well, as we learn to report our findings without bias or confusion because of language and custom differences.

4. Learning what the culture decides is appropriate has powerful effects on the behaviors and direction of the child in every phase of his life.

5. In Japan, the family provides a different kind of base from which the child operates than in Western societies. Be sure you can discuss the effects of the physical closeness and early childhood experiences on later behavior and needs. Compare the education of the Japanese children and their resulting work habits to ours. There are some fascinating differences in many respects. Knowing the proper terms given to children's attitudes is not only fun but useful in this discussion.

6. Children in the newly formed states of Russia are of great interest to us as the world gets smaller and smaller. Russian children were socialized from nursery school on to learn the attitudes important to their principles of government. Studies of children raised in post Soviet schools indicate they are more like their Western counterparts. They recognize that success comes as a result of their own efforts rather than group efforts or government dictates. Remember, this area of the world is

undergoing immense political and socio-economic changes.   There will be more research forthcoming.

7.   The fun (!) of cross cultural studies is in comparing the familiar with what is unfamiliar. The children of the Fore, raised so differently until their contact with the outside world, provide fascinating contrasts. Notice the flexibility of humans here, and how new learning can make such a difference in attitudes, values, and behaviors.

8.   The contrasting society of the Ik, a culture in disintegration, gives us pause for thought about where our society is going. Have we taken for granted that humans have some built-in attitudes in terms of survival and human values that will survive without attention?

9.   You may want to develop a comparison chart for these societies to help you define the differences for the sake of keeping them straight for tests. In any event, do plan to discuss the issues brought into play in this chapter with friends and family. As you do, think of the recent political events in Europe and China. The chances for more complete and scientific comparisons of children are exciting to contemplate.

CHAPTER OUTLINE

Just the major headings this time! You'll want to fill in the details.

Chapter Preview: The fascinating study illustrating the early and lasting effects of culture on personality development.

I.   Cross Cultural Research
    A.   Problems in Cross Cultural Research: the Researcher;
        1.   Adjustment to new culture
        2.   Locals' adjustment to a stranger watching them
        3.   Language translation problems--idioms and concepts
        4.   Limiting investigation methods
    B.   Theory expansion and refining theories.
        1.   Piaget
            a.   Language and experience effects on entry into concrete operations
    C.   Increasing the Range of Variables
        1.   Studies of the same behaviors in other cultures reveal diversity of variables as determinants
    D.   Unconfounding variables
        1.   Separating variables which occur, and finding effects
            a.   study of groups who move away from culture and back after several years
            b.   study of groups moving from one culture to another
    E   Studying the behavior in the context of surroundings
        1.   Variables stand out as influential to researchers who come into a new culture to study and can provide new insights to follow
2.   Cross cultural comparisons - generalizations beyond the culture examined to help understand similar developmental issues

II.   The Culture as Teacher
    A.   Comparisons of the merchant and agricultural tribes
    B.   Schools differ greatly: formal, informal
    C.   Out of school experiences reach into adulthood
        1.   Modeling use of tools, way of making livelihood, observational learning

At Issue: The Development of Minority Children.
    A.   Eurocentric Bias has stifled research into the diversity of cultural influences until now
    B.   The new researcher studies, among other factors,
        1.   poverty effects
        2.   complexities in extended family influences
        3.   stereotyping and the variables which enter that picture

III.   The Effect of Culture
    A.   Why the study of these four cultures
        1.   Japan; highest educational achievers, provides naturalistic observations, country undergoing radical changes
        2.   The former Soviet Union; once the other major power in the world, important to understand basic differences in child rearing practices and values
        3.   Fore; contrast to Western culture, opportunity to see drastic effects of equally drastic cultural change
        4.   Ik; contrasting culture, culture in disintegration, attempts to understand reasons for behaviors

IV.   The Children of Japan
    A.   The effects of close physical contact and "Amae" --
        1.   Doi -- groupness leading to vertical social organization
    B   Few regulations in childhood, increasing as child grows older
    C.   Ittaikan, the measure of maturity
    D.   Japanese school system exacts excellence. "shiken jigoku," "examination hell", "Juku" cram schools
    E.   "Shinkeishitsu"
    F.   Group cohesion continues into adulthood and careers

V.   The Children of the former Soviet Union
    A.   State provision of nursery schools very different from ours
        1.   Peer grouping toward communal atmosphere
        2.   Emphasis on language and social skills
        3.   Early stimulation, training toward self reliance and peer relationships
    B.   Education toward communist morality   Table 16.1
    C.   Objectives for younger children compared to older children reminiscent of Piaget's concepts
    D.   Urie Bronfenbrenner study of children's egalitarian concepts
    E.   New studies of postSoviet schools show children's attitudes about themselves are changing
    F.   The changing face of Russian states economy and politics may be predicted from the way children develop their values.

VI.   Children of the Fore (New Guinea), Richard Sorensen
    A.   Children raised in indulgent atmosphere

        B.   Physical contact and trust of environment
        C.   Changes as exposed to outside world
VII.   The Ik of Uganda, Colin Turnbull
        A.   Forced to arid land and new way to survive
        B.   Disruption of previous lifestyle, kinship ended
        C.   Drastic effects and disintegration of society
Applications: My First Impressionism
        A.   Drawings by children from six different countries reflect culture.
                1.   Howard Gardner, Alexander Alland, *Playing with Form: Children Draw in Six Cultures*
                2.   This is beautiful and fascinating. I'm sure you'll enjoy this discussion.

■ ■ ■ ■

NAMES TO REMEMBER

The Inuit of Baffin Island
Triandis and Brislin
Takeo Doi
The Anatomy of Dependence
Urie Bronfenbrenner
E. Richard Sorenson

Colin Turnbull
Howard Gardner
Alexander Alland
the Fore
the Ik

■ ■ ■ ■

TERMS AND CONCEPTS

cross cultural research
ethnocentric
amae
skinship
ittaikan
shiken jigoku
Juku

shinkeishitsu
collective belonging
upbringer
communist morality
egalitarian communist ethic
egalitarian (Fore)

GUIDED REVIEW

1. The Japanese "orphans" left as young children in the Manchurian province of China after World War Two, surprised researchers. Although exposed to _____ culture for less than 7 years of their 40 or more years, the orphans _____ many of the attitudes and _____ _____ of their original culture.

2. Although genetic influences on their personality cannot be ruled out, the research on these "orphans" illustrates the profound effects of culture on _____ _____ _____.

3. Perhaps the most important result reinforced by cross sectional research is that there is no such thing as a _____ culture.

4. One major benefit of cross cultural research is to _____ and _____ theories by comparing development in various cultures. Examples of these comparisons include the testing of _____ cognitive theory.

5. Research to date has shown a tendency to base developmental information on _____, _____ _____ Western children, rather than considering the effect of diverse _____ and _____ .

6. Researchers' problems with cross cultural research include language differences, _____ of the stranger-researcher, and the limitations in _____ which may allow important cultural factors to be missed.

7. One of the problems in cross-cultural research is the use of only _____ method, which can lead to _____ _____ in an unfamiliar culture.

8. An important benefit of this research is the opportunity to expand and _____-_____ theories to help separate the _____ from the _____ variables.

9. By studying behaviors in other cultures, researchers can identify a broad range of _____ as determinants of _____ _____.

10. These studies offer researchers an opportunity to compare and contrast the _____ _____ which may affect people's behaviors. The differences may help us to understand the roles of both _____ and _____ in determining behaviors.

11. Earlier studies of minority children have used Anglo-American children as the norm for measurement and comparison. This is an example of _____ _____.

12. Previous studies of white, middle-class children will not suffice in our child development studies since. by the year 2000, today's minority children will become the new _____ of young people.

13. Present researchers examine the cultural diversity found in and within minority members, finding both _____ in minority families as well as _____.

14. One factor minority families often have in common is illustrated by the problems of poverty suffered by African-Americans. Three related problems felt proportionately by these children include _____ _____ in school, peer relationship diffuculties, and _____ _____ _____.

15. One area of common experience in minority families requiring more research is that of the rearing of children by _____ _____. These relationships can be quite different from family to family.

16. Lastly, _____ so often associated with minority families can be examined for accuracy. Further, through these examinations, variables will be tested to see which contribute to the development of all children.

17. Children learn from their culture without formal schooling. This is seen in societies where children learn skills needed in _____ through their _____ models.

18. Studies of infants in Japan show parent-child relationships are far more _____ _____ than in the United States. This "skinship" results in close family and group dependency called _____, which extends to peer and work relationships, reflecting what Doi calls _____.

19. Children in Japan enjoy considerable freedom in the early years and have increasing _____ _____ as they approach adulthood.

20. Maturity is measured in Japan by the child's ability to feel at _____ _____ _____, which is called _____.

21. The rigorous school system in Japan prepares children through _____ days of school every week, and tough bi-yearly exams requiring additional school preparation. Japanese schools show an impressive _____% graduation rate from 12th grade.

22. Failure at school is met with such disapproval, and pressures toward success and belonging are so high, that there are high rates of _____ - related disorders and _____ in college-aged students.

23. In the former Soviet Union, nursery schools provide early training toward _____ _____ and promote close collective feelings for peers.

24. Urie Bronfenbrenner's experiments show how Russian education and socialization is centered on _____ closeness, and _____ _____.

25. In contrast to civilization in Western countries, the Fore tribe in New Guinea had a completely _____ society in which children were no more _____ in their behavior than

adults.

26. Fore children grew up in an unstructured society where _____ was considered more important than _____.

27. _____ physical contact, freedom of _____, and complete trust of others in the tribe led the children toward safe _____ of many different adult activities.

28. When the roads opened their village, profound differences in the Fores' society occurred, including the end of the _____ society, and the appearance of _____, _____, and _____.

29. Turnbull's study of the Ik tribe of Uganda, revealed the effects of relocation and a complete change of life-style. Children were not _____ _____ beyond the age of _____. Adults who were _____ or _____ were ridiculed, and abandoned without care.

30. Comparing the Ik with the Fore, shows the profound effect of _____ on _____ values and _____.

31. Alexander Alland, in studying the drawings of children from six different cultures, found that the culture has a _____ _____. This conclusion disagrees with the earlier belief that all children's drawings progress through a _____ _____ _____.

■ ■ ■ ■   ◀
                                                                                               ◀
PRACTICE TEST 1   ◀

1. Difficulties in separating variables that occur together in a particular race or ethnic group are remedied by studying the example in Japan of
   a. members of a culture who remain in Japan for their lifetimes
   b. comparing adjustments to a specific situation of Japanese children who have been raised in another culture with those who have remained in Japan for their lifetime
   c. comparing adjustments to a situation of members of two different cultures who have stayed with their culture for a lifetime
   d. comparing adjustments of members of the same culture who move within their culture

2. The recent cross cultural studies of child development have provided information regarding
   a. the effects of a wide range of cultural variables as they relate to biological development and behavior
   b. the expansion and refinement of theories posited in Western cultures
   c. the effects of contextual factors as they may or may not modify conclusions formed in Western cultures
   d. all of these and more

3.   One problem with the methods used by researchers in cultures other than their own
      a.   are the many methods available to measure behaviors in other cultures
      b.   is the tendency to measure only one of the many variables occurring sequentially.
      c.   is the tendency to use only one research method to measure the variables which may affect child development.
      d.   the lack of objectivity in the method which may ignore variables unfamiliar to the researcher.

4.   Reasons given for studying the children of Japan include
      a.   that children there are among the highest achievers
      b.   that children are reared very differently from those in Western cultures
      c.   that the culture itself is undergoing rapid sociocultural changes
      d.   all of the above

5.   Researchers in Japan found that the physical closeness between parents and their children
      a.   results in a lifetime preference to belong to other groups as closely as the family
      b.   encourages independence in children as they get older
      c.   discourages "amae" in families and/or groups
      d.   encourages parents to impose more rules and regulations on the children

6.   Education in Japanese schools is so demanding
      a.   that children frequently drop out because of rigorous examinations
      b.   that additional school hours are often added to encourage "ittaikan" levels of maturity
      c.   that special additional schools help children cram for the rigorous biannual examination schedule
      d.   that support is offered by teachers and universities to encourage high achievement in school

7.   Similarities between day-care facilities in the U.S. and in states in the former Soviet Union end with the custodial functions, as the latter's nurseries
      a.   began almost immediately to orient children to their peers and collective belonging rather than family kinship
      b.   provided cooperative arrangements where mothers and fathers can continue close relationships with their children
      c.   encouraged competition with class mates rather than toward social humanism
      d.   emphasized physical skills rather than language or social skills

8.   Illustrating peer centeredness and national pride, the Bronfenbrenner study comparing Russian children to Western children, showed that
      a.   Russian children were more likely to misbehave if they thought only their peers would see the results of their work
      b.   Russian children displayed far less antisocial behaviors across each condition than the children from the other three countries
      c.   Russian children displayed far more antisocial behaviors across each condition than the children from the other three countries
      d.   there were no differences between Russian children and those of West Germany

9. Fore children and adults exhibited _____ when roads in and out of their village brought money and social change to their society.
    a.   egalitarian structure
    b.   increased leadership by adults to protect their traditions
    c.   anger, frustration, withdrawal, and selfishness
    d.   caring for the children ceased

10. The Ik's disintegrating society showed members had turned incredibly hard and cruel to one another. Comparing this tribe to the Fore, illustrates the profound effect of
    a.   parenting methods
    b.   the culture
    c.   encroachment of other societies
    d.   money

11. A major reason attributed to the cruel treatment of the Ik to one another is that
    a.   they were too permissive as parents
    b.   they were so isolated they practice incest and so certain behaviors were inbred
    c.   they were forced to move to a barren part of land with little food and shelter supply
    d.   they were genetically predisposed to harsh treatment

12. Compared to drawings of American children, those of Japanese children showed
    a.   less knowledge of form and color
    b.   more primitive choices in subject matter
    c.   more sophisticated use of brushes and color
    d.   use of many small brush stokes to cover the paper

13. French children's artwork was striking in its use of
    a.   nature scenes
    b.   large areas of color
    c.   more angular shapes
    d.   black and white rather than color

14. Howard Gardner suggests that children's drawings depend mostly on
    a.   their culture
    b.   their stage of cognitive development
    c.   their desire to conform to teacher's expectations
    d.   their exposure to stimuli of various kinds

15. In contrast to Gardner's opinion, Alland's studies proposed that children's drawings are most affected by
    a.   their intelligence
    b.   learning and reinforcement
    c.   inherent abilities
    d.   cultural factors

PRACTICE TEST 2

1.   As an example of theory expansion and refinement using cross-cultural research:
      a.   Piaget's theory of cognitive development has been discounted, as it is rooted in biological maturation.
      b.   entrance into Piaget's concrete operational stage has been modified as we find language and experience have considerable effects
      c.   Kohlberg's theory of moral development has been discounted as a result of its biological orientation.
      d.   Kohlberg's theory has been accepted completely as a cross-cultural representation.

2.   Although a researcher may run into some difficulties in adjusting to a new culture, he or she may have the advantage of
      a.   gaining objective insights into aspects of the culture because they differ from the researcher's own experience
      b.   comparing and contrasting the contextual factors to better understand the roles of both nature and nurture
      c.   not being confused by the different connotations and concepts of language translations
      d.   both a and b

3.   To teach children the skills and values needed for adulthood, many cultures across the world
      a.   use formal schools which teach values and technologies
      b.   conduct informal classes of education by parents for their children
      c.   may use formal schools, but some depend only on learning acquired through observation and imitation
      d.   teach their children in informal schools where adults model skills needed

4.   Until recently, studies of child development have centered on the white, middle-class children, using Anglo-American standards to measure all others. This practice illustrates the
      a.   Anglocentric bias
      b.   Eurocentric bias
      c.   Middle-class white bias
      d.   culture-blind bias

5.   Typically, minority families are younger, and are more likely to
      a.   be poorer than majority families
      b.   live in an extended family situation
      c.   show great family differences in their own culture
      d.   all of the above

6.   Minority families in the U.S. provide a rich diversity of cultures. By the year 2000, minority young people will be
      a.   absorbed into the Anglo-American society through racial mixing
      b.   considered isolated because of their special cultures

c.   the new majority in this country

d.   likely to continue to raise their families in poverty

7.   How the culture shapes children's attitudes and behavior in the former Soviet Union is important to study, since

a.   we must understand the sociocultural influence on children if we are to know how to develop good relations

b.   we must understand the sociocultural influence on children if we are to defend ourselves against them

c.   we must understand the sociocultural influence on children if we are to understand the drastic changes they've encountered in recent years

d.   we must understand the sociocultural influence on children if we are to understand the stark contrast to most industrialized nations

8.   Children in Japan differ from Western children in that they

a.   have strict regulations on their behavior in early years but enjoy increasing freedom in later years

b.   have few regulations on their behavior in childhood, but have increasing limitations as they get older

c.   have equally strict regulations on their behavior throughout their entire childhood

d.   have equally permissive allowances in behavior throughout their childhood

9.   Students educated in the demanding school system in Japan

a.   may suffer tremendous pressures to succeed

b.   may exhibit disorders referred to as "skinkeishitsu"

c.   show comparatively high suicide rates

d.   all of the above and still receive little support or help if they are failing

10.   When the Fore tribe was discovered, the most singular aspect of their society was

a.   the competency of the leadership in the tribe

b.   the equal status and cooperation of all members of the tribe no matter what the age

c.   the scheduled activities of the tribe to survive the environmental conditions

d.   the lack of caring for the children of the tribe

11.   As civilization was experienced by the Fore people

a.   they began to plant and own coffee plantations

b.   they became interested and finally used to western kinds of goods

c.   they became less egalitarian

d.   all of the above

12.   Forced from their natural environment, the Ik show us the saddest example of the flexibility of human beings. Scarcities of food and space resulted in

a.   abandonment of children by 2 or 3 years of age

b.   bands of children uniting to protect themselves from attack by tribe-mates

c.   dreadful cruelty to the elderly and injured by both children and adults in the tribe

d.   all of the above

13.   When Ik gangs formed to protect themselves,
        a.   they were kind to members of other gangs
        b.   they often killed their leader
        c.   they prevented cruelty to the elders
        d.   they attempted to restore their former culture

14.   Alland's work in studying the differences in children's art across the world shows that
        a.   there are noticeable differences in choices of colors and shapes
        b.   the pictures and techniques reflect the culture in which the young artists live
        c.   though of six different cultures, there do not appear to be obvious developmental
                age-related sequences in the drawings
        d.   all of these

15.   The children of Bali preferred to
        a.   fill their drawings with small brightly colored marks
        b.   paint large color areas with little form
        c.   draw very specific well disciplined forms
        d.   draw many small colorful marks all over the page

You may not agree with the answers to these questions. Good! Better now than at test time. Now, you have a time to explore and discuss these questions carefully, rather than think in terms of test answers.

ANSWER SECTION

Guided Review

1. Japanese, retained, personality characteristics
2. very early childhood
3. neutral
4. expand, refine, Piaget's
5. white, middle class, environments, cultures
6. distrust, methods or techniques
7. one, false conclusions
8. fine-tune, biological, cultural
9. variables, specific behaviors
10. social context, nature, nurture
11. Eurocentric Bias
12. majority
13. commonalities, differences
14. lowered competence, behavior conduct problems.
15. extended family
16. stereotypes
17. adulthood, adult
18. physically close, amae, groupness
19. social regulations
20. one with others, ittaikan
21. 5 1/2, 90
22. anxiety, suicide
23. communal morality
24. peer, national pride
25. egalitarian, restricted
26. friendship, kinship
27. close, movement, imitation
28. egalitarian, frustration, anger, selfishness
29. cared for, two or three, sick, injured
30. society or culture, human, behavior
31. pronounced effect, standard developmental sequence

Practice Test 1

1. b
2. d
3. c
4. d
5. a
6. c
7. a
8. b

9. c
10. b
11. c
12. c
13. b
14. b
15. d

<u>*Practice Test 2*</u>

1.	*b*
2.	*b*
3.	*c*
4.	*b*
5.	*d*
6.	*c*
7.	*a*
8.	*b*

9.	*d*
10.	*b*
11.	*d*
12.	*d*
13.	*b*
14.	*d*
15.	*a*

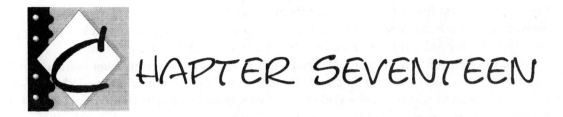

CHAPTER SEVENTEEN

CHILDREN WITH SPECIAL NEEDS

■ ■ ■ ■

LEARNING OBJECTIVES

This chapter gives us an opportunity to study the genetic and environmental influences on the problems of development. The dysfunctions seen in children are not simple to describe and understand, nor is it easy to pinpoint the causes of these problems. They are as varied as the nature and the nurturing aspects of individuals described here. As you read this chapter, make a mental note to watch for news releases and journal articles reporting the progress made to spare children from the disorders which attack them. Pay special attention to the plight of the poor and homeless children. In the meantime, know about the following to help you with the immediate future in this course!

1. Know the factors involved in the study of developmental psychopathology. Understanding the terms is important here.

2. Schizophrenia, a serious and common disorder, can begin in childhood. What are the symptoms? What do we know about the etiology of this disease? Be able to describe the "two-strike" theory. Know how schizophrenia differs from other disorders.

3. Depression in children is equally heartbreaking. Know the symptoms and etiology of depression. Be aware that children of all ages, even infants, have experienced serious depression disorder. As you read about the high incidence of suicide, recognize that there are distinctions between depressed individuals who do not attempt and those who are not clinically depressed who do.

4. Learning disabilities are of great interest to us, especially parents and/or future teachers. Some of these are caused by environmental toxins which could be avoided if we had knowledge of the risks.

5. Dyslexia and attention deficit disorders are two separate learning disabilities which are studied in this chapter. Although much needs to be known, you should be able to discuss what is known now, and be aware of what treatments are available in your school system and community. Need to write a special report? Here's an idea.

6. Some learning problems can be caused by environmental toxins. Only when these dangers become common knowledge will we begin to defeat these threats such as cadmium, lead and mercury.

7. Early infantile autism seems to be related to biogenetic factors. Other possibilities include brain damage from various viral and bacterial diseases. Know the problems encountered by these children.

Describe the latest findings in treating this disorder.

8. Sensory deficits affect many of our children. Imagine the problem the child has whose problem goes undetected. Know about the special disadvantages these children experience.

9. At least 100,000 children sleep in welfare facilities, cars, or even somewhere outside in this modern, wealthy country. Know how this affects them presently and in their future, Why does this happen? What can we do to address these complicated problems more effectively than present programs?

10. Being too poor to have well balanced and sufficient meals each day, a place to call home without old lead pipes that are poisonous, or a run down hotel room without a stove or refrigerator, is a situation that effects all too many Americans. What will it take to do something about those whose jobs are obsolete and who are willing to work to take care of their families whether they are single parents or live in an intact family?

11. Look at how both biological and environmental factors interact to determine how developmental disabilities occur.

12. How is helplessness learned? Understanding this section may help us to understand how it is so easy to give up when we believe we are powerless to change our circumstances. The more we believe we are helpless, the more we become helpless.

13. Many children and adults are shy or remember being shy and have suffered the isolation that occurs as a result. What can families, friends and teachers do to help them?

14. Both the At Issue and the Applications sections provide worthwhile subjects for discussion and study.

■ ■ ■ ■

CHAPTER OUTLINE

Are you ready to do this on your own? Try it, you'll like it!

Chapter Preview: Something Was Wrong! Looking for early warning signs of schizophrenia.

I.   Developmental Psychopathology; Definition: _____

II. Disorders with Probable Genetic Involvement
     A.   Schizophrenia: Definition and frequency _____
          1.   symptoms
               a.   personality _____
               b.   emotion _____
               c.   language and behavior _____
               d.   thinking and believing _____
          2.   causes examined
               a.   genetic links:
                    (1)   family studies _____
                    (2)   twin studies _____
                    (3)   Kety study, Copenhagen
                          (a)   _____

3. the Two-Strike Theory: Developmental brain pathology
    a. abnormal neural connections during second trimester

        _____

    b. environmental influence - influenza virus

        _____

B. Depression; definition and frequency _____
  1. symptoms
    a. _____
    b. _____
    c. _____
    d. _____
  2. age of onset _____
  3. Kety study: adoptees, biological and adopted families

    _____

  4. environmental correlates _____
  5. suicide and suicide attempts _____
  6. prevention and treatment _____
    a. distinction between depressed and suicidal child

    _____

    b. early treatment _____

III Learning Disabilities:
A. Dyslexia; definition _____
  1. symptoms
    a. _____
    b. _____
    c. _____
  2. etiology
    a. _____
    b. _____
  3. treatment _____
B. Attention Deficit Disorder: definition _____
  1. symptoms
    a. _____
    b. _____
    c. _____
    d. _____
  2. etiology, what's suspected
    a. biological _____
    b. environmental _____
  3. treatment
    a. drugs _____
      (1) problems with drugs
    b. behavior modification _____
    c. value of group support _____
  4. numbers of children affected
    a. _____

        b.   labels _____

C.   Hyperactivity disorder: definition _____
sometimes but not always seen with ADD.

    1.   symptoms
        a.   _____
        b.   _____
        c.   _____
        d.   _____
    2.   etiology, what's suspected
        a.   biological _____
    3.   treatment
        a.   Drugs _____
        b.   Behavior modification _____
    4.   numbers of children affected
        a.   _____
        b.   labels _____

IV.   Toxic Induction of Learning Problems

A.   Cadmium, mercury, and Lead: definition and frequency
    1.   living conditions relationship _____
    2.   economic level relationship _____
    3.   symptoms
        a.   IQ scores _____
        b.   _____
    4.   sources of heavy metal contamination _____
    5.   testing underway

V.   Early Infantile Autism; definition and frequency

A.   symptoms: autism a broad category
    1.   aloof and unresponsive _____
    2.   social skills _____
    3.   language development _____
    4.   motor skills _____

B.   Causes investigated
    1.   genetic _____
    2.   sex link suggested _____
    3.   correlation with Fragile X _____
    4.   brain chemistry _____
    5.   brain damage _____
    6.   environment _____

At Issue: Baby Jane Doe and Baby Doe: Ethical issues and legal issues get tangled. Parents must be told of severity of birth defects and the outcomes for child's life.

VI.   Physical and Sensory Disabilities

A.   The CNS and musculature: epilepsy, cerebral palsy, birth defects, disorders connected to accidents and illness
    1.   emphasis on using all available technologies to help children function better with disability
    2.   education of public to meet children's needs

B.   Sensory Exceptionality: define _____
        1.   visual _____
               a.   _____
               b.   _____
        2.   auditory _____
               a.   _____
               b.   _____
               c.   _____
C.   Treatment and aides _____

II.   Homelessness definition and frequency
     A.   Effects: hunger, malnutrition, health problems, lack of mental and physical health care, delays in development, psychological problems, academic underachievement
     B.   Not just "houseless", also without community
         1.   "Robert's" feelings _____
         2.   hotels, shelters _____
         3.   malnutrition _____
         4.   missed inoculations _____
         5.   learning and attention problems _____
         6.   social behavior poor _____
         7.   poor school attendance _____
     C.   Causes and contributions
         1.   although adults outnumber children, children receive less support

               _____
         2.   breakdown in family structure _____
         3.   decline in church and religious influence _____
         4.   divorce, single parent families increase, 34% of homeless

               _____
         5.   rising housing costs _____
         6.   government aid programs buy 26% less per person than 20 years ago
         7.   US economy declines
     E.   Help for the homeless
         1.   affordable housing
         2.   effective drug and alcohol abusers programs
         3.   schools adaptable to children who move often
         4.   education for homeless to rights and services, with   caseworkers to help make connections
         5.   a nation that cares enough to reclaim its children

VIII. Poverty 1963-69 funds for War on Poverty are diminished
     A.   21% American children living with families below poverty line
         1.   comparison to Canada and Sweden _____
     B.   Problems continue
         1.   fewer blue collar jobs
                a.   half of jobs created in 1980' pay less than poverty level
         2.   government benefits have declined
     C.   Effects on children
         1.   cognitive impairments

        a.   poverty best predictor of IQ scores. Better than race, ethnicity, or number of parents in home

    2.   health issues _____

    3.   emotional effects _____

    4.   effects on family structure _____

        a.   stresses _____

        b.   children's behavior _____

    5.   environment's role _____

D.   When family income improves steps taken to better children's lives

    1.   Marybeth Shinn and Yvonne Rafferty studies

    2.   cost of meeting children's needs now less than combating poverty and homelessness later

IX.   Learning and Early Experience

    A.   Learned Helplessness; definition _____

        1.   Seligman and Maier work with dogs _____

        2.   infant-mobile demonstrations _____

            a.   immediate results _____

            b.   later results _____

        3.   minority group beliefs -- U.S. Office of Education

        4.   school children who fail at school _____

        5.   parent /child relationships _____

    B.   Shyness; definition _____

        1.   the vicious cycle _____

        2.   statistics _____

    C.   Retraining

        1.   Public Law 94-142, 1975 in school _____

        2.   modeling, reinforcement, group involvement in regular classroom _____

Applications: Born To Be Wild. An Evolutionary Theory of Hard Times

■ ■ ■ ■

NAMES TO REMEMBER

Seymour Kety

Watson and Ramey

Walker and Lewine

Rafferty and Shinn

Case Western Reserve Laboratory

U.S. Office of Education

Centers for Disease Control

National Institutes of Health

National Alliance to End Homeless

Robert

Conference of Mayors

Partnership for the Homeless

Public Law 94-142

Kagan and Klein

Jay Belsky

Baby Jane Doe

■■■■

◄
◄
◄

TERMS AND CONCEPTS

therapist monkeys
developmental psychopathology
developmental pathology
schizophrenia
the two-strike theory
depression
child suicide
learning disabilities
dyslexia
attention deficit disorders
hyperactivity
infantile autism
Ritalin

American Sign Language
autism
echolalia
Fragile X
fenfluramine
sensory exceptionality
toxic induction of learning disorders
plasticity
homelessness
poverty
welfare hotels
learned helplessness
shyness

■■■■

◄
◄
◄

GUIDED REVIEW

1. "The study of abnormal behavior within the context of measuring the effects of genetic, ontogenetic, cognitive, affective, social, or any other ongoing developmental influence on behavior" defines _____ _____.

2. It has been shown that there is probable genetic involvement in the childhood disorders of _____, _____, and _____ _____.

3. Schizophrenia has a profound effect on the child's ability to _____ and _____ reality, to _____ _____, and it involves a breakdown of _____ _____.

4. A theory of schizophrenia's heritability, held by Seymour Kety, states that there is a _____ _____, as he found the disease 8 to 10 times more often in _____ relatives as compared to 2 or 3 times as often in _____ relatives.

5. A promising direction of research into the cause of schizophrenia, the two-strike theory proposes that there is developmental _____ in the emotion and memory regions of the brain which occurred during the _____ _____ of _____. The second "strike" in the theory is that the environment contributes its influence in the form of the

_____ virus which causes severe disruption in the formation of neural connections in the brain at that time.

6. The text defines depression as a long lasting wide-range of _____ disorders, ranging from _____ to a _____ _____ state.

7. Recent studies support Kety's work, and have found a significant association between childhood depression and depression in _____ _____.

8. Although some depressed children become suicidal, more children who attempt or commit suicide are likely to have _____ suicide, or been exposed to suicide. All threats or talk of suicide must be taken _____.

9. Learning disabilities include difficulties in listening, _____, _____, _____, _____, _____, _____. (try for 5 or 6).

10. _____ children are not suffering from a sensory defect. They have trouble making sense of conceptual information given to them in written form.

11. Although the conclusions are not definite, certain forms of dyslexia may be the result of genetically based problems in _____ _____ and the lack of proper _____ of the neurons.

12. Attention deficit disorders are exhibited in children who are unable to control _____ and who are unable to _____. This deficit frequently occurs in conjunction with _____, in which the child is constantly active.

13. Hyperactivity disorder involves some symptoms similar to ADD but also the child will exhibit a constant whirl of activity, as if _____ by a _____.

14. Although the causes of ADD and hyperactivity are not fully known, signs of brain disfunction are supported by research. Success in many cases involves the use of the drug _____. Other treatments for both disorders that have been helpful are _____ _____ and, for the parents, _____ _____.

15. Some learning difficulties are linked to contamination from the heavy metals _____, _____ and _____, especially in children from lower incomes homes. _____ paints and old _____ are sources of contamination.

16. The term autism describes a group of related behaviors, including aloofness, _____, and severely retarded _____ development. Although autistic children are rarely clumsy or awkward they often engage in restricted, _____, and _____ behaviors.

17. A key feature that distinguishes autism from schizophrenia or other psychotic disorders, is the extremely _____ _____ of the disorder. It is seen even seen at birth or soon

after.

18. There is a strong suggestion that autism is a sex-linked genetic disorder. There is evidence of a concordance rate of 36% in _____ _____, compared to a 0% rate in _____ _____.

19. Additional data shows that there may be biochemical brain involvement in autism, as is evidenced by the positive response shown to the diet drug _____.

20. Two special considerations when a child is disadvantaged by epilepsy, cerebral palsy, birth defects, or other physical disorders caused by illness or accident are to
   1.
   2.

21. The case study of _____ _____ _____ illustrates the problems that occur when there is a conflict between the parents of a handicapped child and the government which is trying to protect the child.

22. The Bowen vs American Hospital Association case points out the need for parents to be given _____ _____ about their child's condition and the prospects for the child's _____ _____.

23. Sensory exceptionality refers to children with _____ or _____ dysfunctions. Although sight impairment involves many problems, the hearing impaired child may suffer even more because of the inherent _____ problems.

24. Along with Braille writers, taped books and magazines and other aides for the blind, and sign language, ASL, hearing aides and speech training for the hearing handicapped, perhaps the best that lay people can offer is _____, not rejection.

25. At least _____ children are presently living in welfare hotels, shelters, cars, or even _____ _____ _____.

26. Some of the devastating effects experienced by these homeless children are:
   1.
   2.
   3.
   4.
   5.
   6.

27. More than "houseless", these children suffer from the lack of community support, loss of contact with _____ and _____, dreadful _____ _____ and lack of _____ in the places they sleep.

28. Children who are deprived of rest, food and sleep, have additional difficulty in _____,

_____ _____, and _____ _____.

29.   Because of the breakdown of families, and the dramatic increase in divorce, _____
       _____ families, and expensive _____, children in need may not receive the
       services they need.

30.   The first priority in solving the homeless crisis is affordable housing. Other solutions include:
       1.
       2.
       3.
       4.
       5.

31.   The best predictor of I.Q. Test scores for children, better than ethnic background, race, or status of
       parents in the home, is _____.

32.   Poverty affects at least 21% of our children and the problems are continuing for all the reasons
       given for homelessness and also because:
       1.
       2.

33.   Rafferty and Shinn point out that it will cost _____ to combat poverty and
       homelessness now than to pay later for the consequences of _____ _____.

34.   Children who find that no amount of effort on their part will make any change in the
       environment, have experienced _____ _____ and come to believe that they are
       controlled by _____ _____.

35.   When children encounter one failure after another in school, they come to think of themselves as
       _____, resulting in lessening of _____ _____ to succeed.

36.   _____ becomes a vicious cycle as the child structures his environment to
       _____ the very learning skills which would help alleviate this deficit.

37.   Frequently, these discouraged children have learned not to learn, and are often labeled
       _____ _____ or _____ _____.

38.   Public Law _____ has allowed disadvantaged children to experience the regular
       classroom.

■ ■ ■ ■

◀
◀
◀

PRACTICE TEST 1

1. By studying the vast range of information in several cultures, it has become possible to predict development as it progresses abnormally under certain circumstances. This study is known as
    a.   ontogenetics
    b.   developmental psychopathology
    c.   developmental disorders
    d.   influential development

2. Schizophrenia's major effects include distorted thoughts, language, behaviors, and
    a.   an inability to monitor and test reality as they experience hallucinations and delusions
    b.   sleep difficulties, deep emotional lows, and apathetic attitudes
    c.   superior language abilities
    d.   all of the above

3. The two-strike theory of the causes of schizophrenia includes
    a.   genetic susceptibility and posrnatal brain damage
    b.   brain pathology and chromosome damage
    c.   the flu virus and environmental influences
    d.   genetic susceptibility and environmental influence

4. In children, depression
    a.   affects 1 to 6 percent of all children
    b.   is a lasting and continuous state of unhappiness and apathy without obvious cause
    c.   both a and b
    d.   seldom occurs after a significant time of stress

5. That suicides are committed by children under 15 years of age points to the need for parents to
    a.   help their depressed child cope with sadness and stress
    b.   help their depressed child use effective problem solving methods
    c.   join the depressed child in family therapy
    d.   all of these

6. A learning disability is defined as an intellectual handicap
    a.   that is not caused by damage to specific areas of the brain or nonmyelination of certain neurons
    b.   that is not caused by environmental factors, mental retardation, or emotional disturbance
    c.   that is caused by a sensory defect involving sight
    d.   that is limited to deficiencies in the ability to read and write language

7. Dyslexia is
    a.   a disorder of the visual system
    b.   a disorder involving making sense of written information
    c.   a maturational disorder

       d.   all of these

8.   Attention deficit disorder
       a.   is marked by inappropriate levels of attention and by impulsivity
       b.   is marked by easy distractibility and the need for careful supervision
       c.   often occurs with hyperactivity
       d.   all of the above

9.   Heavy metal toxic substances related to learning problems are found
       a.   in lead-based paints and old plumbing in old lower socioeconomic neighborhoods
       b.   in the air pollution of congested areas in big cities
       c.   in old homes of higher and lower socioeconomic neighborhoods
       d.   all of the above

10.   Causes of autism examined by researchers indicate
       a.   parental neglect
       b.   a strong genetic component
       c.   a chromosomal disorder
       d.   no relationship between it and brain functioning

11.   Among the behaviors of early infantile autism is severely retarded language development. Some children develop the habit of repeating everything that is said to them. This is known as
       a.   repeatism
       b.   echolalia
       c.   self talk
       d.   antisocial language

12.   100,000 homeless children will sleep in a shelter, car, or on the streets tonight. Factors contributing to the situation include
       a.   the breakdown of family structure
       b.   housing costs have risen as the economy and job availabilies have declined
       c.   federal, state and agency aid which once aided children must now be shared with increasing numbers of needy adults
       d.   all of the above

13.   Rafferty and Shinn, in their studies of the economics of homeless families have stated that
       a.   children are without safety and food
       b.   children missed out on inoculations and therefore are more prone to avoidable diseases
       c.   in the long run, it is more economical to combat poverty and homelessness now than to pay the cost of neglecting the problems in the future
       d.   none of the above

14.   Shyness is experienced by children who
       a.   fail to learn to socialize with others and avoid exposure to opportunities to learn socialization behaviors
       b.   are often thought of as learning disabled or emotionally disturbed

 c. can be taught socialization behaviors and benefit from acceptance by others

 d. all of these

15. Public Law 94-142 has given learning opportunities to shy and "helpless" children through

 a. placing handicapped children in separate classes for special training

 b. using special techniques such as peer modeling, reinforcement, and group involvement in the regular classroom

 c. individual teaching situations where the child does not have to interact with others

 d. a visiting teacher's training program at home

■ ■ ■ ■

PRACTiCE TEST 2

1. Developmental psychopathology includes abnormal behavior in the context of the effects of

 a. genetic and ontogenetic factors

 b. cognitive and affective factors

 c. biochemical, social, and cultural influences

 d. all of the above

2. Seymour Kety's investigation of the relatives of schizophrenic adoptees in Denmark showed the likelihood of becoming schizophrenic increases in proportion to the closeness of the biological relative affected,

 a. and he found the chances of schizophrenia in brothers, sisters, and parents were 10 times more likely, and only 2 or 3 times as likely in distant relatives

 b. which indicates all schizophrenia is genetically linked

 c. and fraternal twins are most likely to be schizophrenic

 d. and close relatives of schizophrenics were 3 times more likely to be depressed than were members of the adopted families

3. The seriousness of childhood depression is seen in statistics (which could even be higher) that show

 a. environmental factors are the primary cause of depression

 b. 12,000 children between 5 and 14 are admitted to psychiatric hospitals in the U.S. because of suicidal behavior

 c. most depressed children attempt suicide

 d. children who talk about suicide are not likely to commit suicide

4. As an example of a wide range of learning disabilities, dyslexia

 a. is caused by a sensory defect, specifically a vision problem

 b. is definitely determined by a specific gene

 c. is a problem of making sense of conceptual information in a written form

 d. shows no damage to brain areas

5.   Attention deficit disorder when accompanied by hyperactivity
        a.   has been treated with stimulants to lengthen the attention span and help the child become more calm
        b.   is characterized by the child's constant activity, lack of attention, and impulsivity
        c.   has sometimes been mistreated by unwise use of drugs
        d.   all of the above

6.   Infantile autism differs from psychotic disorders in that
        a.   autism has an extremely early onset, often appearing at birth or soon after
        b.   autism is characterized by severely retarded language development, often including echolalia
        c.   both a and b
        d.   the label describes a constellation of related unobservable behaviors

7.   Sensory exceptionality refers to
        a.   sight and hearing deficiencies which require special equipment and assistance
        b.   sight and hearing abilities which are better than that of the average child
        c.   lack of competent intellectual skills
        d.   lack of public awareness of the needs of the exceptional child

8.   The Baby Jane Doe study points to the recognition that
        a.   no matter how each state handles the solutions, a devastating blow has been dealt to the parents and siblings in every way
        b.   parents should have the right to know all information concerning their handicapped child's present condition and the prognosis for the future
        c.   that Baby Doe regulations should be posted in all hospitals
        d.   a and b

9.   Considering the large numbers of homeless children in the U.S., we know that the same aid from agencies, the state and federal governments given now buys _____% per person of what it did 20 years ago.
        a.   20
        b.   26
        c.   31
        d.   16

10.   Besides helping the homeless to obtain affordable and decent housing, what can be done to help homeless families?
        a.   rehabilitation programs for drug and alcohol abusers
        b.   establish schools which can accommodate children who move frequently
        c.   educate the homeless to their rights and services, and provide caseworkers who make sure they are being served
        d.   all of these, and for all of us to care!

11.   Poverty can have many effects including
        a.   children express more fear and anxiety

b.   children are seen to have more temper tantrums than non-poor children
c.   children show poorer test scores in school
d.   all of these

12. The rate of poverty in the United States is
a.   twice as high as in other industrialized countries
b.   four times as high as in other industrialized countries
c.   one half as high as in other industrialized countries
d.   about even with other industrialized countries

13. Discovering that one has no control over events in one's environment and believing that the environment is therefore in control of the individual is known as
a.   shyness
b.   learned helplessness
c.   environmental determinism
d.   lack of plasticity

14. Often when children encounter failure at school, they begin to feel like failures. This feeling can lead to
a.   harder efforts on their part to succeed
b.   a vicious cycle of failure leading to more failures
c.   feelings that they are controlled by their environment, rather than the other way around
d.   both b and c

15. As shyness becomes cyclic in childhood and can continue into adulthood, surveys have found
a.   over 80% of Americans have considered themselves to be shy at one time or another
b.   over 60% of Americans have considered themselves to be shy at one time or another
c.   over 50% of Americans have considered themselves to be shy at one time or another
d.   over 10% of Americans have considered themselves to be shy at one time or another

ANSWER SECTION

<u>Guided Review</u>

1.   developmental psychopathology
2.   schizophrenia, depression, learning disabilities
3.   recognize, test, function socially, personality integration
4.   genetic predisposition, primary, distant
5.   pathology, second trimester, pregnancy, influenza
6.   mood, sadness, severely suicidal
7.   biological relatives
8.   discussed suicide, seriously
9.   talking, reading, writing, spelling, arithmetic, communication
10. dyslexic
11. brain structure, myelination
12. impulsivity, concentrate, hyperactivity
13. driven, motor
14. Ritalin, behavior modification, support groups.
15. lead, cadmium, mercury, lead, plumbing
16. unresponsiveness, language, persistent, repetitive
17. early onset
18. identical twins, fraternal twins
19. fenfluramine
20. provide technology to overcome the handicaps, provide education to the public to meet the child's special
     needs
21. Baby Jane Doe
22. full information, future development
23. sight, hearing, language
24. respect
25. 100,00, on the street
26. hunger and malnutrition, health problems, lack of mental or physical care, delayed development,
     psychological problems, academic underachievement
27. family, friends, sanitary conditions, safety
28. learning, school attendance, social skills
29. single parent, housing
30. rehabilitation of drug and alcohol abusers, schools geared for children who move often, education for the
     homeless to know rights and services, caseworkers to connect them to needed services, government funding
     to meet homeless family needs.
31. poverty
32. fewer blue collar jobs, half jobs created since 1980 pay less than poverty level, government benefits have
     declined, more single parent homes
33. less, neglecting children
34. learned helplessness, their environment
35. failures, their efforts
36. shyness, avoid

37.   *learning disabled, emotionally disturbed*
38.   94-142

Practice Test 1

1.	b		9.	d
2.	a		10.	b
3.	d		11.	b
4.	c		12.	d
5.	d		13.	c
6.	b		14.	d
7.	b		15.	b
8.	d			

Practice Test 2

1.	d		9.	b
2.	a		10.	d
3.	b		11.	d
4.	c		12.	a
5.	d		13.	b
6.	c		14.	d
7.	a		15.	a
8.	b			

CHAPTER EIGHTEEN

ADOLESCENT PHYSICAL
AND COGNITIVE DEVELOPMENT

■ ■ ■ ■   ◀
                                                                           ◀
LEARNING OBJECTIVES   ◀

All the questions you always wanted to ask about why teenagers' legs are longer than the floor-space in your living room and why they bring clothes home for approval, only to take them back if you do approve, are answered in this chapter! Surely the members of your study group are as bewildered as you have been all this time. Now, at last, you can discover the answers to these mysteries together. Read carefully, and be able to give feedback on the issues to follow.

1. Remember the agony of all those physical changes in adolescence? You weren't alone. At this stage every bit of the child's emotions, skills, aptitudes, and much of his self concept is related in some way to the body and its developmental changes now.

2. Know about the variations in the adolescent's maturity rates. Differences within a sex, between the sexes, and early and late maturation are all important to teens and their social interactions. Know about the growth spurt and when it occurs.

3. You should be able to describe the secondary sex characteristics, and the difference in boys and girls concerning their occurrence. Your own experience will remind you of some of the problems with this. Need I remind you of your first school dance?

4. Be able to discuss the secular trend with your friends as a phenomena of this century and the reasons for it. Talk about very athletic girls who have a different experience than those who choose less strenuous activities than world class sports and ballet dancing.

5. There is also a difference in muscle growth and strength between girls and boys, for very good reasons. Know the differences and what some can do to compensate if they want to.

6. Discuss nutrition with your friends. The eating habits of our teens are noteworthy, as are the eating disorders and weight problems we see at this age.

7. Erik Erikson talked about "Who am I " and "Where do I go from here?" in an earlier chapter. Be able to talk about the movement through Piaget's stages of cognitive development described in this chapter. First there is the job of dealing with logical combinations, then that of using abstract concepts, and finally, that of appreciating and using hypotheses to consider the most complicated

kinds of thought. You should be able to give examples of these.

8.   Now, as cognitive processes mature, the adolescent looks at the world and national events. Religions and political views are re-examined and may change as the adolescent understands more and more.

■ ■ ■ ■   ◄
                                                                                                     ◄
CHAPTER OUTLiNE   ◄

Chapter Preview: Algebra and formal operations
With this one I'll just hit the high points so you can fill in the details. You'll need to use paper from your notebook. Have fun.

I.   Physical growth
          A.   Feelings about body image are important psychologically and socially.
                    1.   Emotional maturity develops more slowly than physical maturity
                    2.   Early maturation in boys _____
                    3.   Early maturation in girls _____
                    4.   Late maturation in boys _____
                    5.   Late maturation in girl _____
          B.   Puberty and the Growth Spurt
                    1.   Decreased melatonin _____
                    2.   the Growth Spurt
                              a.   lasts about 2 to 3 years
                              b.   begins 2 years earlier in girls
                              c.   boys reach full height at age _____
                              d.   girls reach full height at _____
                              e.   changes such as acne, voice lowering and ____
          C.   The onset of puberty
                    1.   The Secular Trend
                              a.   Menarche average age decreased from: ____ to: _____
                                        (1)   diet, sanitation, medical care
          D.   Exercise and menarche
                    1.   strenuous exercise daily _____
                    2.   disruption of menstrual cycle _____
                    3.   trend has reached biological limit
          E.   Muscle development and strength
                    1.   girls by 45% and boys by __ %
                    2.   boys have more testosterone for muscle development
                    3.   what girls can do
          F.   Nutrition and its effects
                    1.   energy needed for growth
                    2.   U.S. adolescents more prone to consume mass carbohydrates
                    3.   Malnourishment
                              a.   self imposed diets _____

4.   Obesity
    a.   increase of 39% in 12 to 17 year olds
        (1)   the kilocalorie
        (2)   less activity (television watching again)
    b.   diet
    c.   inheritance
        (1)   fat cells _____
    d.   the social problem
        (1)   social isolation
        (2)   self or other initiated _____
        (3)   serious health risks

            _____
            _____
            _____

At Issue: The Pursuit of Thinness; Eating Disorders
        Anorexia Nervosa and Bulimia

II.   Cognitive Development Erik Erikson's "Who am I?" and "What is my role in life?"
    Exploring these questions depend on cognitive changes
    A.   The Logic of Combinations
        1.   Inhelder and Piaget chemistry problem shows progress from concrete operational stage to formal operations
        2.   Inhelder and Piaget pendulum problem; formal operational children logically examine possible combinations to understand which four factors will affect the rate of swing.
    B.   Use of Abstract Concepts
        1.   Preadolescent is preoperational
        2.   Adolescents can deal with concepts of objects and ideas
        3.   can analyze logic and even algebra
    C.   Using and Understanding the Hypothetical
        1.   Concepts of morality, religion and politics
        2.   Can consider potential outcomes of decisions
        3.   NOT uncommon for teens and adults to fail to reach period of formal operations
        4.   Specific experiences can improve use of formal operations
        5.   May use concrete operations on one task and formal operations on another
        6.   An information-processing view of advanced cognitive thinking
    D.   Post formal operational thinking
        1.   Metasystematic reasoning

Applications: Adolescent Egocentrism: Since I'm looking at my faults, everyone else is too.

NAMES TO REMEMBER

Michelle Warren   Erik Erikson
the Pima Indians of Arizona   Inhelder and Piaget

Galileo   Einstein
Gottfried Wilhelm von Leibnitz

■ ■ ■ ■

TERMS AND CONCEPTS

adolescence   malnourishment
puberty   obesity
growth spurt   anorexia nervosa
early maturation   bulimia
late maturation   the logic of combinations
melatonin   formal operational stage
pineal gland   abstract concepts
the secular trend   hypothetical thinking
menarche   post formal operational thinking
menstrual cycle   metasystematic thinking
testosterone   adolescent egocentrism
acne

■ ■ ■ ■

GUIDED REVIEW

1. As an adolescent's body changes at puberty, psychologists are aware of the interactions of
    _____ _____ with emotions and behavior.

2. Evidence of the interaction of physical and emotional maturity is seen in the effects of
    _____ and _____ physical maturation.

3. Early physical maturity in boys is _____ stressful than for girls because boys'
    emerging secondary sex characteristics enhance their _____ with their peers as well as
    their _____ ability.

4. New and difficult expectations of performance in early maturing girls and boys can lead to the
    development of _____-_____ and _____.

5. Early maturation may be difficult for girls even though they too enjoy increased status through
    _____. However, they may find themselves attracted to older males and lack the
    _____ _____ to deal with the problems that may occur.

6. Boys who mature later than their peers may be the target of _____ and _____. The resulting _____ _____ _____ can continue into adulthood.

7. Girls who mature later than their peers tend to score as less _____ _____ on personality tests. They do have the advantage, however, of growing _____ and _____ as adults than early maturers.

8. The physical changes that occur at adolescence are controlled by _____ and _____ and mark the beginning of the period called _____.

9. The hormone _____ from the pineal gland shows a _____ in production just prior to puberty.

10. The dramatic change in size and body proportion, called the _____ _____, lasts about _____ years and occurs about _____ to _____ years earlier in girls than in boys. As _____ and _____ grow faster than the _____, teens may have an awkward time managing their new proportions.
    (Remember how you complained about your "flood" pants, almost the day after you bought them too long! And how you were convinced your feet would fit into clown shoes any minute!)

11. In boys, typical secondary sex characteristics include; (name 4 or 5)
    1. _____
    2. _____
    3. _____
    4. _____

12. In girls, typical secondary sex characteristics include; (name 4 or 5)
    1. _____
    2. _____
    3. _____
    4. _____

13. In this century the earlier average onset of physical maturity is known as the _____ _____.

14. Compared to the non-athletic teenage girls, the onset of _____ can occur as much as _____ years later in girls who engage in strenuous exercise. In addition, the _____ _____ can be disrupted.

15. Generally boys increase their strength _____ more than girls in puberty, and are better able to maintain sustained effort because of their higher levels of _____. However, girls can increase their strength impressively through _____, despite their lack of muscle mass.

16. One problem of United States' adolescents is the maintenance of proper nutrition. The two major

problems associated with this are _____ and _____.

17.   The concern for "becoming fat" finds teenagers _____ unwisely, and suffering from
       _____ _____ _____.

18.   Such excessive and self imposed dieting is believed to be responsible for _____% of the
       stunted growth and _____ _____ found in underdeveloped children. Long
       term and extreme dieting during adolescence may result in a lack of ability to _____
       _____ for lost normal growth.

19.   Obesity is a problem which has _____ by 39% among young teens.   Causes include
       not only inheritance, but also _____ of _____ and simply taking in
       _____ _____ than the body can use.

20.   The disorder involving starving one's self to lose weight is known as _____
       _____ and that of purging through vomiting and using strong laxatives is known as
       _____. Both are characterized by the victims' view of themselves as _____.

21.   An adolescent suffering from continued anorexia nervosa risk serious effects such as; (name 4 or
       5)
       1.   _____
       2.   _____
       3.   _____
       4.   _____

22.   Bulimics also suffer serious effects in their pursuit of thinness; (name 4 or 5)
       1.   _____
       2.   _____
       3.   _____
       4.   _____

23.   Prerequisites of the ability of adolescents to work through the identity crisis are those related to
       _____ _____. Piaget called this last stage _____
       _____.

24.   The first cognitive step occurs when adolescents are able to examine all the _____ of
       _____ of a problem in a logical way to discover their _____ and the answer
       to the problem.

25.   The second step is to think and analyze problems by understanding _____ concepts.
       This advancement involves movement from the _____ _____ stage to
       understand the factors of the problem that are not in view.

26.   At about _____ years old, the child reaches the most advanced thinking level, and is
       capable of using _____ constructs. For example, this ability is useful in thoughts about
       _____ and _____ issues, and the child's concerns about the potential

outcomes of decisions made by _____.

27. In tasks developed by Inhelder and Piaget to test formal operations, only 2% of the _____ to _____ year olds, who could perform at the level of _____ _____ on one of the tasks, could perform them on all tasks.

28. "If I'm thinking about me, everyone else must be thinking about me." This "on stage" belief illustrates the concept of _____ _____.

29. The adolescent is finally able to _____ as the period of formal operations becomes established, and she realizes that she is no longer the _____ of _____.

30. To help adolescents decenter, it is helpful for them to discuss their feelings with understanding _____ and to develop close relationships with _____. Comparing notes helps!

■ ■ ■ ■

PRACTICE TEST 1

1. A good understanding of the adolescent's changes in physical growth and development is essential
   a. to understand the teen's emotions and behaviors.
   b. to make allowances for the teen's "bizarre" behaviors.
   c. to understand the variations in puberty development within the same age range.
   d. both a and c.

2. Each generation until this one has grown taller and has entered puberty at a younger age. This phenomenon is known as
   a. the menarche trend
   b. the secular trend
   c. the Tanner trend
   d. the maturity trend

3. During the growth spurt, we witness
   a. the trunk of the body growing longer first, giving the teenager a disproportionate look
   b. the weight and height growth leveling off
   c. the arms and legs growing more rapidly than the trunk, contributing to clumsiness at times
   d. the growth spurt is completed before the occurrence of secondary sex characteristics

4. According to the text, boys who mature early
   a. lose status with their male peers
   b. gain status with peers of both sexes

    c.   find early maturation stressful because their clumsiness interferes with their athletic ability

    d.   enjoy higher status with adults

5.   Whereas early maturation in boys has certain advantages, late maturation can lead to

    a.   worries about ever developing further

    b.   ridicule by more mature friends

    c.   negative self image which can last into adulthood

    d.   well sure, you remember, all of the above

6.   Girls who mature early may enjoy increased status with peers, and

    a.   may find new confidence in their athletic ability

    b.   may find older boys attractive and be found attractive by them

    c.   may not be emotionally mature enough to deal with dating older males

    d.   all of the above

7.   Boys usually reach full height between ____ years, while girls reach their full height between _____ years.

    a.   20 and 22; 17 and 19

    b.   16 and 17; 18 and 20

    c.   18 and 20; 16 and 17

    d.   23 and 25; 19 and 20

8.   Muscle strength increases in adolescents differs between boys and girls. Measurements show increases average

    a.   girls at 10%, boys at 75%

    b.   girls at 45%, boys at 65%

    c.   girls at 25%, boys at 50%

    d.   girls at 35%, boys at 75%

9.   Malnutrition, a problem in the United States, is seen in teenagers

    a.   in about 7% of those with stunted growth and delayed puberty suggesting a causal relationship

    b.   at an increased rate, occurring in 39% of 12 to 17 year olds

    c.   perhaps because they are afraid of becoming "fat"

    d.   all of these

10.   Obesity during adolescence presents special problems, including

    a.   self imposed social isolation

    b.   eating to provide comfort

    c.   both a and b

    d.   neither a nor b

11.   Two eating disorders now under study occur more often in females than males. They are

    a.   obesity and malnutrition

    b.   malnutrition and anorexia nervosa

    c.   anorexia nervosa and bulimia
    d.   obesity and bulimia

12.   Which statement about the anorexia nervosa patient is WRONG?
    a.   by starving herself, she loses significant amounts of weight
    b.   she will most likely suffer amenorrhea
    c.   she will become dangerously thin but will see herself as fat
    d.   none of these is incorrect

13.   Psychologists and physicians searching for possible causes of eating disorders, are investigating
    a.   a hypothalamic disorder
    b.   lack of self control
    c.   a schizophrenic tendency
    d.   a side issue of childhood depression

14.   During adolescent cognitive development, we see the child move from
    a.   the concrete operational to metasystematic stage
    b.   the concrete operations to formal operations stage
    c.   the preoperational stage to formal operations stage
    d.   the hypothetical stage to formal operations

15.   Adolescents who understand the concept that the poker chip is either green or not green have achieved
    a.   the ability to use logical combinations
    b.   the ability to use abstract concepts
    c.   the ability to theorize
    d.   metasystematic thinking

This is not really a question, but a suggestion for observation. Why do you suppose researchers have difficulty measuring the limits of intelligence? Are there any? Look around you.

■ ■ ■ ■

PRACTICE TEST 2

1.   Genetics, hormones, and a decrease in the hormone _____ secreted by the _____ gland are responsible for the onset of puberty.
    a.   growth hormone, pituitary
    b.   melatonin, pineal
    c.   estrogen, sebaceous
    d.   testosterone, ovaries

2.   Predictions about the continuation of the secular trend suggest:
    a.   that it has reached its biological limit.

b.   that it will continue at least another generation.

c.   that it reached its limit at the turn of this century.

d.   that the studies are not conclusive.

3.   The dramatic and apparently sudden increase in weight and height, and the change in body proportion is known as

a.   the secular trend

b.   the adolescent spurt

c.   the growth spurt

d.   the onset of puberty

4.   Although early maturation for girls may be more stressful than for boys, late maturing girls

a.   fear they'll never develop further.

b.   tend to grow taller and slimmer than their earlier maturing friends.

c.   both a and b.

d.   are less socially mature than early maturing girls.

5.   Although boys have an advantage of having larger hearts, lungs and increased muscle mass, girls

a.   with training, may become as strong as boys

b.   can't ever be as strong as boys even with training

c.   with training, can develop stronger muscles than boys

d.   can sustain athletic efforts for longer periods of time

6.   Strenuous exercise

a.   can delay menarche by a few months

b.   can delay menarche by up to three years

c.   will have no effect on the timing of menarche

d.   can bring on an early onset of menarche

7.   The prevalence of obesity has increased by 39% in teenagers due in large measure to

a.   heredity

b.   preparation for famine and increased muscle mass

c.   unwise eating habits and television watching

d.   none of the above

8.   Adolescents who diet for long periods of time

a.   often over eat at one meal to make up for dieting on others

b.   are fighting a losing battle against inherited fat cells

c.   may never make up for lost growth

d.   are known as bulimics

9.   Bulimia patients are often

a.   secretive about vomiting after meals to keep from gaining weight

b.   female rather than male

c.   suffering from dental and digestive problems

d.   all of these and more

10.   A strong motivating factor in anorexia nervosa and bulimia is
    a.   the accent in society on thinness as synonymous with attractiveness.
    b.   the adolescent's attempt to gain control and self worth in spite of a family in conflict.
    c.   the self image of being "fat" no matter how underweight the child is.
    d.   a, b, and too sadly, c

11.   Many researchers argue that society must change its emphasis on being thin by
    a.   publicizing the dangers of eating disorders
    b.   ignoring the patients, thereby not reinforcing their disordered behavior
    c.   emphasizing health education, including the weight which is most appropriate for good health
    d.   emphasizing a change in styles in clothing to flatter the normal figure rather than the slim model

12.   The movement from trial and error solutions to being able to examine combinations of information logically toward a solution, is referred to as
    a.   understanding the hypothetical
    b.   understanding the use of logical combinations
    c.   understanding abstract concepts
    d.   metasystematic thinking

13.   An adolescent who suddenly announces to her family that she is going to volunteer for the "other" political party
    a.   may be advancing into the formal operations stage
    b.   may be influenced by media information and changes in the social climate
    c.   both a and b
    d.   neither a nor b

14.   Comprehensive studies of cognitive development in adolescents and adults show
    a.   90% are in the formal operations stage
    b.   30% are in the formal operations stage
    c.   70% are in the formal operations stage
    d.   50% are in the formal operation stage

15.   One complexity of measuring the extent of cognitive development in adolescents and adults is
    a.   that they are not necessarily consistent in the levels at which they function.
    b.   that no one reaches the formal operational stage.
    c.   that only a few people can think in abstract terms.
    d.   that most people are at the metasystematic stage.

ANSWER SECTION

Guided Review
1.   body image
2.   early, late
3.   less, status, athletic
4.   self-doubt, insecurity
5.   athletics, emotional maturity
6.   teasing, ridicule, negative self image
7.   socially mature, taller, slimmer
8.   genetics, hormones, puberty
9.   melatonin, decrease
10.   growth spurt, 3, 2, 3, arms, legs, trunk
11.   lower voice pitch, facial and pubic hair, increased muscle and muscle strength, height and weight increases, cognitive advancement
12.   breast development, widening of hips, narrowing of waist, pubic hair, increase in strength with training, height and weight increases, menarche and regulation of menstrual periods, cognitive advancement
13.   secular trend
14.   menarche, three, menstrual cycle
15.   20%, testosterone, training
16.   malnutrition, obesity
17.   dieting, self imposed malnourishment
18.   7, delayed puberty, make up
19.   increased, lack, exercise, more calories
20.   anorexia nervosa, bulimia, fat
21.   death from starvation, heart disorders, amenorrhea, hyperactivity, a distortion of body image, low self esteem
22.   dental and digestive problems, anxiety and depression, difficulty in keeping their vomiting a secret, low self esteem, distorted body image, danger of choking when vomiting
23.   cognitive development, formal operations
24.   combinations, factors, consequences
25.   abstract, concrete operational
26.   15, hypothetical, religious, moral, government or politicians
27.   11, 18, formal operations
28.   adolescent egocentrism
29.   decenter, center, attention
30.   adults, peers

Practice Test 1
1.   d   6.   d
2.   b   7.   c
3.   c   8.   b
4.   b   9.   d
5.   d   10.   c

11.	*c*		*14.*	*b*
12.	*d*		*15.*	*b*
13.	*a*			

<u>Practice Test 2</u>

1.	*b*		9.	d
2.	*a*		10.	d
3.	*c*		11.	c
4.	*c*		12.	b
5.	*a*		13.	c
6.	*b*		14.	b
7.	*c*		15.	a
8.	*c*			

# CHAPTER NiNETEEN

ADOLESCENT SOCiAL AND PERSONALiTY DEVELOPMENT

■ ■ ■ ■

◀
◀
◀

LEARNiNG OBJECTiVES

We're coming down the home stretch! Has it been an interesting semester? I hope so. In this chapter, we see how the time of adolescence marks adjustments in personality and the way teens make the transition from childhood to adulthood. These are the times that try parents' patience and sanity, but even more, the times when the child has the most reason to be confused about who she is. Talk to teenagers to get their direct experience.

1. Be aware of the cultural effects on the adjustments and treatments of adolescents. An interesting special project might be to look at the relevant differences in each of the last few decades in the values and encouraged behaviors in the teen years.
2. Know what specific decisions must be made during the teen years regarding present and future behaviors.
3. Now that we understand the cognitive advances made in adolescence, what kinds of emotions and social behaviors result from the new understandings? What messages are they receiving about sex-role behavior, independence, marriage, having children, deciding on and pursuing a career? How does the prolonged schooling and dependence on parents affect our teens?
4. Know how Erik Erikson looks at adolescent development. How do kids develop a stable self concept, and what happens to those who succeed as well as those who don't make it?
5. Since teen-age suicide is such a major issue in America, know as much as you can about who, why, where, and when this is liable to happen. What can we do to prevent this tragedy?
6. As you saw in the study of peer groups in older children, peer groups become more and more important to children. How do they figure in the teenager's life? A fascinating extra report might be to study different kinds of groups, ranging from church clubs to inner city gangs, to compare their influence and functions.
7. To what lengths will children go to be accepted by their peers? We see so much literature about drug use, we'd better know more about what drugs are used and why. Those of you who are parents of teens, or ever plan to be, can't get too much information on this topic.
8. The dating scene is all important to the teens I talk to. Are kids really irresponsible in their sexual

activities?   How much do they really know? How involved should the community be in sex-education? How can we, and they, prevent STD's?

9.   The remarkable increase in teen-age pregnancies can't be ignored. What can be done for both the teen-age mother and the young father? Why don't kids use birth control? Why do some use abortion as a solution?

■ ■ ■ ■

CHAPTER OUTLiNE

The semester or quarter is almost over! Here we go with our best effort! This outline will leave even more up to you. I'll suggest headings, but don't feel you have to do it this way. If you've developed your own style, and I hope you have, do it your way. I'm proud of you!

Chapter Preview: Rites de Passage: Cultural differences and similarities!

I.   The Emergence of Adolescence
    A.   Why such a turbulent time?
        1.   or is it?
        2.   A wide range of adjustment patterns
        3.   Stressors differ from those in adulthood
    B.   A changing philosophy
        1.   Developmental tasks: I counted at least seven!

            _____

            _____

            _____

            _____

    C.   Choosing a Career
        1.   Piaget and Inhelder's statement - a "real" job
            a.   Piaget's input in terms of cognitive development
            b.   summer or part-time jobs
        2.   The reality of economics and need for community intervention
    D.   A Crisis of Identity
        1.   Erikson discussion of an acceptable, functional, self concept
            a.   stability versus role confusion
                (1)   changes in relationship to parents
            b.   foreclosure
            c.   identity diffusion
            d.   negative identity
            e.   moratorium
                (1)   Linda, a case of role confusion
        2.   Genetics and self worth
            a.   genetic contributions
                (1)   scholastic success through large vocabulary

(2)   sociability
- E.   Adolescent suicide
    1.   Why? Who? The shocking numbers!
    2.   Warning signs
    3.   LISTEN

At Issue: Is Suicide Contagious
       Clusters
       Prevention
       Prevention of imitative suicides
       More research needed

II.   The Peer Group
- A.   The desire to belong
- B.   The peer group influence
    1.   How the individual uses the group
    2.   How the group influences the teen
    3.   The choice of peer group
    4.   Where parental influence fits in the peer group picture
        a.   age related
        b.   shared views
    5.   Cultural differences
- C.   Drug Use and Abuse See Table 19.2, major correlates
    1.   Why use drugs?
        a.   for the excitement and daring
        b.   gaining prestige by knowing about drugs
        c.   quick money and status
    2.   Each factor in Table 19.2 carries its own impact but can be accumulative
        a.   helps in understanding through short and longitudinal studies
        b.   hopefully will help address areas of   prevention and treatment
    3.   Commonly used drugs, alcohol, marijuana, stimulants, cocaine, psychedelics
        a.   predictors of use
        b.   dangers of use
        c.   _____

III.   Sex and the Adolescent
- A.   Changes in sexual attitudes
- B.   Actual sexual practices
- C.   Masturbation
- D.   Homosexuality
- E.   Sexually transmitted diseases
- F.   Control and prevention

APPLICATIONS; Preventing Teenage Pregnancy:
       Present trends
       Differences between the U.S. and other countries
       Why, what happens?
       Abortion issues
       What to do?

NAMES TO REMEMBER

Mandan boys
G. Stanley Hall
Offer, Ostrov, Howard
Jean Piaget
Erik Erikson
Rotheram-Borus

Janet Hardy and Theodore King
Johns Hopkins Program
Alan Guttmacher Institute
National Academy of Sciences Panel on Early
Pregnancy

TERMS AND CONCEPTS

Rites de Passage
teenager
identity
role confusion
foreclosure
identity diffusion
negative identity
moratorium
adolescent suicide
imitative suicide
alcohol, tobacco

marijuana, stimulants
cocaine
sexual behaviors
permissiveness
masturbation
homosexuality
teenage pregnancy
birth control
sexually transmitted diseases
STD's

GUIDED REVIEW

1. Rather than a period of _____ and _____ the University of Michigan 8 year
    study of adolescent males found that _____-_____, _____ on
    _____, and many other attitudes showed little change between 10th grade and the age
    of 20.

2. Offer, Ostrov and Howard report teenagers feeling _____, _____, and
    _____-_____, rather than in turmoil and rebellion.

3.   Perhaps the period of adolescence gained the reputation for turbulence because of the wide range and _____ of _____ needing to be made during these years. Decisions about _____ , _____ , and _____ issues are just a few of the adjustment decisions to be made by teenagers.

4.   Inhelder and Piaget described the entrance into adulthood as incorporating the teenager's acceptance of the reality of the _____ _____ .

5.   According to Piaget, summer and vacation jobs appear to be helpful in the maturation of the _____ _____ .

6.   Erik Erikson noted than teens who fail to achieve the establishment of an acceptable, functional, and stable self concept, will suffer from _____ _____ .

7.   Erikson's definition is summarized in the text as the teen's ability to form a meaningful connection with the _____ , establish stable goals for the _____ , and keep up adequate interpersonal relationships in the _____ .

8.   Erikson believes that it is necessity for the teenager to integrate a _____ sense of individual uniqueness with an _____ striving for a continuity of experience.

9.   It appears that mature adolescent identity is achieved when, in a redefinition of parent-child relationship, parents and children can share their own perspectives in a _____ _____ way. (This sounds like the formation of a friendship, doesn't it?)

10. In Erikson's terms, _____ occurs when the adolescent has prematurely adopted an identity without questioning alternative values.

11. Adolescents who become apathetic about searching for their own goals and identity experience _____ _____ . Others adopt an identity which is the opposite of what might be expected, called a _____ _____ . Teens who are still searching for their identity are said to be in _____ .

12. The case of Linda C. illustrated the problem of _____ _____ , as she was never able to succeed in this major developmental task.

13. _____ _____ for those between 15 and 24 are alarmingly high, and increased sharply in the 1960's and 1970's. One researcher found that _____ of all college students had thought seriously of suicide.

14. Although more females _____ suicide than males, more males _____ suicide because they use more _____ _____ .

15. Warning signals of a potential suicide attempt must always be treated seriously. Among these signs are: Try for at least four.

     1.   _____

2. _____

3. _____

4. _____

16. On At Issue: Is Suicide Contagious? This is what I call a thinker question!
Since a correlation has been found between publicity of suicides and the incidence of suicide, network programs depicting fictional suicides have been broadcast in hopes of preventing suicides through education. Since that hasn't really been effective, how would you design a program to decrease suicide as an option? (I know this is not a typical guided review item, but do talk to friends, think about this, and draft a letter to the networks with suggestions you believe will help. They really do read and use ideas submitted by viewers.)

17. Two functions of adolescent peer groups are to provide a reference for the teenager to compare his _____ and to provide _____. A study by Brown, Lohr, and McClenahan, shows the groups can influence teenagers to engage in either _____ _____ or _____.

18. Among 12 year olds, advice of parents is valued _____ _____ than that of peers, but by the age of 17, friends' opinions come in a _____ _____. influence.

19. Adolescent drug use is reportedly due to three major reasons which may operate independently or in combination. They are:

1. _____

2. _____

3. _____

20. The person possessing a drug-prone personality is described as one who uses drugs for the _____ that they provide and/or one who becomes _____ _____ to drugs or almost any behavior.

21. We still see teens smoking or chewing tobacco, especially if a _____ or _____ _____ smokes.

22. Use of alcohol, on the other hand, is most influenced by whether the child's _____ drink alcohol.

23. In order of their usage by adolescents, the three most frequently used drugs are: 1._____
2._____ 3._____

24. By the end of their senior year, _____ of high school seniors have experienced the use of alcohol. Alcohol related vehicular deaths among teens are estimated in a range from _____ to _____.

25. Permissive attitudes regarding sexual behaviors are reflected in 1970 statistics showing that _____ of women under 20 were virgins.

26. Evidence that teenagers are not as promiscuous as the statistics imply is provided by the fact that the majority of young people report they only engage in sex with the person they consider to be their _____ _____ _____ .

27. Sexual orientation according to Ellis and Ames, begins with biochemical changes in _____ . Even so, researchers don't agree except to say that sexual orientation begins _____ and is _____ to change.

28. Although attitudes toward homosexuality have become more accepting, homosexual behavior _____ _____ .

29. The text lists 6 major STD's, including AIDS. Based on an intensive program conducted in five New York shelters, Rotheram-Borus and her associates recommend:

30. The sad fact that teen-age pregnancies in the United States have increased more than in many other countries becomes even more tragic when we see that American teens are less likely to _____ _____ _____ than those in six other countries with which they were compared.

■ ■ ■ ■

PRACTICE TEST 1

1. Rites de Passage can be measured by
   a. tribal rituals involving a specific challenge to a boy's abilities showing bravery and endurance
   b. a transition into adulthood marked by several behaviors such as reaching the age to vote, marry, drive etc.
   c. a bar mitzvah or other religious ceremony
   d. both a and b.

2. Among the developmental tasks of adolescence are
   a. to achieve emotional independence from parents and other adults
   b. to recognize one's gender role and face responsible sexual relationships
   c. both a and b
   d. neither a nor b

3. Although most teenagers get through adolescence without undue difficulty, some have specific adjustment problems in
   a. adopting a philosophy incorporating religious, political, and social concepts
   b. progressing toward choosing a career by entering, at least part-time, the reality of the world of work
   c. establishing a sense of personal identity
   d. some or all three of these.

4.   Piaget and Inhelder believe that _____ is a major step from adolescence to adulthood.
       a.   marrying and having children
       b.   attaining and accepting a career
       c.   accepting one's physical development
       d.   taking a political and/or religious stance

5.   Research has indicated that the resolution of the identity crisis depends greatly on the adolescent's
       a.   society, peers and family
       b.   redefinition of the parent-child relationship
       c.   acceptance of parents' beliefs and expectations
       d.   a and b

6.   Erik Erikson's term for the experience of being apathetic to commit to goals or searching for identity is
       a.   foreclosure
       b.   identity diffusion
       c.   negative identity
       d.   moratorium

7.   Some adolescents who find themselves still searching for an individual identity are said to be _____, while others who adopt the opposite values of family and society are described as choosing _____.
       a.   in foreclosure, moratorium
       b.   in moratorium, a negative identity
       c.   in negative identity, identity diffusion
       d.   in identity diffusion, foreclosure

8.   Rates of suicide in adolescents and young adults of ages 15 to 14
       a.   have tripled in the last 20 years
       b.   have stabilized over the last 20 years
       c.   have doubled over the last 20 years
       d.   have decreased in the last 20 years

9.   Signs of withdrawal, feelings of rejection, feelings of academic failure, and spoken hints about self destruction
       a.   should be ignored since they are all signs of feeling sorry for one's self
       b.   should be attended to, since these may indicate a potentiality for suicide
       c.   should be treated as signs of role confusion
       d.   should be ignored, because time will take care of these adjustment problems anyway

10.   Peer groups provide important social structure for adolescents when
       a.   the teen goes to extremes to avoid rejection by the peer group
       b.   the teen uses the group as a reference to compare his or her own values and behaviors
       c.   the teen considers peer opinions second only to those of his or her parents
       d.   all of the above

11.   Adolescents who are without adult supervision after school are
    a.   more receptive to influences of peers to engage in antisocial behaviors
    b.   less receptive to peers influence to engage in antisocial behaviors
    c.   are neither more or less receptive to peer influence toward antisocial behavior
    d.   none of the above

12.   Among adolescents of every age the advice of parents is more valued than that of peers; however, by the time a child reaches 17 years old
    a.   peer advice is valued more than parents'
    b.   peer advice runs a close second to parents' advice
    c.   peer and parental advice are equally valued
    d.   peer advice on war, religion, and law are valued more than parents'

13.   The seriousness of alcohol use in teens is seen in the statistics showing
    a.   3 out of 5 graduating seniors in high school report having used it within the last month
    b.   alcohol is related to 30 to 50% of all teenage vehicular deaths
    c.   both a and b
    d.   it is used more than tobacco

14.   The most widely used drugs by adolescents are, in order,
    a.   tobacco, marijuana, alcohol
    b.   alcohol, cocaine stimulants
    c.   tobacco, alcohol, marijuana
    d.   alcohol, tobacco, stimulants

15.   While the numbers of virgins have dropped dramatically in young men and women
    a.   the resulting early choice of partners pays off with a good record of lasting marriages
    b.   permissive attitudes are responsible for this statistic because of wide spread promiscuity
    c.   permissive attitudes promote the increase in homosexual behaviors
    d.   research shows they are not promiscuous, rather they chose a partner in a sort of pseudo marriage

■ ■ ■ ■

PRACTICE TEST 2

1.   Rather than a time of turbulence and conflict, the University of Michigan 8 year study showed adolescence as a time when most teenagers
    a.   feel confident, happy and well satisfied
    b.   feel torn between societal and peer influences
    c.   have attitudes in the tenth grade which are consistent with those at the age of 20
    d.   both a and c

2.   Erikson describes the failure to establish self concept as distinctive from others as
      a.   role confusion
      b.   identity diffusion
      c.   negative identity
      d.   foreclosure

3.   The case of Linda C., who failed most of the developmental tasks of adolescence, illustrates
      a.   foreclosure
      b.   identity diffusion
      c.   role confusion
      d.   negative identity

4.   Boys are _____ more likely to _____ suicide than girls, where girls are _____ more
      likely to _____ suicide than boys.
      a.   10 times, commit; 2 to 8 times, attempt
      b.   4 to 5 times, commit; 10 times, attempt
      c.   5 times attempt; 8 times commit
      d.   10 times attempt; 10 times commit

5.   The relationship between television programs depicting suicide and imitation suicides of those
      who watch suggests
      a.   that we should ignore the relationships and hope kids will see the effects on loved ones
      b.   that we should take all such programs off television
      c.   a need for research into what kind of programs can help inhibit rather than provoke such
              imitation
      d.   that we should limit issuance of driver's licenses to those 21 years old or older

6.   The peer and group behaviors chosen by a teenager often depend on
      a.   the opinions of the adolescent's parents
      b.   how the adolescent evaluates herself
      c.   the peer group's vocation skills
      d.   all of the above

7.   In studies of peer influence on misconduct, susceptible teens were most likely to
      a.   accept the pressure of the group to either avoid or perform misconduct
      b.   accept pressure to socialize with other peers rather than perform misconduct
      c.   accept the influence of parents to avoid misconduct
      d.   accept society's influence and refuse to perform misconduct

8.   Three major reasons given for adolescent drug use include
      a.   for the sake of the excitement
      b.   to demonstrate knowledge of drugs thereby gaining acceptance by peers
      c.   to obtain quick money and status
      d.   all of these

9.   Although the use of many of the drugs seems to be leveling or dropping off, one remains in

steady use.
    a.   alcohol
    b.   marijuana
    c.   tobacco
    d.   LSD

10.   Through longitudinal studies, we find that those who used drugs as adolescents because their friends did, or who experimented briefly with them, are most likely to
    a.   give them up in adulthood
    b.   continue to use them as adults
    c.   changed their drug(s) of choice
    d.   alienated themselves and suffered physical and emotional distress until death

11.   If the present trend continues, 40% of today's 14 year old girls will have been pregnant at least once before the age of 20. The major difference between the U.S. teens and those of other countries appears to be
    a.   that the U.S. leads in the number of teens who become pregnant
    b.   that U.S. teens have the lowest level of contraceptive use
    c.   that the U.S. teens have effective education programs available
    d.   both a and b

12.   One of the most frightening consequences of the increase in sexual activity among adolescents is
    a.   the danger of breakups in the pseudo marriage
    b.   the loss of the teenager's "good" reputation
    c.   the infection by serious sexually transmitted diseases
    e.   the casual treatment taken when the adolescent does finally choose a marriage partner

13.   The Johns Hopkins program, developed by Hardy and King, has at its core
    a.   medical and psychological services for pregnant teenagers
    b.   follow up classes and care for three years after delivery
    c.   a close supportive relationship between staff and teen mother
    d.   all of these

14, 15 and more! Here's another "thinker" for you! No, I don't want to know how you'd spell it! Having read the application section, if YOU were to be in charge of a program to reduce teenage pregnancies, how, where, and when would you institute a more effective program than exists now. On this one, meet with three other students and submit the outline of a program proposal to your teacher and/or the rest of the class.

For your consideration:
1.   What information would you present?
2.   How would you involve parents, PTA's, and community organizations
3.   How old is the target population?
4.   What would be the setting of the program? Health center, small groups, after school, homes, school, local hospital, etc.
5.   Would you provide information about contraceptives?

6.   Would you provide contraceptives?
7.   What will you tell kids about abortion, adoption, birth control, abstaining and sexually transmitted diseases?
8.   How long would your program last in terms of the teens' ages?
9.   Does your program include unwed parents and follow-up such as in the Johns Hopkins' program?
10.   Who else should be a part of your program? (E.g., parent education, religious leaders etc.)
11.   How will you deal with parents who want no part of your program?
12.   What problems do you anticipate, and how would you handle them?

It's time to say good-bye. Thanks for sticking with the course and the study-guide. I wish you the very best happiness in the years to come.

ANSWER SECTION

<u>Guided Review</u>

1. *turmoil, conflict, self-concept, outlook, life*
2. *confident, happy, self-satisfied*
3. *complexities, adjustments, identity, values, sexual*
4. *occupational world*
5. *adolescent ego*
6. *role confusion*
7. *past, future, present*
8. *conscious, unconscious*
9. *mutually supportive*
10. *foreclosure*
11. *identity diffusion, negative identity, moratorium*
12. *role confusion*
13. *suicide rates, 65%*
14. *attempt, complete or commit, lethal means*
15. *perceived or actual failure in school; withdrawal from social relationships; feelings of rejection by family, teachers, or friends; the end of a sexual relationship; difficulty dealing with sad or angry feelings; talk or jokes about wanting to commit suicide*
16. *you're on your own!*
17. *standards, companionship, prosocial behaviors, misconduct*
18. *far more, close second*
19. *peer acceptance and drug use; the existence of a drug prone personality; an unsatisfactory parent-child relationship*
20. *effect, easily addicted*
21. *parent, older sibling*
22. *peers*
23. *alcohol, tobacco, marijuana,*
24. *92%, 30-50%*
25. *45%*
26. *future marriage partner*
27. *utero, early, resistant*
28. *hasn't changed*
29. *HIV prevention programs in shelters, foster care, group homes, and other special agencies*
30. *use birth control*

<u>Practice Test 1</u>

1.	*a*		7.	*b*
2.	*c*		8.	*c*
3.	*d*		9.	*b*
4.	*b*		10.	*d*
5.	*d*		11.	*a*
6.	*b*		12.	*b*

13.   *c*   15.   *d*
14.   *c*

Practice Test 2
1.   *d*
2.   *a*   8.   *d*
3.   *c*   9.   *c*
4.   *b*   10.   *a*
5.   *c*   11.   *b*
6.   *b*   12.   *c*
7.   *a*   13.   *d*